Astrology Plays Detective

In *Astrology Looks at History*, six astrologers take on the role of detective, using the advanced astrological technique of rectification. In their sleuthing of the famous, they make some startling discoveries that upset established literary or historical tradition.

For example, literary historians are undeniably one day off for Shakespeare's birth, as well. For the bard, while there is so little to go on, the astrology emerges and comes through extraordinarily. From that astrology, we can also contribute to history powerful evidence that Shakespeare was murdered, and by none other than a member of his own family!

Rectification means making it right, working backward through the characterological waves and cadenced events of a person's life to determine the birth time meaningfully for the beginning of it all. In the process, we reinforce the miracle of astrology that keeps us all enthralled and studying.

Welcome to the scholarly studies ahead: fascinating times with historical dates, with times created by astrologers using the myth-magic and measurement-might of astrology. For the most part, the studies focus on genius personalities. This is because, by definition, these individuals are so extremely well-defined, capturing in their life experience and memorial the essence of the times in which they lived.

To Write to the Authors

If you wish to contact the authors or would like more information about this book, please write to the authors in care of Llewellyn Worldwide, and we will forward your request. Both the authors and publisher appreciate hearing from you and learning of your enjoyment of this book and how it has helped you. Llewellyn Worldwide cannot guarantee that every letter written to the authors can be answered, but all will be forwarded. Please write to:

Llewellyn's New Worlds of Mind and Spirit
P.O. Box 64383-K868, St. Paul, MN 55164-0383, U.S.A.
Please enclose a self-addressed, stamped envelope for reply, or $1.00 to cover costs. If outside U.S.A., enclose international postal reply coupon.

Free Catalog from Llewellyn

For more than ninety years Llewellyn has brought its readers knowledge in the fields of metaphysics and human potential. Learn about the newest books in spiritual guidance, natural healing, astrology, occult philosophy, and more. Enjoy book reviews, New Age articles, a calendar of events, plus current advertised products and services. To get your free copy of *Llewellyn's New Worlds*, send your name and address to:

Llewellyn's New Worlds of Mind and Spirit
P.O. Box 64383-K868, St. Paul, MN 55164-0383, U.S.A.

Llewellyn's New World Astrology Series—Book 16

Astrology Looks at History

edited by

Noel Tyl

1995
Llewellyn Publications
St. Paul, Minnesota, 55164-0383, U.S.A.

FIRST EDITION, 1995
First Printing

Cover Design by Anne Marie Garrison
Editing and Interior Design by Connie Hill

Library of Congress Cataloging-in-Publication Data
Astrology looks at history / edited by Noel Tyl. — 1st ed.
     p.   cm. — (Llewellyn's new world astrology series: bk. 16)
    Includes bibliographical references.
    ISBN 1-56718-868-0 (alk. paper)
    1. Gifted persons—Miscellanea. 2. Horoscopes. 3. Astrology.
I. Tyl, Noel, 1936–   . II. Series.
BF1728.2.G54A88   1995
133.5—dc20   95-12689
                                                      CIP

Llewellyn Publications
A Division of Llewellyn Worldwide, Ltd.
St. Paul, Minnesota 55164-0383, U.S.A.

The New World Astrology Series

This series is designed to give all who are interested and involved in astrology the latest information on a variety of subjects. Llewellyn has given much thought to the prevailing trends and to the topics that are most important to our readers.

This project has evolved because of the lack of information on these subjects and because we wanted to offer our readers the viewpoints of the best experts in each field in one volume. Other titles in this series include: *Astrological Counseling*, edited by Joan McEvers; *Astrology of the Macrocosm*, edited by Joan McEvers; *Astrology's Special Measurements*, edited by Noel Tyl; *Communicating the Horoscope*, edited by Noel Tyl; *Exploring Consciousness in the Horoscope*, edited by Noel Tyl; *Intimate Relationships*, edited by Joan McEvers; *Planets*, edited by Joan McEvers; *Sexuality in the Horoscope*, edited by Noel Tyl; *Spiritual, Metaphysical & New Trends in Modern Astrology*, edited by Joan McEvers;

Llewellyn's New World Astrology Series will be a welcome addition to the novice, student, and professional alike. We know this series will fill a gap in your astrological library.

Enjoy, and feel free to write to Llewellyn with your suggestions or comments.

Other Books in this Series

Dedication

The plans for this book included astrologer Jim Lewis,
who was to study the extraordinary dynamics
of the historical focus in Dallas in 1963.

Jim Lewis died on February 21, 1995.

—In my last conversation with him,
he was decidedly conscientious about this work;
he was determined to complete it, but he couldn't.

As friend, colleague, innovator, leader,
Jim Lewis gave astrology so much.
He touched our time and space emphatically and lastingly.

This book is dedicated to his memory.

Noel Tyl

Contents

Noel Tyl

For over twenty years, Noel Tyl has been one of the most prominent astrologers in the western world. His seventeen textbooks,
built around the twelve-volume *Principles and Practice of Astrology*,
were extraordinaily popular throughout the 1970s, teaching
astrology with a new and practical sensitivity to modern psy-
chotherapeutic methodology. At the same time, Noel presented
lectures and seminars throughout the United States, appearing in
practically every metropolitan area and on well over 100 radio
and television shows. He also founded and edited *Astrology Now*
magazine.

He is one of astrology's most sought-after lecturers in the
United States, and internationally in Denmark, Norway, Ger-
many, South Africa, and Switzerland, where for the first three
World Congresses of Astrology he was a keynote speaker.

Noel wrote *Prediction in Astrology* (Llewellyn Publications), a
master volume of technique and practice, and has edited Books 9
through 15 of the Llewellyn New World Astrology Series, *How to
Use Vocational Astrology*, *How to Personalize the Outer Planets*, *How
to Manage the Astrology of Crisis*, *Exploring Consciousness in the
Horoscope*, *Astrology's Special Measurements*, *Sexuality in the Horoscope*, and *Communicating the Horoscope*. In the spring of 1994, his
master opus, *Synthesis and Counseling in Astrology—The Professional Manual* (almost 1,000 pages of analytical technique in practice),
was published. Noel is a graduate of Harvard University in psychology and lives in Fountain Hills, Arizona.

Noel Tyl

Trying to Make it Right!

This book is certainly one of the most interesting astrology books *I've* ever read! Its scholarship shows astrology working at its very best through rectification, capturing in the astrological terms near and dear to us the fascinating lives of geniuses who have touched the development of arts, sciences, and government in Western history. It reveals the details of their personal development and illuminates their interaction with the world as they changed it.

Rectification means *making it right,* working backwards through the characterlogical weaves and cadenced events of a person's life to determine the birthtime meaningfully for the beginning of it all. Clearly and alluringly, the premise is that astrology *can* do this—more specifically, that *astrologers* can do this with astrology. In the process, we reinforce the miracle of astrology that keeps us all enthralled and studying.

Rectification is difficult; it presumes an outstandingly secure knowledge and an artistically facile use of *all* theories and techniques in astrology. The process is continuously a series of "what if" propositions, hypotheses of planetary placements and movements in relation to what we expect in theory and what actually happened in life. When we multiply this process by so many planets and measurements and movements and tie them to so

1

many happenings in a lifetime, the dimensionality of rectification becomes multi-layered, easily bewildering, always challenging. Then there is the breakthrough; seeing the light; the spheres within the spheres within the spheres harmonizing beautifully in the astrologer's awareness.

In this process, the danger within the rectification process is that astrologers engineer the astrology to show *what they expect to see*, what they *want* to see. We seek the sense of "rightness" that is directly related to the quality of knowledge we have. A caution that experts learn is always to guard against the danger of accepting the "easy" hit, if you will, that arc or transit or natal aspect placement that "says it all perfectly." Highly skilled astrologers are seasoned with the objectivity to say, "this is too good to be true, something's wrong. Life doesn't work that way. Let's rethink the possibilities."

This is another way of saying that life moments are not "simply" created by nifty measurements; there must be a place made in our awareness of any horoscope for the reality that most of what happens in life is less than ideal, less than what we dream of, that there are delays more often than not, that things don't always work out the way they should; that there are values and influences outside the horoscope that enter into change; and, perhaps most importantly, that the security of our routine in life tends to keep things as they are, actually *to resist* upheaval and change. Development in life does not occur simply with the flick of one astrological measurement. One or two monumentally clear measurements can indeed establish *the signal* of potential and start our inquiry into more detail, but the reality of development involves many dimensions, which often camouflage or inhibit life circumstance.

For example, especially with historical figures of enormous reputations, we must beware the gloss of the reputation, cut through the Cecil B. DeMille dimensions of drama, romanticism, and fictionalized traditions that grow up quickly (and naturally) about the celebrated; and we must push away out-and-out wish fulfillment on our own parts. Machiavelli was *not* a demon; he "simply" methodized the political ways he saw around him; he was never late for work, so to speak, and he never took a penny under the table! The core truths come first in the rectification process; the pine tree and its branches before the holiday glitter.

Achievements in life have a very important dimension beyond their moment of crystallization: being on top of Everest is a moment that rewards the time of ascent, the time of preparation, the long, long time of planning and training ... in short, a whole lifetime. This is the dimension of *duration:* things take time to be conceived, adjusted, tested, presented, refined, fulfilled, and routined. Astrology can center dramatically on the measurement moment, but the astrologer must, as well, always acknowledge the sense of duration. *Many* measurements and meanings, talents and times must work together in every horoscope.

The existential reality of duration is perhaps why *applying* aspects in transit and arc measurement are often apparently more powerful demarcations of reality than exact measurements (partile) are. Separating aspects also have their place in the scheme of duration. In my work, I like to refer to this span of duration as Time Orb; one-half of a degree in Solar Arc, for example, is tight indeed, equating to six months of life time development; and so it is for the average Secondary motions of Mercury and Venus, but longer for Mars and Jupiter, etc.

This concept of duration is inexorably linked with the concept of *potential.* Potential is registered supremely within the birth moment, through the birth moment (and even before it, in terms of pre-Natal eclipses, converse arcs, and other measurements!). The whole life duration is taken up with working out the potentials: duration marks the whole of life passage. When did Nelson Mandela begin his development to give rebirth to South Africa? When he was born; when he became a lawyer, went to prison, was released from prison, ran for president, when he became president?

Duration conditions potential. Similarly, the individual is included in and conditioned by the collective; specifically, *the individual's horoscope works with the horoscope of others,* against a backdrop of history: Nelson Mandela's idealism and particular personal strengths to project and fulfill that idealism could not flourish in a society that did not need him as hero or antagonist. People, cities, states, movements all work together in the realm of socio-cultural leaders, and on down to the hierarchy of neighborhood leadership, on-the-job stewardship, etc.

It is simply astounding how the horoscopes of the issue of slavery, the state of South Carolina, the organization of the Confederacy, and the Civil War were "needed" by Lincoln (and his horoscope) in order to make much of American history. In fact, from this vital, dynamic synastry, perhaps yet another possible United States chart emerges for further study. The astrology for all this is simply extraordinary: See "Lincoln, the South, and Slavery" by Marc Penfield in this volume for a shelf-full of data description in this direction.

In the rectification process, astrology plays detective and, in the sleuthing of the famous, astrology often upsets established literary or historical tradition. Astrological proofs are becoming valid more and more as astrologers step forward to be recognized and counted as circumspect social observers.

Literary historians are undeniably one day off for Shakespeare's birth! For the bard, while there is so little to go on—just six signatures that don't match and lots of "stories" that contradict— the astrology emerges and comes through extraordinarily. And from that astrology, we can also contribute to history powerful evidence that *Shakespeare was murdered*, and by whom (his son-in-law)! The astrology in this volume shows all that (see "Shakespeare's Time to Be," by Maurice McCann). The astrologer's resourceful, deductive creativity captures the practically nonexistent to establish something meaningful and significant in terms of Shakespeare's birth.

In the rectification process, ideally, we engineer measurements to see what others saw about the person we study and to parallel what actually did happen in the life. In this book, dealing with geniuses of world history, the astrologers did work with historians, and became historians themselves with their very powerful research tool. Objectivity is uppermost in importance in the presentation. In the end, this objectivity reveals the beauty of astrology, gives disciplined abandon to the astrologer's imagination, and unveils the realism of the subject's life.

Beginners in astrology should not be put off by the masterful job these astrologers did in this volume—and I do not know of any other text in astrology that has been devoted to such in-depth, high-level application of astrology by so many researchers. Study *the process*, how the thinking developed. It is very much like a mystery plot: when you are doing a rectification for someone— usually it's an adjustment of perhaps four or five or ten minutes (see below)—you are looking for clues all the time and, in that search, you are constantly theorizing, constantly trying to put things together to have everything make sense. For people born long ago, the rectification time-span may be several days or a year or two, as you will see in some of the cases in this volume.

Signs of the times help the process. The background supports the individualistic thrust to development. For example, the times in which a genius lived (or anybody, for that matter, i.e., a black in the South at certain times in certain cities; a Japanese born in California around 1940; people now approaching forty, born of parents caught up in the Hippy Power times of the 1960s) are vitally important and strongly conditioning. Those times are vital to the light in the life as it develops through the person, his or her family life and values, socio-economic level, community expectations, education, job level, and so forth.

For example, if you read Charles Nicholl's fascinating biography focused on the murder of Christopher Marlowe (*The Reckoning,* Harcourt Brace 1992), you learn extraordinary details of religious allegiances, suspicions, treachery, torture, and treason in life in Elizabethan England (the second half of the sixteenth century) that temper the life background of Shakespeare as well. Or perusing John Hales' *The Civilization of Europe in the Renaissance* (Athenum, NY 1994), a brilliant and detailed travelogue for the mind and spirit, the textures and values of life then color the lives of the people we study.

When you savor Basil Fearrington's rectification of Machiavelli's life in this volume, you will see unfolded the billowing velour of late fifteenth-century political intrigue in Italy—the Borgias, the Popes with their mistresses, the villainy—that became the antecedent backdrop for Galileo, for example (and so many brilliant artists and theoreticians). The genius astronomer/philosopher/writer (with Mars-Neptune opposed Uranus, the axis squared by the Pisces Sun) pressed his vision of the real universe rebelliously into establishment sensibility in the face of the garotted corpses of cardinals, priests, and teachers who, through knowledge itself, were thought in defiance of God! Does Machiavelli's Neptune in Scorpio conjunct the Midheaven reflect that professional milieu?

Thanks to the computer and the superb software resources we have, working with dates long in the past is no longer difficult (just be sure to enter birth times as "Local Mean Time" before time zones were established[1]). We can generate an ephemeris for any time period in the past in a minute or two!

What *is* difficult, however, in working with the lives of people long dead, is the absence of dialogue! We can't ask them questions, and we have to trust that biographers captured personal vignettes and important dialogues closely enough to truth to feed deductions and give reliable substance to our measurements. We need the biographer-historians, at best the primary sources, who were exact with dates: "in 1294" is not as good as "in the spring of 1294," which is not as good as in "March of 1294, just three days before the Equinox!"—And that brings up another concern for the historical astrologer: the Equinox in 1294 was *not* March 21 or March 22. (It occurred about 5:31 A.M. GMT on March 13!) Then, in addition to the Precession of the Equinoxes (that backward movement of a little over 8 minutes of arc every ten years into the past from any time mark), there is the change of calendars at different times in different countries! All of this is managed in our computers—thank goodness!—and it is covered in the research chapters that follow.

The authors in this book are strongly convinced by what they have "discovered" about their subject's birth time. Going through the rectification process makes the astrologer feel that way; you have used all you know to do the job and there is a total faith in yourself; you are the ultimate authority of your rectification. Through long study and work, each author is now extremely informed and expert about the life of the special individual studied. It is a superb feeling to be so full of awareness of someone so special, to have shared in such detail so much of an important time in history. It is astrology that makes that enrichment possible. Rectification astrology is exultant astrology.

All the researchers were very careful as well to be comfortable with measurement *inexactness*. We know that big changes in

---

1   The concept of a 24-Meridian world-time organization was proposed in 1878 by Sir Sanford Fleming, a Canadian Civil Engineer and scientist. In America, William Frederik Allen worked with Fleming. Their system, called "standard time," was adopted by Canadian and U.S. railroads at noon on November 13, 1883 (Sunday).

There was resistance to the change. It took about two years for most states to adopt the plan. Congress finally stepped in and passed the Standard Time Act on March 19, 1918. Astrology is in debt still to the research and published reports by Doris Chase Doane in the mid-1960s on this very important matter, which has complications throughout every country in the world.

life take time; allow me to repeat in a different way the concept of *duration* introduced earlier: there is the inception of an idea (something important; "Eureka!"); there is the building of the idea, Columbus gathering the money and resources for his voyage—a support process that took years; there is the moment of accomplishment itself, the discovery of New World landfall; the completion of *the* symphony; there is the significance of the discovery thereafter, the meaning of discovering another planet, of seeing other worlds clearly. Measurements must embrace the living process of inception, building, completion, and significance. Astrology is a clock ... but it is not necessarily a stopwatch.

So there is a "feel" to rectification, a human touch that is very important within the process to capture building, culmination, dissemination. It is just the same within historical research: just how much was so and so's account of the master's death romanticized? Were those really so and so's last words? Didn't George Washington tell one lie in his life? Did Benjamin Franklin really fly a kite during a thunderstorm? (Yes, Franklin did, and Tim Lyons tells us about it in "Franklin's Electric Spark.")

And always, when dealing with famous horoscopes especially, we must remember that other souls were born at very close to the same time in the same place—or at slightly adjusted times and place—and have horoscopes very, very similar to one another, and yet only one of those souls enters history. We can acknowledge this but we can not understand the "why." The soul's journey carries with it something beyond schedule; it has an inscrutable mission. Astrology is just part of the architecture of greatness. Not knowing all about this keeps all of us human.

The Process

You will see that, while our experts in this volume use slightly different combinations of techniques to accomplish rectification, they do proceed very similarly: the background of the birth in its time-period and social circumstance is established; the outstanding attributes that describe the person are listed concisely and objectively; this list is then structured developmentally with key dates. Next, the general astrological lay-of-the-sky is inspected, being very aware of the tell-tale, speeding Moon's aspect and sign-change potential within the particular timespan.

Then, the "if's" begin, usually relating planets to tenancy of Houses (natal Saturn in the 1st will be clearly different in manifestation from natal Saturn in the 7th (a 12-hour time shift), with a special eye to grasping the Moon's sign in relation to the Sun's sign *and then adding conjecturally a synthesizing Ascendant.* The Ascendant is conditioned by location as well as time, and the Midheaven responds to adjustments to the actual birth time.

The major aspects are carefully analyzed, and two astrological maxims begin to emerge: the first is that *a strongly evident characterlogical dimension will be corroborated often (several ways) in the horoscope,* i.e., different measurements will seem to suggest the same thing. For example: a Mars square with the Moon in Mutable signs will suggest hyper-reaction, perhaps extreme sensitivity, as will a square between Neptune and a proposed Ascendant and/or a Mercury-Venus conjunction in Mutable Signs, Cancer, or Scorpio, or … The maxim acknowledges that the well-defined personality, the highly focused individual, is matched by similarly focused, unifiedly organized horoscope dimensions.

Gradually, the astrologer zeroes in on hypotheses born out of the person's reputation or characterlogical profile, which are then hooked onto the astrological structure of the day, and then hung on the coordinates of the birthplace and a specific time. Refinement then starts with Arcs (and Progressions) and "heavy" transits over and/or in square or opposition to the angles. The second astrological maxim is *that every major change in life involves activation of the angles of the horoscope.* It is the angles that establish time and place. One's occurrence in life changes "angularly." It is the angles that lead the proof of a rectification.

Astrologers learn little "tricks" of technique in the process of rectification, just as detectives do collecting clues and solving cases deductively. For example, every astrologer will raise an eyebrow to a birth time that is on the hour, on the half-hour, or even on the quarter-hour. It looks too neat and, from experience, it *is* too neat. The chances are high—and statistically easy to prove— that more births occur *away from* rounded quarter-hour intervals on the clock than at those times, and, very important, the chances are high (empirically) that most births listed at apparently rounded-off times *took place **earlier** than at the time listed.*

A second "trick" astrologers learn is to look for a mighty arc or transit quickly, to spot a major "hit," i.e., a major life development, with which to begin chart hypothesis. For example, the Solar Arc of Saturn, Uranus, Neptune, or Pluto over or opposed a trial Midheaven or over or opposed an Ascendant is most often the first line of conjecture. If it's close enough to possible occurrence within the early homelife years, say, from eight to thirteen or in the early adult years, say, from age seventeen to twenty-five, this "hit" becomes a prime, early hypothesis: the angles are established, the planets fall into houses, and test analysis against the list of characteristics and historical occurrences can take place.

The age spans suggested above clearly avoid transits of Saturn to its own position: six to seven, fourteen to fifteen, and twenty-eight to thirty years of age (the spans do not exclude twenty-one when transiting Saturn makes the closing square to its natal position and transiting Uranus makes the opening square to its natal position). The point here is that if something happens *without transit activity being clearly core-involved* (not having major transit or arc activity to the Sun either) *then the arc or progression itself is touching a vital point; the angles—the time and place—mean something.*

Then, astrologers find that transits will echo the angular arc or progression powerfully *within the orb of duration* represented by the arc or progression leading up to and separating from the major measurement center. Indeed, sometimes they all work together brilliantly, more often than not, it seems, in the lives of the famous. Perhaps accuracy of measurement-response *is* part of the profile of the emphatic personality.

Astrologers remember that in 4 minutes of clock time, the Midheaven will change 1 degree, which is 1 year of life in Solar Arcs and Secondary Progressed Sun movement (the arcs for the Sun and Midheaven are the same). Major transits of the Midheaven (and Ascendant) can click into place within particular time orbs. Then, just as a fix on the Secondary Progressed Moon position can be moved (adjusted) at a rate of *1 degree* per month of life time, Solar Arcs can be subdivided to *5 minutes* of arc per month in life. The timing is refined more and more.

The Secondary Progressed Moon is a powerful rectification measurement-proof: the Moon moves so many degrees each day (each year in progressions) that its Secondary passage over the angles is *extremely telling to the month of life.* Then, transits take over (especially Mars) for dates within the month. And then, quite the icing of proof mechanisms, there are Tertiary Progressions (each day after birth equaling one Lunar month in life). Computers now bring this technique easily and quickly into the foreground of testing. Tertiaries can reveal *the day* when major events are focused powerfully: we look for Tertiary angles to conjoin natal planets especially (shifting a birth time 8 minutes later will add 8 degrees to the T. Midheaven and to the T. Ascendant; thus, 1 minute of clock time moves the Tertiary angles 1 degree; this helps using one Tertiary chart as a reference forward and backward in time during the rectification time span. Familiarity with, say, three or four Tertiary charts, each 1 month from the other in real time, will show the principle clearly.

The point is that the rectifier goes through a good bit of *mental* generalization and approximation to begin the process. The mind makes major leaps of "what if" proposals, and it helps greatly to know about cycles and measurement shifts *in relation to birth time adjustment.* The astrologer's measurement know-how is pressed into streamlined organization and facile development.

Let's take as an example—not for complete life study, but for orientation to the procedural considerations discussed above— the horoscope of Nelson Mandela.

The primary general-profile descriptions of Mandela before his inauguration as President of the New South Africa on May 10, 1994 (at precisely 12:18 P.M. EET in Pretoria, SAFR) were as follows: tall, lean, broad-smiling; lawyer, statesman-dignified, apparently a natural leader from a family of tribal leaders; slow speaking and philosophical; extremely private personal life; athletic, amateur boxer; humanitarian and modern thinking in a rigidly segregated society; dramatic, confrontational trouble with the government because of his outspoken views during his early legal career; victimized by the political regime and imprisoned for life (the life sentence pronounced on December 6, 1964); freed by F. W. DeKlerk, white Apartheid president of South Africa, on November 2, 1990, after twenty-five years. Then, three years and six months later, Mandela is inaugurated the new president of South Africa.

Figure 1 (page 12) shows the planetary lay-of-the-sky (the Solar Chart) for Mandela's birthday, July 18, 1918, for noon in

Umtata, SAFR (and just wait until you study Nicholas Campion's theoretical and practical management of Solar Charts in the first chapter of this volume!). Most conspicuous is the Mercury-Saturn conjunction: deliberate, perhaps slow speaking; philosophical; residually wise; in Leo, reinforcement of leadership potential, ambition through dramatic means. Mercury-Saturn is sextiled by Mars in Libra, giving an energetic support in the name of fairness and equanimity, perhaps bucking the organization; and a potential square with the Moon in Scorpio (definitely in Scorpio on the day of his birth) which would add driving conviction to the tightly-reined ideas and their strategic projection.

Jupiter is conjunct Pluto: extreme resourcefulness, a fighter.

Neptune is peregrine (not making a Ptolemaic aspect), except perhaps a square with the Moon if Mandela were born just after midnight at the beginning of this day (i.e., 6 degrees or 12 hours earlier back from this noon mark—think this through; see it in your mind—for the Moon to be within orb of the square to Neptune; and if he were born then, the test chart would have been upside down (12 hours, one-half day), roughly from the noon mark position, perhaps giving an early Taurus Ascendant, which certainly does not fit the general image of Mandela. (An *Aries* Ascendant could fit; the fire part of it, the sense of mission and ego projection; but the Moon would be in the 7th and Mandela appears too private. But then again, his wife, Winnie (7th House), became a powerful woman over the years. We keep this all in mind.)

Neptune peregrine (though semisquare Venus) suggests that an idealism will run away with the personality and commandeer its resources to achieve a dream or a delusion. (Perhaps the Moon-Neptune aspect is not needed, or maybe this would be important corroboration that idealism *must* be emphasized somehow in the life); Uranus is the final dispositor of the horoscope, in Aquarius, appropriate for a humanitarian focus of individuality. Uranus is trine the resourceful Jupiter and cerebral, idealistic, socially-orientated Venus in Gemini.

When I visited South Africa for a lecture tour in November 1993, I discovered that the South African astrologers, in the main, were using a rounded-off chart for Mandela, set at 8:45 A.M. See Figure 2 (page 15). This horoscope was impressive upon first study, *but was it a too-easy congruence with the Mandela profile?*

• His penchant for privacy and the "destiny" for prison suggested the 12th House emphasis so decided in this 8:45 A.M. horoscope. The Moon rules the 12th and would be square to Saturn in the 12th.

• The Sun would be just peregrine, wanting to express the Cancerian humanitarian energies but apparently lost in the 12th unconnected. That does not feel right for the Messianic figure Mandela was to become.

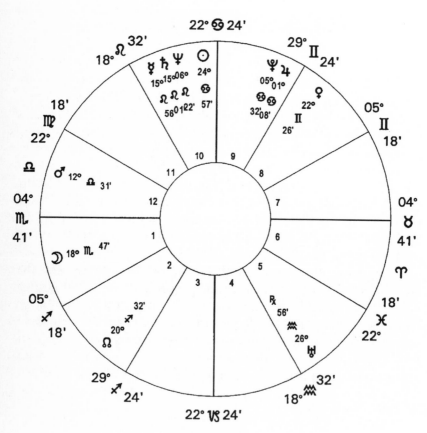

Figure 1
Nelson Mandela
July 18, 1918 12:00 P.M. EET
Umtata, SAFR
28E47 31S35
Placidus Houses

• The humanitarian thrust was all exposed to the world in the 7th on the horizon through Uranus, trine (across the signline) to the resourcefulness in the Jupiter-Pluto conjunction and trine Venus, but that is the only placement in the Western hemisphere, and Uranus is retrograde. Might this be *too much* withdrawal, i.e., all in the East focused on the 12th; we must know that Mandela *did* emerge from prison into public prominence worldwide!

• The Leo Ascendant is suggested to counterbalance the 12th, establishing leadership, but the ruler of the Ascendant in the 12th? Again, the easy fit: in jail for life; but development continues within life duration: Mandela *was* freed.

• The Moon fell nicely into the ideas-and-communication 3rd. But ruling the 12th? Yes, the Moon would be square Mercury, ruler of the Midheaven; someone who writes political philosophy from a confined position? Not unfamiliar historically.

• Again the privacy situation was emphasized through the Moon-Venus trine embracing, retaining all planets except Uranus within the Eastern hemisphere, definitely a self-defensive position. Where was the fighter?

Now, let's just work with three events: the pronouncement of his life-imprisonment at age forty-six and one-half (December 6, 1964; which would correspond to the accumulated semisquare Solar Arc, slow for July birth); his extraordinary grant of freedom twenty-six years later at age seventy-two (November 2, 1990); and his inauguration as president of the country three and one-half years after that at age seventy-five (May 10, 1994). Figure 2 does not create arc formation to conjunction, square, or opposition with *an angle* for any one of these life-crucial time periods! [Just add the age-arcs mentally to the key hypothetical planetary positions: Uranus at 26 Aquarius, for example, plus 46 is 72 Aquarius or 12 Aries, opposite Mars (and meaningful) but not in contact with an angle; Pluto to the Ascendant angle measures 49 degrees/years, but there is no significant life event at that time.]

Figure 2 shows almost no transit formation to conjunction, square, or opposition an angle for either the first (46-1/2) or second (72) time period. Only one major transit *which would not occur if the time were changed* (i.e., to an angle or to the Moon) occurs for each event: for imprisonment, transiting Neptune was at 17 Scorpio conjunct Mandela's Moon as presented in the 8:45 A.M. chart, the Moon ruling the 12th. For Mandela's freedom, transiting Pluto was also at 17 Scorpio conjunct this Moon! This is remarkable, telling us that *the 18th degree of Scorpio may be an ultra-sensitive degree in Mandela's astrology.*

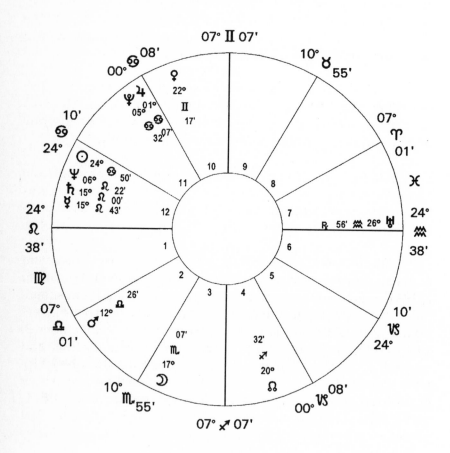

Figure 2
Nelson Mandela
July 18, 1918 8:45 A.M. EET
Umtata, SAFR
28E47 31S35
Placidus Houses

Then, for the inauguration, transiting Pluto was at 27 Scorpio, a 3-degree orb square to the 8:45 Ascendant, and transiting Saturn was square this Midheaven. Since these inauguration transits occurred together, they increase in importance, but instinct told me that there was not enough for such a remarkable career; where are the angles as keystone symbolisms of the confinement, the resurrection, the power and the glory?

The "feel" I had every time I saw Mandela speaking, when reading about his past, experiencing first-hand the thrust to freedom that thrilled this country, was *Sagittarius:* he appears Sagittarian, his athleticism, his statesmanship, international celebrity, lawyer-isms, dignities, the fire of opinionation; all reinforced enormously by the Pluto conjunction with Jupiter. This is where the astrologer's imagination leads to new hypothesis. Could Sagittarius be on the Midheaven, making the birth at about 9:30 P.M. (just turning the 8:45 A.M. chart around until Sagittarius is on the MC) which would probably put the Sun in the 5th House, i.e., between 8 and 10 P.M.)?

A test-chart for 9:20 P.M. is shown in Figure 3, with an Ascendant-Descendant axis of 16 Pisces-Virgo. At the time of life-imprisonment sentencing, transiting Mars, Uranus, and Pluto were at 15 Virgo applying exactly to this Descendant axis and squaring the Midheaven! Uranus—the chart's final dispositor—was natally now in the 12th, the House it rules, an appropriate symbolism of the rebel incarcerated, fighting to be free (the square with the Moon and the trine with Jupiter).

In the natal configuration, the Moon was still square Saturn and Mercury, but now was nicely trine the Sun.

For the freedom time, there is no major transit (and we have lost signification of the 18th degree of Scorpio). And for the Inauguration, there is no angular transit either. In terms of Solar Arcs, there is *no angular contact* in the 4th harmonic for any of the major events. Something is wrong. This chart looks very good with the Uranus position, the peregrine Neptune ruling the Ascendant (idealism), with the powerful Scorpio Moon (the need to know and convince) strong in the 9th House (legal, international, etc.), feeding a trine to the Sun. The Mercury rulership of the 7th and its conjunction with Saturn corresponded to the public dignity of the leader. Mars there could suggest his wife; along with Mercury conjunct Saturn, their troubled marriage, Winnie's accumulation of power—but with no angular contacts within arcs and progressions, there was something missing once again.

The next hypothesis: could Sagittarius be on the *Ascendant?*

By the time I was this far with this issue, I learned that Boston astrologer Frances McEvoy had reported that her son had actually interviewed Mandela and asked him for his birth data—I believe that's the story. Mandela had said "mid-afternoon." Mid-afternoon is midway between 12 and 6 P.M. or 3 o'clock. A horoscope for 3 o'clock gives *Sagittarius rising!*

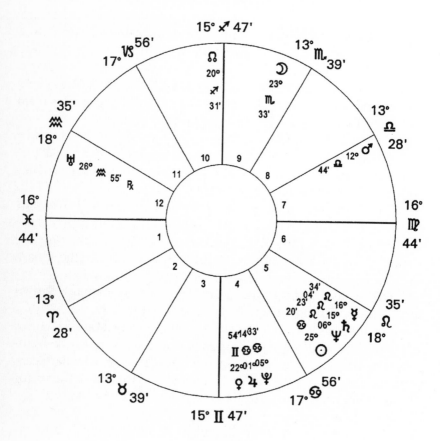

Figure 3
Nelson Mandela
July 18, 1918 9:20 A.M. EET
Umtata, SAFR
28E47 31S35
Placidus Houses

I began to test the 3:00 P.M. time, and I was astounded how everything began to click in, as if all the spheres of Mandela's personal heavens geared themselves into synchronization, especially with the adjustment I made away from the rounded-off 3:00 P.M. hour to the specific time of *2:54 P.M., July 18, 1918*. See Figure 4, page 18.

A selection of these "hits":

• On the day of life-sentencing and imprisonment (December 6, 1964), Mandela's SA Moon was at 4 Capricorn 47, just 46' of arc applying to opposition with natal Pluto, ruler of Mandela's rectified 12th, holding his Moon. This corroborated the privacy of the man, put the image of public resourcefulness and dedication into the 7th, and allowed for the symbolism of incarceration. Additionally, natal Pluto conjunct Jupiter in the 7th, ruled by Mercury conjunct Saturn profiled Mandela's marriage to powerful Winnie.

Mandela's SP Moon at 11 Leo 06 was exactly on the midpoint of Sun/Uranus and Saturn/Neptune.

Transiting Neptune was at 18 Scorpio, within 2 degrees of conjunction with Moon in the 12th House.

• On the day when Mandela received his freedom (November 2, 1990), his Solar Arc Mars was at 22 Sagittarius 23 applying tightly to his Ascendant (the fighter freed from the long stay in the 12th). And his Secondary Progressed Moon—always conditioned acutely by any rectified birthtime—was *exactly* conjunct his natal Sun. Literally, through these measurements, Mandela was born again.

Additionally, transiting Pluto was at *18 Scorpio* (see transiting Neptune above, twenty-six years earlier), conjoining Mandela's Moon, sensitizing that degree, emphasizing it upon Mandela's freedom. In this rectified birth chart, that degree area 17–19 Scorpio becomes the natal midpoint of Mars/Ascendant, definable so aptly with the concept of "fighting spirit!"

• At the Inauguration (May 10, 1994), Mandela's Solar Arc Venus was at 5 Virgo 50, only 11' of arc from precise conjunction with this rectified Midheaven angle!

The Secondary Progressed Moon was at 7 Virgo 51, tightly upon his Midheaven as well, precisely there just the month before (back one degree) when Mandela won the election!

The Solar Arc (and SP) Midheaven was exactly at *19 Scorpio 17* tightly conjunct the natal Moon!

And *finally,* as polish on the apple (to test finitely the meaning sensitivity and measurement response of the rectification

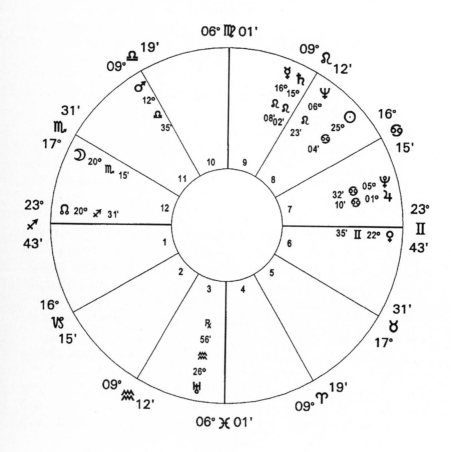

Figure 4
Nelson Mandela
July 18, 1918 2:54 P.M. EET
Umtata, SAFR
28E47 31S35
Placidus Houses

time), Tertiary Progressions (Figures 5, 6, 7, page 20) for these three events are absolutely astonishing, depicting the *actual* day of each event in the tightest symbolism:

• Mandela was given his life sentence in prison (Figure 5) when Tertiary *Saturn was at 6 Virgo 02, precisely conjunct the rectified Midheaven!* Tertiary Mercury, ruler of the rectified Midheaven was at 22 Pisces 30, tightly square (within one week of time) the Ascendant.

• Mandela was given his freedom from prison (Figure 6) when Tertiary *Uranus was at 6 Pisces 26, exactly opposite his Midheaven,* suddenly and dramatically starting a new life on the fourth cusp. The Tertiary Ascendant squared his Mars exactly.

• Mandela became president of his country (Figure 7) with the extremely time-sensitive Tertiary Moon at 1 Capricorn 33, exactly opposite natal Jupiter; Tertiary Jupiter in turn had just crossed his Midheaven; and *Tertiary Sun at 6 Taurus 12 was exactly square Mandela's idealistic, peregrine natal Neptune! A dream illuminated, fulfilled.*

Additionally, SP Venus was at 24 Virgo exactly square the rectified natal Ascendant.

Wow! I sent the notes for this rectification to Rod Suskin, one of South Africa's premiere astrologers, in Cape Town. He checked this time of 2:54 P.M. against—not three—but fifteen events in Mandela's life over the past fifty-three years. He was "astonished" at how everything fit, and I thank him for his study and confirmation. The chart has meaning.

That is the mainstream process of rectification in today's astrology with the sophistication of our times now and the aid of computer accuracy and speed.

In rectification—while we can be proud as punch and confident to the extreme, because of our total involvement with the process—*we do not know if the result is correct.* We do not know that Nelson Mandela was indeed born out of his mother's uterus at precisely 2:54 that afternoon in 1918. But we do know that this birth time is valid, to a great extent, in rich detail, and in fascinating revelation.

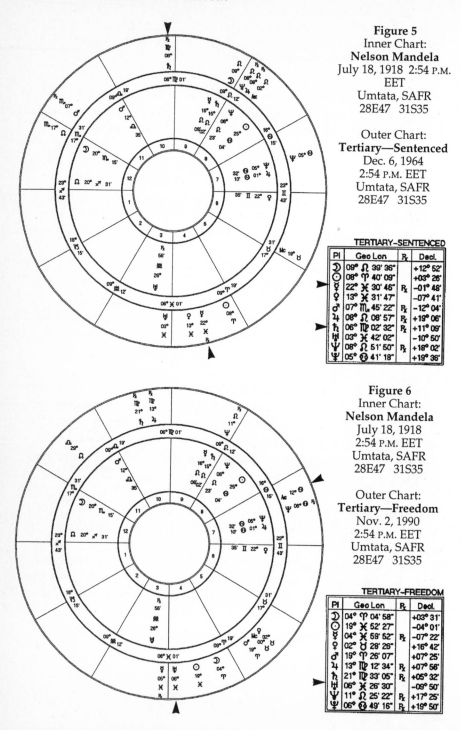

Figure 5
Inner Chart:
Nelson Mandela
July 18, 1918 2:54 P.M.
EET
Umtata, SAFR
28E47 31S35

Outer Chart:
Tertiary—Sentenced
Dec. 6, 1964
2:54 P.M. EET
Umtata, SAFR
28E47 31S35

TERTIARY—SENTENCED

Pl	Geo Lon	R	Decl.
☽	09° ♌ 39' 36"		+12° 52'
☉	08° ♈ 40' 09"		+03° 26'
☿	22° ♓ 30' 46"	R	−01° 48'
♀	13° ♓ 31' 47"		−07° 41'
♂	07° ♏ 45' 22"	R	−12° 04'
♃	08° ♌ 08' 57"	R	+19° 06'
♄	06° ♍ 02' 32"	R	+11° 09'
♅	03° ♓ 42' 02"		−10° 50'
♆	08° ♌ 51' 50"	R	+18° 02'
♇	05° ♋ 41' 18"		+19° 36'

Figure 6
Inner Chart:
Nelson Mandela
July 18, 1918
2:54 P.M. EET
Umtata, SAFR
28E47 31S35

Outer Chart:
Tertiary—Freedom
Nov. 2, 1990
2:54 P.M. EET
Umtata, SAFR
28E47 31S35

TERTIARY—FREEDOM

Pl	Geo Lon	R	Decl.
☽	04° ♈ 04' 58"		+03° 31'
☉	19° ♓ 52' 27"		−04° 01'
☿	04° ♓ 59' 52"	R	−07° 22'
♀	02° ♉ 28' 26"		+16° 42'
♂	19° ♈ 26' 07"		+07° 25'
♃	13° ♍ 12' 34"	R	+07° 56'
♄	21° ♍ 33' 05"	R	+05° 32'
♅	06° ♓ 26' 30"		−09° 50'
♆	11° ♌ 25' 22"	R	+17° 25'
♇	06° ♋ 49' 16"	R	+19° 50'

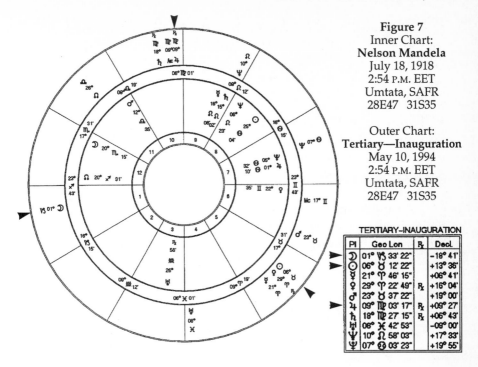

Figure 7
Inner Chart:
Nelson Mandela
July 18, 1918
2:54 P.M. EET
Umtata, SAFR
28E47 31S35

Outer Chart:
Tertiary—Inauguration
May 10, 1994
2:54 P.M. EET
Umtata, SAFR
28E47 31S35

TERTIARY–INAUGURATION

Pl	Geo Lon	R	Decl.
☽	01° ♑ 33' 22"		−18° 41'
☉	06° ♉ 12' 22"		+13° 36'
☿	21° ♈ 46' 15"		+06° 41'
♀	29° ♈ 22' 49"	R	+16° 04'
♂	23° ♉ 37' 22"		+19° 00'
♃	09° ♍ 03' 17"	R	+09° 27'
♄	18° ♍ 27' 15"	R	+06° 43'
♅	06° ♓ 42' 53"		−09° 00'
♆	10° ♌ 58' 03"		+17° 33'
♇	07° ♋ 03' 23"		+19° 55'

Now we can look ahead *into Mandela's future,* through this lens that has shown its potential for well over half a century of his life. As we study, we have to keep certain special circumstances in mind to test the rectification further:

• The inauguration chart (12:18 P.M. EET May 10, 1994 in Pretoria; there was *no* Daylight Saving Time in South Africa) came into being *one hour later* than was scheduled! Why? Why of all days, in full view of billions watching throughout the world, was Mandela late to this world-important event? Was fate pushing a particular time into being?

If this inauguration is geared to tell us something, we must note that the Aries Point (the tie with the public at 0 Aries, or 0 of any Cardinal sign) is 19' from exactly at the midpoint of Mars-Saturn in the 8th House. The Aries point in Mandela's natal horoscope as we have rectified it is the midpoint of Pluto/Ascendant just 22' of arc from 0 Libra. This can suggest a concern for public death or death in office for the head of the government.

• In the new South Africa chart (April 27, 1994 at 00:01 A.M. EET in Cape Town, SAFR[2])[3], the Aries Point=Pluto/ASC, South Africa's ultra-public position. Fascinatingly, Mandela's rectified Moon at 20 Scorpio is conjunct the new South Africa's Moon at 21 Scorpio!

• Throughout 1995, transiting Neptune will oppose Mandela's Sun and, in October, his SA Neptune comes to a semisquare with his MC, while transiting Saturn squares his rectified 23-Sagittarius Ascendant, a very important time to test this rectification further.

A punctuation of this set of measurements is definitely Mandela's Tertiary picture for October 1, 1995 during the measurements just noted (Figure 8): T. Moon at 5 Virgo exactly conjunct

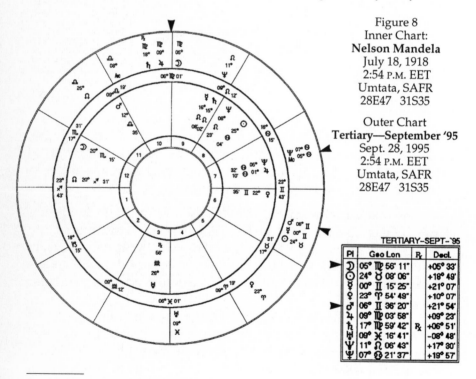

Figure 8
Inner Chart:
Nelson Mandela
July 18, 1918
2:54 P.M. EET
Umtata, SAFR
28E47 31S35

Outer Chart
Tertiary—September '95
Sept. 28, 1995
2:54 P.M. EET
Umtata, SAFR
28E47 31S35

	TERTIARY-SEPT-'95		
Pl	Geo Lon	R	Decl.
☽	05° ♍ 56' 11"		+05° 33'
☉	24° ♉ 08' 06"		+18° 49'
☿	00° ♊ 15' 25"		+21° 07'
♀	23° ♈ 54' 49"		+10° 07'
♂	06° ♊ 36' 20"		+21° 54'
♃	09° ♍ 03' 58"		+09° 23'
♄	17° ♍ 59' 42"	R	+06° 51'
♅	09° ♓ 16' 41"		−08° 48'
♆	11° ♌ 06' 43"		+17° 30'
♇	07° ♋ 21' 37"		+19° 57'

---

2 South Africa has two capital cities: Pretoria in the northeast, just north of Johannesburg; and Cape Town at the very southwest tip of the African continent. The two are some 1,500 miles apart; the reason suggested is that the government can pick different climates at different seasons to conduct business and certain ceremonies.

3 At the time of Mandela's inauguration, a new constitution was being written, to be ratified within two years, i.e., May, 1996. This new chart will be a very important, new component in the astrological mix.

his rectified Midheaven, T. Mars precisely square his Midheaven, and his Tertiary Midheaven itself exactly conjunct his natal Pluto. This is a time of major change in Mandela's life, at a point seventy-seven and one-half years into its duration and potential.

So, welcome to the studies ahead: fascinating times with historical times, times created by astrologers using the myth-magic and measurement-might of astrology. Yes, for the most part—beyond Campion's extraordinary choice of charts that takes us from the Creation of the World to Jack the Ripper by way of the Astrological Lodge of London(!)—the studies focus on genius personalities. This is because, by definition, these individuals are so extremely well-defined, capturing in their life experience and memorial the essence of the times in which they lived.

But I want to repeat that there were other children born the same day, time, and location as Benjamin Franklin for example. They all flew kites as children, but only one continued to take a prominent place in history. So let us never overlook that there is *something else* at work in astrology that is beyond astrology and beyond astrologers. While our next grand frontier may be a syntaxual marriage between astrology and genetic engineering, bringing us closer to that further light, we must at present appreciate and respect our extraordinary position as astrologers: *we are mediums of time*, and every time we work with a horoscope we engineer that time to create meaning ... and we come ever closer to the miracle.

Nicholas Campion

Nicholas Campion is the President of the Astrological Association and a past president of the Astrological Lodge of London. In fact, he is the only British astrologer to have held both posts. He is also the only British astrologer to have edited the country's two most prestigious astrological journals, *Astrology Quarterly* and the *Astrological Journal* (he guest-edited three special issues).

He began studying astrology in 1971 while reading history at Queen's College, Cambridge, and became a professional in 1975, prior to completing his studies at the School of Oriental and African Studies and the London School of Economics, where he received his MA in 1976.

After graduating, Nicholas taught history and English for some years, and has also taught astrology for London's Camden Institute, for the Faculty of Astrological Studies, and the Centre for Psychological Astrology, and has lectured around the world.

His books include *An Introduction to the History of Astrology*, the classic *Mundane Astrology* (with Michael Baigent and Charles Harvey), *The Book of World Horoscopes* (for which he received the 1992 Marc Edmund Jones Award), *The Practical Astrologer*, his popular students' guide, and *The Great Year*, his seminal work on the place of astrological ideas in history.

Nicholas Campion

Mythical Moments in the Rectification of History

 Astrology, the Past and the Future—The sharpest test of skilled astrologer is the ability to predict the future, but the value of astrology often lies in its ability to confer understanding of the eternal present, the bridge between the future and all the past events which brought us to our current situation. In this spirit, the astrologers of the Islamic world of the ninth to thirteenth centuries, to whom we owe so much, regarded astrology's ability to give meaning *to the past* as one if its greatest gifts. They were historians, but not in the sense that they believed in an objective account of human affairs for their own sake. In their view, the model for all human behaviour lay in the heavens, and human past had to be studied in the light of the stars and planets. In addition, when the past was *re*constructed, the evidence provided by the duration of planetary orbits was taken as *equal to other historical evidence.* What's more, dating derived from planetary evidence often overruled more conventional historical evidence! This practice by which astrology, rather than written records, determines the timing of past events is known as rectification.

The astrologers of the Islamic world believed that they were rectifying history. However, bearing in mind the fact that views of the past are frequently mythologized in order to justify a view of the present, it would be more accurate to say that they were rectifying mythology. This is the practice I wish to explore. It raises important questions such as the apparent "reality" mythological perspectives bear in relation to "historical" ones, and it stands at the heart of most astrological practice.

Rectifying Events

This is a deeply practical essay. Rectification is not something that most of us are taught; it is an application of astrology which we have to find out for ourselves by trial and error. Technique is important, but I have always believed that technique is nothing without theory. If, for example, technique is represented by the notes of the musical scale, then theory represents the composing skills necessary to work these into a melody. It doesn't matter how many techniques we have in astrology (and we have many—too many, I would say), we will not know what to do with them unless we have a model or theory with which we may apply them to promote understanding of the subject of enquiry. This is a simple point, for we all know, for example, that Secondary Progressions possess a significance which is quite different to that expressed by natal planets. Yet it is one which is overlooked all too often, and that is why so many astrologers get in such a muddle using so many different techniques, jumping randomly from tertiary progressions to asteroids and hypothetical planets like so many headless chickens.

My advice to the confused student is always to:

(1) Slow down and start interpretation with the Sun, Moon, Ascendant and major planetary aspects;

(2) Always interpret the radical (natal) chart first and never jump off into wild speculation on the basis of natal alignments which are not related to the subject under discussion;

(3) Always think about what you're doing;

(4) And always remember that, as time is ruled by Saturn, so astrological interpretation, the study of our relationship with time, should proceed in an orderly and disciplined manner.

I would like to start with some thoughts about the nature of rectification. What are we doing with it? What does it say about our astrology? And where does it fit in to an overall theory of history, of our relationship with the past.

Astrology and History

The use of astrology to analyze history dates back to the earliest recorded history in the Mesopotamia (modern Iraq) of the third millenium B.C. Indeed the study of history itself may have developed in order to increase the efficacy and accuracy of astrology. This is the argument I presented in my book, *The Great Year*.[1] Astrology was used to forecast likely futures, which were then modified via the use of *namburbis* (prophylactic rituals designed to ward off evil) and any practical or ritual action which might affect the consequences of current behaviour.

From earliest times though, the relationship between the two studies, history and astrology, contained certain paradoxes. It is important to be clear about what these were, especially as they were rooted in the contradictions within astrology itself.

On the one hand, astrology seemed to offer insights into a world which was superior to or more perfect than, the physical environment on earth. To the Mesopotamians, astrology was a means of communicating with the goddesses and gods who were the world's original inhabitants. In the centuries before Christ, when the Greeks produced a systematic abstract philosophy of astrology, it was to be dominated by Plato's doctrine that the physical world was but a pale and deeply flawed reflection of a superior, perfect world. Plato called these two dimensions Becoming and Being: on the earth everything is in a state of flux continually *becoming* something else, while in the perfect dimension everything is in a state of perfect non-change, or *being*. Being, according to Plato, contained the Ideas, the Ideal Forms, which were the perfect model of everything we experience in the physical, material world. It is the home and source of perfection.

Plato believed that the planets existed midway between Becoming and Being. On the one hand, they moved, and thus changed, and so were like imperfect Becoming. On the other hand, they moved slowly through the zodiac (the slower they

---

1   See especially Chapters 1–3, *The Great Year*, Penguin, UK 1994, USA 1995.

moved, the more perfect they were, he believed), and hence were close to perfect Being. From this belief arose a simple theory of planetary motions, namely that these were perfect circles, or were composed of series of interlocking perfect circles, the circle itself being a perfect shape.

This model, which dominated European astronomy until the seventeenth century, was in direct contradiction to the observation that each planet varies in speed, moving direct, stationary and retrograde, and changes in latitude and declination. In other words, in Platonic terms they were profoundly *imperfect*. The contradiction between the theory and reality of planetary motions was to be a major problem for ancient and medieval astrologers. Yet, rather than study planetary orbits as-they-were (unsatisfactory and imperfect), *they produced models based on the way they-should-have-been* (uniform and perfect). This attempt to force measurable planetary orbits into the straight-jacket of a model of perfect circles was pursued by the giants of ancient astronomy, Aristotle and Ptolemy. It was only finally rejected as a result of Kepler's formulation of the laws of planetary motion in the 1600s.

The unresolved contradiction between the theoretical model and the observed data had a direct result in two rival approaches to astrological history. On the one hand, there was an ideal history-as-it-should-have-been, on the other history-as-it-was. A gulf had opened between the subjective desire that the world should be one thing, and the objective experience that it was another. There was only one way to convert the latter into the former, and that was through rectification.

History As It Should Have Been

The first approach, the study of history-as-it-should-have-been, reveals an attempt by many ancient historians to discern the perfect patterns in history. While the Mesopotamian records reveal just such a programme, it becomes clearest in the work of the "idealist" historians of the late Greek and classical Roman worlds, around 2,000 years ago. Heavily influenced by Plato (c. 427–348 B.C.), they wished to discern the working of perfect Being in the imperfect world of Becoming. They believed that, if they could succeed, they would be able to organize society more efficiently, and hence direct the future on to a more suitable course. Their history was didactic, designed to teach moral lessons rather than merely impart information. As a result, their written histories combine a record of the past as-it-was together with a view of the past *as-it-should-have-been*. In short, history itself was rectified.[2]

This belief in history-as-it-should-have-been also emerged significantly in the histories compiled in the Islamic world after about the eighth century onward, especially by men such as Abu Ma'shar and Masha Allah. These scholars were engaged in an audacious attempt to understand history according to the will of God manifested through the heavens and expressed through the major planetary cycles. They started by attempting to locate in time the great mythical events of biblical history. By defining these according to the most suitable astronomical alignments, instead of according to the available records, they were, indeed, rectifying history.

The Flood

One of the greatest examples of rectified history occurs in the work of Abu Ma'shar, who was born in Afghanistan in 787 and died in 886. Abu Ma'shar was one of the most influential mundane astrologers in the Islamic world, and his writings were highly regarded in medieval Europe. He analysed history according to twelve cyclical measures, none of which was dependent on planetary orbits in the normal manner. (NOTE: Abu Ma'shar's system is outlined in *The Thousands of Abu Ma'shar*, by David Pingree, published by the Warburg Institute, London, in 1968). These measures varied in duration from the mighty *qisma*, which moved around the equator at the rate of 1 degree every thousand years, or one complete circuit in 360,000 years, to the small *fardar*, which lasted seventy-five years and moved symbolically through phases represented by the seven traditional planets and the Moon's two nodes. These measures are best compared to the progressions used in ordinary natal astrology in that they have *symbolic* power and are not necessarily tied to a measured observation of physical reality.

---

2 In 1994 Ellen Black and Robert Schmidt became aware of the remarkable work of A. T. Fomenko, the Russian statistician who claims that most western chronology up to about 1600 has been arranged to conform to certain patterns rather than to accurate records of events. Fomenko's work, dauntingly titled *Empirico-Satistical Analysis of Narrative Material and Its Applications to Historical Dating* is published in two volumes by the Kluwer Academic Group in Dordrecht in the Netherlands for $282. It is available in the U.S.A. from Project Hindsight, PO Box 002, Berkeley Springs, WV 25411.

Abu Ma'shar's self-imposed task was therefore to work out when to begin his series of cycles. He decided to use the great flood, the deluge of the Book of Genesis. But when did this happen? He calculated that at midnight at the beginning of February 18, 3101 B.C. a mean conjunction of planets occurred at around zero degrees Pisces (as the final water sign this was regarded as the natural sign of the flood). Then, at dawn, he concluded, the rains began which initiated the flood. I have been unable to replicate Abu Ma'shar's calculations. Using one programme (Electric Ephemeris), the entire conjunction of planets occurs in Aquarius. However, satisfied that he was correct, Abu Ma'shar used midnight on February 18, 3101 B.C. as the starting point for his series of twelve cycles.

How do we regard this work now? Well, even though the deluge myths may find an historical root in the floods which afflicted low lying inhabited areas, such as Mesopotamia, there is yet to be discovered any archaeological evidence of a universal deluge of the type described in Genesis. Such myths can only have a psychological rationale based in a profound longing for collective cleansing and rarely have historical basis. This does not invalidate Abu Ma'shar's work. It does, however, remind us that here is a form of astrology which relies predominantly on the imagination, on deriving abstract and symbolic measures from a mythical event.

We are dealing here with an astrology which is heavily "judicial" in the sense that the astrologer's judgment plays a far more important role than the historical record (see below). The fact that Abu Ma'shar *believed* that the flood *did* occur and that it coincided with a conjunction of all seven planets at the beginning of Pisces makes his work no less an exercise of the imagination. In fact his very belief gives his work its power. Certainly, the attempt to measure world history against long-term cycles became a very important one for astrologers eager to understand the dramatic events of the seventh century when a new world religion, Islam, shook the world to its foundations.

History as It Was
The second approach to history was evident in the Mesopotamians' earliest records, and that is the desire to keep an accurate and literal record of events as they happened. This programme was absolutely essential if astrological prediction was to

be perfected, the future correctly anticipated, evil omens averted, and order maintained. The keeping of precise historical records was therefore a political imperative of the highest order. Eventually, motivated by dissatisfaction with astrology's emphasis on events-as-they-should-have-been, a number of astrologers began once again to emphasize the need for accurate chronology. Chief among these astrologers were Jean Bodin, the sixteenth century French astrologer and political theorist, and Johannes Kepler, who in the seventeenth century attempted to strip astrology of most of its classical and medieval structures, leaving it only with precisely measured planetary cycles. Both Bodin and Kepler are regarded as reformers, but as astrologers they were attempting to turn the clock back to the halcyon days of the Assyrian empire in the eighth–ninth centuries B.C., when it was believed that the keeping of an accurate record of history-as-it-was was essential to the creation of a precise and accurate forecasting astrology. Bodin and Kepler were joined by non-astrologers in their quest, such as James Ussher, Bishop of Armagh. Even the great calendar reform of the sixteenth and seventeenth centuries, when the new, more astronomically correct Gregorian calendar was introduced, was part of this move. However, when astrology lost all intellectual respectability in the seventeenth century, any hope of a reformed astrological study of history was lost.

Astrology—Natural and Judicial

It is clear then, that we have two forms of astrological history. They contradict each other, but then astrology, taken as a whole, is a discipline which contains many internal contradictions. The question is can we have both? Can we have an astrological history which relies primarily on external events which are greater than the individual, and another which explicitly imposes human desires and expectations on external events? The answer lies in Cicero's great study *De Diviniatione* (On Divination) composed 2,000 years ago. Cicero rejected as false the detailed predictive astrology reliant on the reading of horoscopes, yet he took it for granted that the planets possessed general significance over human affairs. For example, he agreed that Mars was a hot planet which might bring drought, Venus a moist and peaceful planet, and that great periods of history were measured by the distances between mean conjunctions of all the planets (a so-called Platonic Year).

The first sort of astrology he classed as judicial divination, the second he included under the umbrella term natural divination. If we adopt these two definitions, then we can isolate two forms of astrology—judicial astrology and natural astrology.

Natural Astrology

Natural astrology rests in the world of observable cycles and influences, and includes at its most obvious such phenomena as lunar gravity and solar radiation. It requires the observation of exact data and exact correlation with planetary cycles. Rectification is completely *il*legitimate within this definition, for we must get to know the world as closely as we can, minimizing our own individual preconceptions. This is the astrology I have been pursuing in my work on mundane astrology.

Judicial Astrology

Judicial astrology allows for a much greater input from the astrologer, especially if the goal is to impart meaning rather than to make correct, precise, and accurate prediction. It is, by the way, important to distinguish correct forecasts made by the clear application of astrological rules from the theoretical possibility of accurate forecasts made on the basis of clairvoyance, intuition, or psychic skills. All astrological interpretation is based on manipulation of the rules of astrology. In judicial astrology, astrology is very much a language of consciousness, a form of poetry in which the astrologer extracts meaning from the natural phenomena of astronomy, and imparts this to others. Judicial astrology does not require accurate birth data and can rely on wrong data, rectified times and solar charts (whether cast for midnight, dawn, or midday, the three most common options). I know that this is a very radical statement. I have heard many astrologers say in private that wrong data can produce a right interpretation, but it has generally been taboo to say it in print. The reason is simple: it undermines one of the cardinal tenets of astrology, which is that exact birth times are essential for accurate readings.

Let me make my position a little clearer. I have absolutely no doubt that objectively speaking I am a creature of my horoscope, rooted psychologically and emotionally in the time and place of my birth. Yet if I, as an astrologer, am called upon to make sense of the world, a different order of reality takes hold. Since astrology is a discipline closely dependent on observation, it is what *I see* that is important. Therefore, it is what comes to me which enables me to make sense of the world. Therefore I must rely on the birth data which comes to me. In astrology we can only work with what we can see, or believe is there.[3] If that data is incorrect, I must then use that data. Correct data is always preferable, but no data can ever be 100 percent accurate. There is always a compromise, even if it's a matter of seconds (and seconds, as we know can substantially change the timing of forecasts made by primary directions).

I am not talking about only my own experience here, but also my observations of the way astrology as a whole works. The plain fact is that much of the data we use is inaccurate. There's no concealing that fact. So what do we make of Jung's aphorism that "Whatever is born or done has the qualities of this moment of time?"[4] This may be true in natural astrology. Indeed, I would say that it is, but in judicial astrology we should adapt Jung's words

---

3 Ironically, Paul Kurtz, founder and chairman of the Committee for the Investigation of Claims of the Paranormal (CSICOP) is spot on when he writes that "the truth of astrology and other paranormal phenomena is found in the eye of the beholder, i.e., it is subjectively validated by a person's preconceptions, his preferences, prejudices and interpretations, rather than by any objective reference to the external world" (Paul Kurtz, "In the Eye of the Beholder: The Psychology of Paranormal Belief" in *Science of Pseudo? The Mars Effect and other Claims*, ed. J. W. Nienhuys, Skeptische Nitiies 8, Stichting SKEPSIS, Postbus 2657, 3500 GR Utrecht, Netherlands, p. 3).

There is a great deal of truth in this proposition as far as judicial astrology is concerned, but while Kurtz then regards astrology as an enemy of science, reason, and freedom, I would say that it is precisely because it can structure the subjective world so effectively that astrology is so useful. Kurtz would also say that no objective truth can be gleaned from subjective experience, but this is really because he is working within the limits of astronomy, his academic discipline.

To any historian, subjective experience is essential evidence. Astrology began as a study based on observation, like any science, and has retained the important emphasis on individual experience and perception which modern science has lost. Kurtz would regard any individual perception as meaningless. Astrology, valuing the individual, would regard it as meaningful. However, as we shall see, judicial astrology moves beyond the purely subjective when its rules, based on objective external appearances, measure mythological moments. This is what makes astrology so remarkable. The question is, then, if astrology is in the eye of the beholder, what is it that it beholds, and what is the nature of the beheld?

4 I do not have an original reference, but this aphorism was quoted at the beginning of Margaret Hone's *Modern Text Book Of Astrology*, and hence was read and absorbed by generations of astrology students in the '50s, '60s and '70s. The book went through thirteen printings or editions from 1951 to 1973.

to read "Whatever is born or done has the qualities of the moment of time at which I (the astrologer or client) think it happened."

When I began studying astrology formally in 1974, about three years after commencing my own, undisciplined studies, I obtained some blank horoscope forms from the Faculty of Astrological Studies in England. On the bottom right-hand side were a series of little boxes where one filled in the data and made the calculations. This was in the dim far-off days before computers. I was always intrigued by the fact that the box where the birth data was to be entered was labeled "birth data as given." Not "birth data," but the data *as given*. That is, not the time when the client was born, but the time when they think they were born. This is a major problem in England and Wales where, unlike Scotland, the United States, and so many other civilized countries, birth times are not entered on birth certificates. Most people in England and Wales know only that they were born "in the early morning," or "after breakfast" or "around tea time." Some people will say they were born at 3:00 A.M. The next time you meet them they have changed their minds to 4:00 A.M., or 4:00 P.M. Others give you a time, such as 11:55 A.M. You read their chart and they go away satisfied. The next time you meet them, they tell you that their mother got it wrong, and they were born at 4:30 P.M. "Does that make any difference?" they ask. The conventional answer is yes, of course it does, for the birth time must be accurate!

The less conventional, but in my view more truthful answer is "No. It doesn't matter." How can we justify such a response? Well, in a meaningful universe, everything is significant. In the astrological solar system, there is no room for meaningless coincidence or chance. Therefore, when people state the wrong birth time, *they are inviting a reading based upon that birth time,* and that is the reading they need at the time. The astrologer gives the reading which is appropriate to the client's needs in the present, and that advice doesn't need to be based on a horoscope cast for the client's birth time.

I know that that is a shocking statement to most astrologers, but it is one which is well within historical tradition. After all, the excessive emphasis on natal astrology is a feature of twentieth-century astrology alone. In the great days of European astrology from the fourteenth to seventeenth centuries, most people had no idea of their time of birth, even of the date. The systematic recording of births was a nineteenth-century invention; in earlier times only baptismal records were kept, and these were no reliable guide, for children might be baptized at *any* age. Therefore, almost all astrological consultations were based on horary charts cast for the moment at which the client arrived and anounced their major concern.[5] In other words, there was no belief that one had to have a precise time of birth in order to benefit from astrological advice.

Astrology and Divination

Most astrologers have experience of other forms of divination, principally the I Ching or Tarot. I began using the I Ching when I was eighteen, shortly before I cast my first horoscope. I also dabbled in the Tarot from 1978 onward, and in 1979 I attended a course in London with Juliet Sharman-Burke, Liz Greene's co-author on *The Mythic Tarot*. One question which rages among Tarot readers is the significance of the different "spreads," as if a "Celtic" spread has an objectively different significance to a "Zodiac" spread. In my work with the Tarot, it became clear that this belief in a spurious objectivity was somewhat naive, and that the important move was to decide subjectively what each card signified before turning it over. Having made this designation, the reading then became fruitful. It was necessary, though, that the reader *trust* that the spread and the card would yield the right information, or provoke the reader into making the appropriate statements. This element of trust is a vital one in astrological readings.

To return to the matter of the Faculty horoscope forms, then, it became clear to me that if both client and astrologer trust that the birth time as given is correct, the reading will proceed

---

5 Event charts cast for the moment the client arrives are essentially Horary consultation charts which reveal the essence of the moment, suggesting the appropriate advice for that time. About 1980, I started casting charts either for the time clients asked me to cast their horoscope, or for the time they arrived, using these to indicate the clients' current concerns. I have since found that a number of other astrologers follow this practice, notably in Denmark. Adrian Duncan's book, *Doing Time on Planet Earth*, includes discussion of consultation charts. [See Christian Borup's chapter on this subject in *Communicating the Horoscope*, Llewellyn Publications, Tyl, 1995. — Ed.]

smoothly and fruitfully. The astrologer will have the confidence
to make useful judgments and the client will trust the astrologer's
words, interpreting them in the light of her or his circumstances
and endowing them with significance.

Wrong and Right Data

I must deal very briefly with the issue of wrong and right horoscopes, in particular with the use of charts based on wrong data to
provide right information. This is a subject rarely addressed in
print, yet the plain fact is that a large proportion of the data available to us is wrong. This particularly applies to the birth data of
public figures available in data collections. The births of the last
three U.S. Presidents offer an ideal example: we have only vague
clues as to Reagan's birth time, there is a measure of doubt over
Bush's exact time, while all initial prognostications concerning
Clinton's chances of winning the 1992 election were based on
inaccurate data. In the United Kingdom, there has been a muddle
over Princess Diana's birth time, which was initially anounced as
2.00 P.M. and then corrected to 7:45 P.M. In 1993, Diana offered me
two birth times via an intermediary. First she said she was born at
2:15 P.M. Then, when I queried this, she said that she was born at
7:45 P.M. Dealing with this problem I decided to abandon the concept of the wrong or right data and return instead to the concept
of the *appropriate* data. If astrology is a matter of signs, the question is what does each of Diana's charts *signify?* I then read the
earlier time, 2:15 P.M. (Libra rising) as representing the private person, especially the shy young girl Prince Charles married. I concluded that 7:45 P.M. (Sagittarius rising), which was the time we
had been using for Diana since her marriage, represented Diana,
the princess.

I have something else to confess. In 1980, I was with a group
of astrologers at the televised opening of an antique shop. The TV
people decided that one of them should have a reading, but we
astrologers had no ephemeris. Now, March 4, 1980, the day in
question, was my twenty-seventh solar return. This gave us the
only significant planetary positions for the day. We therefore created a horoscope using the four outermost planets for the inter-
viewee's year of birth, and the six innermost planets for my solar

return, which were, in any case, the planetary positions for the day. The resulting horoscope was part nativity, part horary, and, loosely calculated as it was, provided an excellent improvised reading. I have never forgotten this experience, which strengthened me in my resolve, in spite of the prevailing ethos of the time, that astrology (as a whole in all its branches) was not and could not be a science in the modern sense, carrying an objective set of verifiable laws.

Principles of Rectification

Where does this all leave us with rectification? Those who regularly rectify horoscopes believe that they are impartially applying the precise rules of astrology to discover an objectively accurate time of birth. I have no doubt that this is not true. Rectification should instead be seen as an important, and in some cases necessary, preparatory step which is undertaken prior to the divinatory act of extracting meaning from the horoscope through the act of judicial astrology. It is quite clear that some astrologers need to rectify horoscopes. While I used to when I saw clients regularly, I do not now.

Let me describe the very simple technical procedure I used. First I purchased for myself a "radionic" pendulum from the Aetherius Society, who sell the best pendulums available. I then prepared two pieces of paper, one with A.M. and one with P.M., written on one side. I then took twenty-four other pieces of paper, twelve of them with the zodiac glyphs and twelve with the numbers 1–12. I then satisfied myself which way the pendulum would swing in order to give a positive indication, and then, turning each piece of paper face down I held the pendulum over each one in turn until I found a time of day which corresponded to a rising sign.

Whenever I state this case to keen rectifiers I find myself lectured on the merits and accuracy of the practice. This only further convinces me that an important element of the judicial process in astrology is the need to trust one's own practices and data.

Solar Charts

One excellent alternative to rectification is provided by the use of solar charts. These are usually set for midnight, dawn, or noon. If I have a vague idea of the time, I will set the chart for the nearest major point on the Sun's diurnal journey, including dusk. In those cases in which I have no knowledge of the time though, I set the chart for noon. I find that the information yielded is invariably *extremely accurate* and that the principle planetary positions describe the essential matter under investigation. Let's look at a few examples.

Example 1 — The First Public Opinion Poll

The first-ever public opinion poll was conducted in Wilmington, Delaware on July 24, 1824 (Source: *Today* newspaper, July 24, 1991). The noon chart for this day places Mercury, the ruler of opinions, exactly on the Midheaven, to within 3 minutes of arc. We could really not wish for a more accurate signature, especially as Mercury is within minutes of a conjunction with Venus, the planet of human relationships. Mercury is also conjunct the Sun, but we can discount that as the Sun is bound to be on the Midheaven at noon local mean time.

We should also check the Moon, the ruler of public opinion. This planet is dignified at 9 degrees, 25 minutes in in Cancer, its own sign, indicating the grip opinion polls have secured over public policy and information. The Moon is also conjunct its south node and in a tight opposition to Neptune, which should warm the hearts of all those who regard public opinion polls as unreliable purveyors of fiction. In addition, the Moon and Neptune are opposed across the 9th–3rd access, in the houses of thought and communication.

So far, we have looked at this chart, set for a speculative though symbolically important moment, in fairly standard terms. We can see how the language of astrology, based in the natural phenomena of astronomy, yields word pictures which describe situations as accurately as any photograph. Yet what is the relevance such an exercise bears to history on the grander scale?

First of all let us define this horoscope. What does it signify? Well, clearly it represents *public opinion*. Let's move forward to the greatest triumph of public opinion in recent times, the opening of the Berlin Wall, the culmination of the European revolutions of 1989. At the moment the Wall was opened (6:59 P.M. CET, November 9, 1989), Saturn and Neptune at 10 degrees Capricorn were in an exact opposition to Jupiter at 10 degrees Cancer, straddling the Moon-Neptune conjunction in the radical "First Poll" chart. In other words, Neptune was making an opposition to its radical place, while Jupiter and Saturn, the principle *chronocrators* (timers of history) were also in opposition over the crucial degrees.

So, what are the conclusions to be drawn from this exercise? First, a speculative chart, set for noon, yields real information about the question under consideration. Second, the chart possesses significance, revealed under transit(s) for future related events.

I would like to digress at the moment and introduce the concept of types and archetypes, devised by Plato as a means of

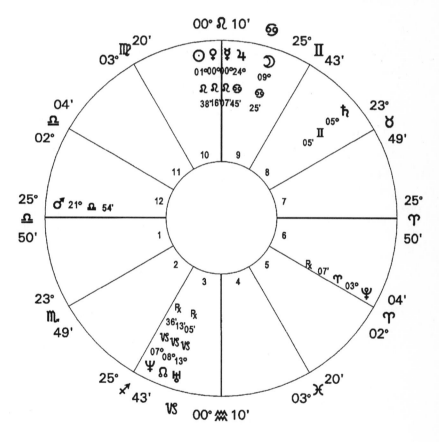

Example 1
First Poll
July 24, 1824 12:00 P.M. LMT
Wilmington, Delaware
75W33 39N45
Placidus Houses

describing cosmic reality. Plato believed that everything in this world was a manifestation of an archetype (one of his Ideal Forms) which existed in the superior, intangible realm of Being, and could be described through numerology. To take Plato's thoughts one step further, there may be an archetype representing "public opinion." In this case, the asking of the first question in the first public opinion poll and the opening of the Berlin Wall both become "types" derived from the original archetype. Both are therefore related, and we should not be surprised to find close planetary links between them.

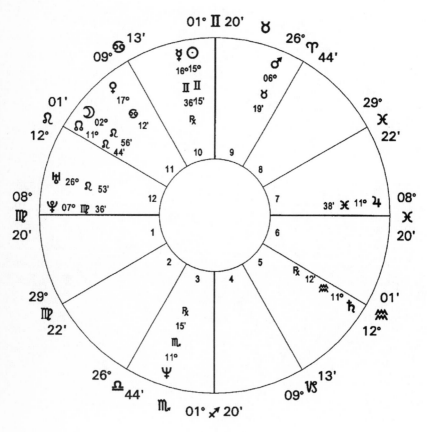

Example 2
Beatles' Recording
June 6, 1962 12:00 P.M. GMD
London, England
00W10 51N30
Placidus Houses

Example 2 — The Beatles' First Recording Session

The Beatles met for the first time to record under the aegis of George Martin at EMI on June 6, 1962. This was not their first recording, but it did inaugurate the "Beatlemania" phase of their existence. Setting a horoscope for noon places Pluto exactly on the Ascendant and Jupiter on the 7th cusp. The first position, Pluto, represents their profoundly revolutionary status at the time as the greatest subversive challenge to contemporary sexual and cultural mores. The second position, Jupiter (dignified in Pisces, its own sign), reveals the extraordinary, almost unique enthusiasm, with which their music was greeted.

Here is another Solar chart that makes an accurate eloquence, what with the Sun-Mercury square that Jupiter; Venus, ruling the 3rd, trine Jupiter; the Leo Moon square Mars in the 9th, etc.

Example 3 — Bob Guccione

Bob Guccione is Hugh Hefner's major rival as the purveyor of sanitized photographic sex. I include him here because I am fascinated by popular culture, as the major bearer of contemporary mythology on the one hand, and its relationship to astrology on the other. Guccione's *Penthouse* empire, founded in 1965, challenged and almost destroyed Hefner's *Playboy* conglomerate in the 1960s–70s, although the two have now settled into a symbiotic rivalry.

Setting Guccione's horoscope for noon (page 42) gives all the signatures we require for his career: the Moon and Venus are conjunct in Scorpio in the 8th House, trine to Jupiter and Pluto exactly on the cusp of the 5th House. Thus the planet which has the greatest significance for public image is utterly and completely tied in to planets of excess, decadence, and pleasure in the houses of sex and lovers and the signs of femininity. Jupiter, the Ascendant ruler, is also in a wide opposition to Mercury and Saturn in Capricorn in the 10th House, indicating publishing (Mercury is natural ruler of communication, is ruler of the 3rd cusp, and is in opposition to Jupiter, lord of the 9th) and business (Saturn is in Capricorn). Patriarchal Saturn's lordship over the publishing enterprise and the presence of the two principle Olympian males, exactly on the fifth cusp, reveals that a standard feminist critique of Guccione's business empire was written into his chart at birth. This is not to say that Guccione is in any way

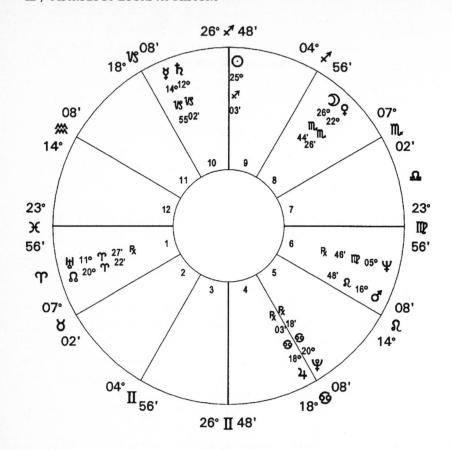

Example 3
Bob Guccione
Dec. 17, 1930 12:00 P.M. EST
Jersey City, New Jersey
74W05 40N44
Placidus Houses

what feminist critics of pornography say he is, but that his chart represents their allegations.

Here then, a speculative chart, set for the birth of an individual, gives us a glimpse into the cultural debates and changes of the last thirty years.

Takes

Time for another theoretical digression into the world of "Takes," an idea developed in the Astrological Lodge in the early 1980s.[6] The phrase was adapted from the world of film in which each scene or shot can be described as a take—as in "Take 1," "Take 2" and so on. In the same way that each shot in a film can reveal a different level of plot or reality, so each interpretation of a horoscope can reveal a different scene. One example, developed by Vernon Wells, drew on the horoscope of Christopher Reeves, the actor who played Superman in the 1980s films. If we look at Reeves as Superman, his horoscope, with Jupiter culminating, does indeed describe a Herculean persona. This is a different matter to looking at the chart as Reeves' own astrologer might, in terms of his psychological processes. The point here is that the horoscope does not carry a fixed set of objectively defined data, but can be used by us to extract the information we need for our own ends. This does not mean that there is no reality in the horoscope, but that we conspire with the astrology to bring out whatever information is relevant and meaningful at the moment, depending on our perspective and prejudices.

The First Known Birth Chart

We can apply the same logic to events in the history of astrology. An excellent example is provided by the first known birth chart, set for April 29, 410 B.C., probably in the region of modern Iraq, south of Baghdad. We have no time for this horoscope, although we know it was cast for the son of Shumar-usa. The surviving reading states only that "things will be good for you, probably in the basis of Saturn's debility, Jupiter and Venus' dignity and the Sun's exaltation."

This is almost certainly not the first birth chart ever cast. It would be astonishing if it were so. However, it is the first known to us, *the first to have survived into our modern astrological consciousness.* Therefore, in line with the proposition that astrological interpretation is based primarily on what we can see, and that the first known instance of any event provides us with a model for all subsequent developments of the same order, this is not just the first

---

6 See Gordon Watson, "Takes and Astrological Interpretation," *Astrology*, 57/4, Winter 1983–4, pp 120–131.

known birth chart. It is, in fact, *the natal horoscope of natal astrology.* This is in a sense a piece of nonsense, for natal astrology is not a person but a concept. This is no problem, however, for astrology is full of non-sense, in that the judicial astrological understanding of the world is derived mainly from reason

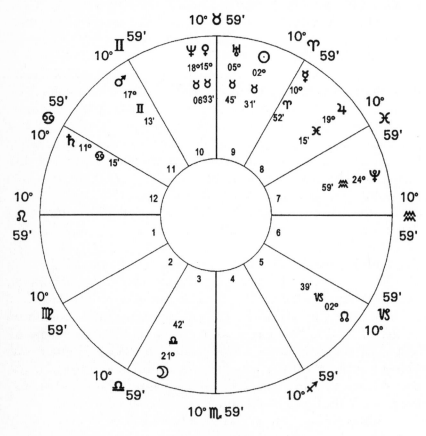

Example 4
First Birth Chart
Apr. 29, −0409* 12:00 P.M. LMT
Baghdad, Iraq
44E25 33N21
Placidus Houses

---

* NOTE: B.C. dates are entered into the computer less one year because there is no "zero" year; i.e., 410 B.C. is entered as −0409; 4004 B.C., −4003, etc.

rather than observation, from thought processes rather than the evidence of the sensual world. [Of course, this first known birth "chart" was preserved in lines of text; without the services of a "cuneiform computer." We present the data here in a circle drawing, which format itself did not come into use until some 2,000 years later! — Ed.]

This horoscope, set for noon and for the assumed coordinates of Baghdad, vividly describes the art and practice of astrology. Indeed, no astrologer could have manufactured more appropriate symbolism. Mercury, Hermes to the Greeks, the lord of wisdom and ancient ruler of astrology, is in an exact square to Saturn, Cronos to the Greeks, and in my opinion related to chronos, or time. The lord of wisdom is therefore linked to time via a quarter division of the zodiac, indicating structure. What does this mean? Only that astrology is the knowledge of time made real; nothing could be more stunningly descriptive. Near the solar Midheaven we find the Sun, the central planet in any modern horoscope, in a tight conjunction with Uranus, the modern ruler of astrology, also culminating. We could go further if we wish: surely Jupiter, symbolizing wealth, dignified in its own sign, Pisces, in the 8th House, representing death, reveals astrology's role as quite possibly the oldest profession, apart from war and prostitution, and as well the astrologer's function as the keeper of the secrets of birth and death.

More astonishing still is this horoscope's ability to reveal through simple transits future developments in the history of astrology. If we look, for example, at recent developments in British astrology, which through the incredible efforts of Alan Leo, restored and transformed astrology across the western world, we find some intriguingly simple contacts.

What sort of man was Leo himself? He was the great popularizer of astrology, dealing in cheap horoscopes (the ancestor of our modern computerised interpretations) on the one hand, and establishing the foundations of twentieth century humanistic, spiritual and psychological astrology on the other. So, if we progress the first horoscope to Leo's birth we should look for lunar contacts, as these indicate popularity. We therefore find that at his birth, on August 7, 1860, the progressed Moon in the 410 B.C. chart, at 8 degrees Scorpio, had passed over the IC (ruling fathers and origins) and was about to form a square to the Ascendant.

There is Alan Leo, the man who took a natal astrology which in substance was still rooted in the mathematical techniques of Claudius Ptolemy, and almost single handedly converted it into its twentieth-century form: even the best, modern Sun sign astrology has adapted Leo's belief that emotions and the internal life matter more than external circumstances.

Let's look very briefly at a few transits. On July 13, 1917, Alan Leo founded the Astrological Lodge, which not only still meets every Monday night in London but is the parent body of almost every British astrological society and school. This moment therefore represents the giving of a permanent structure to British astrology. It is therefore gratifying to find progressed Saturn, representing institutions, at 8 degrees in Cancer closely approaching its return to its 410 position. In addition, the Ascendant at the key moment (7:15 P.M. GMT) was at 5 degrees in Capricorn, in a harmonious trine to this "ancient" Uranus, symbolizing astrology's modern potential: here was Leo the reformer. [Or, as Leo named the planet Uranus, "The Awakener." — Ed.]

Let's do another piece of astrological number-crunching. If we take the 410 Moon (representing public popularity) and progress it to both Leo's birth and his foundation of the Astrological Lodge, the two figures are 8 Scorpio and 14 Scorpio. The midpoint is exactly 11 Scorpio 13, within minutes of arc of a conjunction with the Lodge's MC at 11 Scorpio 35. Thus Leo and the Lodge are brought together with the 410 BC chart in a symbolic trinity.

Another planet which must be examined in the 410 chart is the Moon, the public face. If we look at post-Alan Leo developments in British astrology, we find that both Charles Carter's Moon and the Astrological Association's MC are in a close conjunction with this 410 Moon. The relevance of these contacts has been amply demonstrated. From 1922, when he became President of the Lodge, until his death in 1968, Carter was the towering figure in British astrology, as creative a thinker as Leo and every bit as effective an organiser. The Astrological Association, founded by a group of Lodge members in 1958, was established with the expressed purpose of enhancing astrology's public image: what better way to develop the potential of that 410 Moon?

Urania's Children

The significance of such an approach to astrology is, in my opinion, radical and dramatic. It is, in astrological jargon, Uranian. It moves us away from the assumption that judicial astrology is a science in the sense that there is an objective body of knowledge, existing quite aside from human consciousness, and which we can read and analyse like lab technicians in white coats. Let's be quite clear that this approach to astrology extends beyond that tiny band of researchers who are pursuing statistical investigation into astrology as a whole (including natural astrology), and those who still believe that the rules of judicial astrology themselves constitute a hard science. By this I refer to those people who believe in such simplicities as, for example, the ascendant's ruling physical appearance, devoid of any other factors.

However, I also include as aspiring scientists all those astrologers who are so keen to invent new factors and techniques, from hypothetical planets and asteroids to precession-corrected transits. These additions to astrology are nothing without the human ability to perceive meaning in the world around us, yet I am constantly meeting astrologers who have devised new techniques "which really work." My simple and direct response is that, when dealing with judicial astrology, astrology doesn't work. Let me make that plain: *judicial astrology doesn't work; it's astrologers who work.* In this sense the horoscope usually functions as an ink blot on to which we project our ability to analyse human character and impart meaning to human situations.

However, and this is a very big *however*, there is something out there. Astrology is like a a game of chess with an invisible partner. We set out the board and the rules, make a move, and then find that the pieces are moving themselves, as if by an invisible hand.

To take a simple example, when in September 1994 the asteroid Urania, named after the muse of astrology transited my MC, and Charles Harvey ceremonially handed over to me the Presidency of the Astrological Association, Urania was not causing these events to happen. Urania was named the muse of astrology by the Greeks. The modern asteroid Urania was probably named by an overworked astronomer distributing classical names to insignificant lumps of rock. Yet *there* was the asteroid, culminating in my horoscope when I took over a post which makes me principle representative of British astrology. There were of course other transits as well, connecting myself, Charles and the AA chart in a bizarre triumvirate.

My only conclusion at the time was that we inhabit a series of self-created hallucinations, which come together in a collective delusion, which itself can be observed through the movements of the stars and planets. Not only the stars and planets of course, but also, for most astrologers, in the other parts, points and imaginary factors of judicial astrology. Such a point of view fits well with the philosophy set out by Plato in his great work, *Timaeus,* and which will be well known to anyone who is familiar with Buddhism or Taoism. As I have already set out, Plato's fundamental proposition was that all material forms, the entire physical world of the senses, is derived from, or modeled on, intangible "ideas" emanating from the mind of God. I am arguing here that astrology demonstrates that we are somewhat closer to the realm of Ideas and less rooted in the physical world than we usually imagine. Such is the pressure of daily survival that we overlook the fact that we are creating our own reality in ways which are utterly mysterious, which are to us bizarre and to orthodox scientists incomprehensible.

One book which influenced this way of thinking was Alexandra David-Neal's fascinating work *Magic and Mystery in Tibet,* which I read when I was eighteen, and which gave me much food for thought during my subsequent intense experiments with LSD from 1971–4. David-Neal outlined the practice by which Tibetan Lamas create, though meditation, human-like thought forms, known (if my memory serves me right) as Tulkus. Initially, these are under the control of the creator, but David-Neal described one amusing incident when a Tulku assumed a life of its own and began stealing food and performing an impish Puck-like role. I wish to make no comment on the veracity of this account. However, I did find it thought provoking. It made me aware of the extent to which consciousness and matter interrelate, and it also confirmed my experiences with Christianity when I was thirteen, when I discovered that prayer really does "work": all that's required is faith.

The Creation of the World

The greatest horoscope of all is that for the world, which in the sense the word was used by the ancient Greeks, Jews, and the first Christians, was synonymous with cosmos or universe. I gave a brief summary of these horoscopes in *The Book of World Horoscopes.* The most interesting such chart is set for a moment selected by a non-astrologer, the seventeenth-century theologian Bishop James Ussher. In his *Annals of the World,* published in 1658, Ussher calculated that the Creation commenced at the

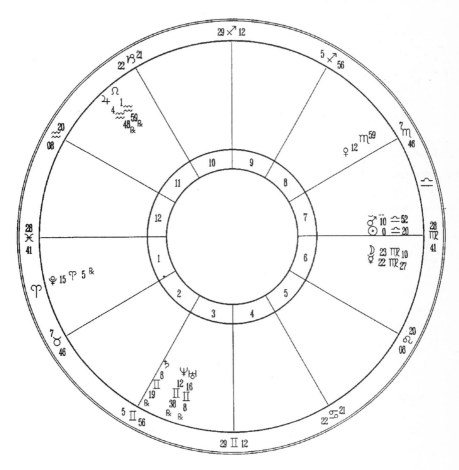

Natal Chart
Creation of the World
Oct. 22, –4003   6:00 P.M. LMT
31N46   35E14

beginning of the night preceding October 23, 4004 B.C., or 6:00
P.M. on the 22nd of October.

To cast a horoscope for this event, we need a set of coordinates for heaven. However, as with time, so with place. If we
don't have a time for a chart we use a solar chart; to find a suitable
location we must follow through the logic of Ussher's own
mythology: if we don't have the latitude and longitude for heav-
en we must therefore find a terrestrial location, and the only fea-
sible option is the Garden of Eden. We don't know where this was
either, so let us assume the Holy Land will do, the capital of
which, of course, is Jerusalem. So, the horoscope for the Creation
should be set for Jerusalem.

This is a wonderfully descriptive horoscope. Let's start with
the MC. This is the degree which rules kings and God, as the king
of kings, is therefore represented by the MC ruler. The MC is at 29
degrees Sagittarius, but according to Ussher's cosmology (he set
the chart for the autumn equinox) the MC should have been zero
Capricorn. This is therefore ruled by Saturn. In other words, the
Christian God is the Greek Cronos, the Roman Saturn, intriguing
in view of the Jew's selection of Saturn's day as their Sabbath.

The pagan gods and goddesses are ruled by the 9th House,
the House of the gods, with Sagittarius on the cusp. Sagittarius is
ruled by Jupiter which is itself in Aquarius, disposited by Saturn,
the ruler of Aquarius. Symbolically then, we see the gods dis-
placed and controled by the one true God. Jupiter, of course, was
also Zeus, the chief Olympian deity.

God, Saturn, is himself in the 3rd House and in Gemini, the
House and sign of ideas. Is this the terrible god of the Old Testament or the kabalistic and Platonic god, initiating the Creation by
the very process of having a thought? Yet, he was retrograde, and
before long his plan came unstuck: the creation was imperfect,
containing the seeds of its own destruction and eventually its
highest pinnacle, man, had to be expelled. However, when he
turns direct he will come into a conjunction with Neptune and
Uranus, two of the planets whose cycles measure the fundamental seed moments of history, when new ideas come into consciousness.

Where is the feminine? Where is Eve? She is obviously
Venus, the planet of Inanna/Ishtar, the supreme goddess of the
Babylonian astrologers, whose chief festival commemorated her

descent to the underworld to rescue her dead lover, Dumuzi, a prototype of Christ. There she is in the cusp of the 8th House of death, in Scorpio, the sign of death. There is Eve, who with Adam, within the teaching, incited the loss of innocence, the origin of guilt, and the fall from grace. Paradise was brought to an end. There is also Mary Magdalene, the lover, spiritual or physical, of Christ; like Inanna, a sacred whore, the all-knowing woman.

If we return for a moment to Saturn, God, we see that he is disposited by Mercury. Mercury is, of course Hermes, the teacher of wisdom and of the esoteric lore of the Hellenistic world, on which all subsequent astrological traditions are based. Mercury is strong, in his own sign, Virgo, and is conjoined with the Moon, herself in classical mythology the representative of heavenly motherhood. This is astonishing symbolism, as the Moon in Virgo becomes the Virgin, Mary the Mother of God, Queen of Heaven, the great goddess of Catholic mythology. And here is Hermes, the teacher of wisdom, perfecting a celestial marriage, a coniunctio, with the Queen of Heaven. What do we have here? Gnosticism?

This probability leads us on to another profound conclusion. According to the Gnostics, the world was created by the god of the Jews, who himself was a somewhat malicious junior divinity, distinctly inferior to the supreme creator. The supreme creator himself, a figure identical to Plato's God or the Buddhists' supreme consciousness, was the source of good and the origin of the consciousness, the Ideas, which animate the physical world. So, in Ussher's creation Saturn, disposited by Mercury, becomes the inferior god who himself came into existence some way down the process of creation. Thus from our modern perspective, Ussher had built into his Creation the gnostic and feminist alternatives to the dogmatic patriarchal conservatism of the mainstream Catholic churches. This is my "Take" on this chart.

Let's go on and look at some recent transits over this chart. The most striking modern transit was the conjunction of Neptune and Pluto in Gemini in the 1890s, and the opposition from Uranus in Sagittarius. This alignment saw one of the greatest cultural revolutions in Europe since the revolution, quite possibly the greatest. If we take the whole period of 1890 to 1905 as that covered by the conjunction, the world witnessed specifically Gemini-Sagittarius developments in communications technology such as the first commercial manufacture of the motor car and the first powered flight. If such conjunctions denote shifts in international relations, it described the British Empire's traumatic encounter with its "Vietnam" in the Boer War and the United States' ascent to imperial power in its conquest of Cuba and the Philippines. In the arts, modernism became the dominant force.

Yet, if we are thinking of the Creation chart, and its religious significance, our minds focus on Freud and Einstein, both of whom developed their initial ideas under this alignment, and between them, through psychoanalysis and relativity, revolution-ized our understanding of inner and outer space. Indeed, it has been said of Freud that he killed God, while in Einstein's relative universe heaven can no longer be "up there."

To move on to the 1960s and the prolonged Uranus-Pluto conjunction in Virgo which symbolized that decade's cultural upheavals, we can see a deepening of the humanistic perspective, and the shift away from God. The New Age movement took deeper roots than ever, spreading the theosophical notion of a dis-tant creator and a universal religious truth. Psychotherapy and counseling became almost universally recognized ways of finding the cause of personal ills in the personality rather than in God or morality. And finally, the sexual revolution of the early sixties had, by 1969, laid the foundations of a new wave of feminism, which in turn led in the early nineties to the widespread success of a new feminist theology, mainly in the protestant churches. By 1994, even the conservative Church of England had ordained woman priests.

But is all this no more than sloppy horoscope interpretation of the anything-can-mean-anything variety? The way to bypass such poor astrology and maintain rigour is by using accurately timed events: not rectified times but times taken from the records. For example, we can check the horoscope for the ordination of the first woman priest by the Church of England, the moment at which the most institutionally conservative bastion of Protes-tantism succumbed decisively to the new theology. This event took place at 5:56:57 P.M. GMT on March 12, 1994 in Bristol, with 19 degrees Virgo on the Ascendant opposing the Creation Moon, which was therefore rising at the moment the bishop laid his hands on the first woman. The symbolism is clear and unmis-takeable: the goddess was rising.

A few hours earlier there had been a New Moon, as the Sun and the Moon, the great masculine and feminine powers of classical astrology, met to begin a new monthly cycle. This New Moon took place at 21 degrees and 29 minutes Pisces, within one minute of arc of opposition of the Creation Moon (as calculated by Astro-Computing services) at 29 degrees and 30 minutes Virgo [Here, calculated by AIR Software at 23 Virgo 10. — Ed.]. In addition, 1993's Uranus-Neptune conjunction in Capricorn had trined the Creation Moon, liberating the female promise of the Creation chart. We thus find both the long and short-term transits necessary to indicate *a precise event arising out of a religious reading on the Creation chart.* Yet the Creation chart is set for a fictitious moment, created by Ussher's literal biblical mythology.[7]

What, then, gives the horoscope set for Ussher's Creation moment its force? The only answer is faith. Ussher, ironically motivated by the new belief in scientific chronology, believed devoutly that he had calculated the objective moment at which the creation began. His dating was then incorporated in many bibles and has entered evangelical Christian mythology. It is precisely this chronology which is accepted by the Creationists, those fundamentalist Christians who accept Genesis at face value. From myth flows belief, and from belief flows a remarkable ability to pinpoint moments which, according to the rules of astrology, are symbolically meaningful. Just as astrologers must trust their data, so Christians must have faith in their dogma. In the horoscope for Ussher's moment, the two versions of subjective, collective truth coincide.

A Modern Myth: Jack the Ripper

I would now like to move from the political and universal to the particular and personal. One of the questions which has long preoccupied me is the overlap between natal and mundane astrology in the problem of what makes some people famous. Why should some people be brought before the public eye while others remain, either voluntarily or against their will, in obscurity. Some become famous through skill. Others are born famous.

---

7   Actually Ussher was interested in history-as-it-was, rather than history-as-it-should-have-been, and his chronology was designed to move historical studies on to a more objective basis, using the literary evidence of the Old Testament.

Some are just in the right place at the right time, and others are thrust into the limelight against their will, and through the force of circumstances. Equally important to me is why certain historical characters are mythologised, taking on the character of fairy tale or legendary beings. The deification of Marylin Monroe and Bridget Bardot as Venus types is an obvious example. Looking at the dark side of history, in these times of serial killers, one of the most feared murderers of all times was Jack the Ripper.

One of the publishing sensations of late 1993 was the release of *The Diary of Jack the Ripper*, a transcript purporting to be the journals of the Ripper himself, as part of a book by Shirley Harrison. The diary itself is a sixty-five page handwritten document which had been lost for 105 years until rediscovered a few years ago. Argument rages as to whether it is genuine or a forgery.[8]

According to this new account, the Ripper was a Liverpool-based cotton broker, James Maybrick. The circumstantial evidence making Maybrick a possible suspect is strong. Most convincing of all, in my opinion, is the fact that the Ripper diaries (learning from the embarrassing experience of the Hitler diaries) have been subjected to extraordinarily rigorous forensic analysis. I was given Maybrick's data, together with those for the five Ripper murders, by Shirley Harrison, in order to offer an astrological opinion. Could Maybrick be the Ripper, the man whose five bestial murders terrorized the East End of London in 1888 and which have since been a bench mark for savagery? To this day, images of Victorian London, with its dark alleys and swirling fog, are seldom complete without some reminder of the Ripper.

Maybrick was a womanizer and drug addict with a history of violence, and he regularly patronized brothels on his visits to cotton ports around the world. Although born in Liverpool, he moved to London at the age of twenty and married before returning north. One of his brothers lived in London at the time of the Ripper killings, and as a cotton merchant he would have made frequent trips to the metropolis. The abrupt end of the Ripper's reign of terror could be explained by his sudden death in July 1889. His wife, Florence, was put on trial, accused of poisoning

---

8 Finally, in July 1994, the alleged forger, Michael Barrett, was exposed by *The Sunday Times* (July 3, 1994). Barrett, though, was just one of a number of people involved in generating the Maybrick-Ripper mythology.

him. She was tried at St. George's Hall, Liverpool, and sentenced to death. However, after a public outcry over conflicting evidence, her sentence was commuted to life imprisonment. She was released in 1904 and moved to the United States, where she wrote her autobiography. Eventually, she died alone and in poverty in Arizona, in 1941.

I realize that there is an extensive literature on astrology and murder, some of which covers the Ripper case. My concern here, though, is solely with Maybrick.

Maybrick's Horoscope

Maybrick was born in Liverpool on October 24, 1838, with the Sun in Scorpio and the Moon in Capricorn, indicating the broadly conservative tendencies appropriate to a well-to-do Liverpool tradesman. Unfortunately we have no record of his time of birth and we are therefore unable to calculate his Ascendant or house cusps. If in doubt I always work with a Solar chart cast for noon, although in this case I didn't feel that the noon cusps were particularly significant.

However, I always look for connections between horoscopes of individuals of similar reputations. It is then, an interesting fact that the Sun at Maybrick's birth occupied almost precisely the degree and minute axis of the zodiac occupied by Hitler's Sun (0 Taurus 48). This is not in itself unusual, although the coincidence develops strongly if we cast Maybrick's horoscope for noon. In this case, as well, we find that Maybrick's Moon conjoined Hitler's Moon (6 Capricorn 38). This connection between the serial killer and the mass murderer offers a symbolic clue that we are on the right track in our suspicions that Maybrick may have been the Ripper.

We should also examine Maybrick's horoscope for indications of exposure to violence. In the first instance, we should check for difficult alignments between the Sun and Moon on the one hand, and Mars, Saturn, Uranus, and Pluto on the other. These four planets, each in its own manner, represent the possibility of violence. In the horoscopes of violent individuals, we would expect them to occur in combination with each other and the Sun and Moon, either in the same degree of the zodiac or separated by either 90 or 180 degrees. In Maybrick's horoscope, no such combination occurs. In addition, due to the uncertainty surrounding his birth time, we are unable to check whether the four planets of violence made the appropriate contacts to the ascending or culminating degrees. Our initial scan of Maybrick's horoscope is therefore not encouraging.

The next step is to analyze the planets of sexual attraction, Venus and Mars. We find here that both are making appropriate alignments. Mars is in a square with Saturn, indicating the threat of violence. However, this alignment is not uncommon and is not sufficiently powerful to suggest that Maybrick was a perpetrator of violent crimes. Venus, however, is very striking, being in a very tight opposition with Pluto, changing the picture quite dramati-

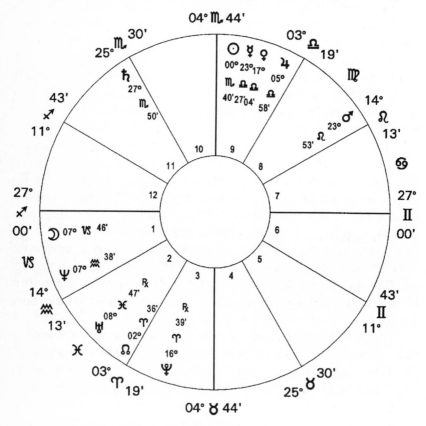

James Maybrick
Oct. 24, 1838 12:00 P.M. LMT
Liverpool, England
02W55 53N25
Placidus Houses

cally. Venus is the symbol of the maiden, while Pluto, in classical mythology was the underworld God who abducted Persephone, a goddess closely associated with Venus. There could be no more powerful evocation than this of the Ripper myth within Maybrick's horoscope, and here we find one of the key astrological symbols of sexual violence. It is well worth quoting extensively on the matter from Liz Greene's *The Astrology of Fate,* chapter 3, "The Astrological Pluto":

> Whenever myth portrays his (Pluto's) entry into the upper world, he is shown persistently acting out one scenario: rape ... Its (Pluto's) intrusion into consciousness feels like a violation, and we, like Persephone, the maiden of the myth, are powerless to resist. Where Pluto is encountered there is often a sense of violent penetration, unwished for yet unavoidable.

Later, Liz discusses the psychological complexes indicated by the astrological alignment of Venus and Pluto at birth. These offer a fascinating insight into Maybrick's personality and the pressures which may have compelled him toward his violent actions. Describing Pluto as the "destroyer rapist," she discusses the dilemmas which occur when Pluto brings its emotional power to the subtle femininity represented by Venus:

> Something or someone is *trying to dismember* the very thing one values and cherishes the most. I believe that this destroyer, which is inherent in the psyche of the individual who is born with Venus-Pluto, is not really intent upon wanton ruin. Perhaps it is intent upon self-revelation, or a discovery of the underworld of one's own emotions ... Only the Olympians can claim goodness and perfection, and even they cannot claim it all the time. What is incarnate is flawed, and shares in the violence and darkness of nature. Rather than accept this, Venus-Pluto will more often try to blame the partner for this fated intrusion into idealised love. One imagines that one sees in the other, male or female, the shadowy woman with the "soul-freezing eyes." It is not that Venus-Pluto is incapable of the gentler face of love, but this comes at a price. *Here fate often intrudes upon love, frequently in the form of an obsessive sexual passion or the breakdown of the sexual relationship between two people* [my italics].

Liz's remarkable analysis of the psychological complexes represented by Maybrick's Venus-Pluto alignment confirm that, even if he was not the Ripper, at least he is an appropriate suspect. She comes remarkably close to proving Maybrick's murderous potential when she concludes that, for the Venus-Pluto individual, death can often be perceived as a variant on sexual initiation.

However, let us draw back from the question of whether Maybrick was or was not the Ripper. We do not and may never know the truth of these allegations. This is not important. What we do know is that he has been accused of the murders, and just as mud sticks, so he will always be associated with them. His name will probably never be cleared. Therefore, regardless of his previous history, he is now, and will forever remain, linked to the mythical person of Jack, the Ripper.

Therefore, Maybrick's horoscope should reveal *his incorporation into Ripper mythology,* and that is what his Venus-Pluto opposition is telling us. This is our "Take" on his chart. Not everyone with Venus-Pluto oppositions is a murderer. That would be a ridiculous claim. Yet we are concerned with Maybrick alone, and our "Take" on him is as a potential Jack, the Ripper. We are not therefore, looking at absolute truth, but at relative truth.

The Ripper Murders

Let us continue though, with the allegation that Maybrick was the Ripper. The essence of any astrological investigation is timing, and if Maybrick is to be accused of the Ripper murders it is necessary that his Mars-Saturn and Venus-Pluto alignments themselves be powerfully aspected by the planets on the night of the first murder. The Ripper's first victim, Mary Ann Nichols, was murdered at 3:00 A.M. on August 31, 1888. Intriguingly, at this moment, Maybrick's Mars-Saturn alignment was indeed powerfully aspected, and the following pattern is apparent:

- Maybrick's birth: Saturn 28 degrees in Scorpio, Mars 23 degrees in Leo

- Mary Ann Nichols Murder: Jupiter 29 degrees in Scorpio, Mars 23 degrees in Scorpio.

Jupiter's involvement represents an exaggeration of Maybrick's basic disposition, and under such alignments his violent tendencies were at a peak. Saturn was not implicated in this pattern, although if we are to pursue the Hitler connection, this planet, considered by ancient astrologers the most unfortunate of all possible influences, had reached exactly the same degree of the zodiac it occupied at Hitler's birth (13 Leo 28). Such coincidences do not tell us that Maybrick was the Ripper, but they do suggest that there may be a common mythology of evil, indicated in certain common planetary positions and connecting the Ripper murders with Hitler's holocaust.

Also, at Nichols' murder, Uranus, at 15 degrees in Libra, had come to the conjunction with Maybrick's natal Venus, and was opposing his natal Pluto. Uranus destabilizes already uncertain situations and is closely associated with erratic and uncontrollable events. We may therefore conclude that Maybrick's psychological obsession with death and sexual initiation was likely to be expressed in a shocking manner. Combine this with the violence of his Mars-Saturn alignment, and we have powerful evidence that, on the night of Mary Ann Nichols' murder, *Maybrick was primed to commit a violent act.* The circumstantial evidence of the horoscopes for his birth and the first murder offer powerful testimony in support of Maybrick's guilt.

There was one other important alignment at Nichols' murder which, at first sight, bore little relationship to Maybrick's horoscope. This was a square between the Moon at 25 degrees in Gemini and Venus at 22 degrees in Virgo. Psychologically this pattern is indicative of extremely unstable emotions, bordering on hysteria. However, both Gemini and Virgo are analytical signs which find it difficult to express feelings. They are more likely to conceive a rational plan by which pent-up emotions may be expressed through practical action. Symbolically, Venus in Virgo represents the maiden, and the Moon represents the mother. Both are therefore female planets. The alignment between them was separating, and therefore growing weaker, but would have been exact about 9:00 P.M. on the previous evening, perhaps around the time when the Ripper was preparing his first murder.

Midpoints

The next level of analysis after examination of Maybrick's planetary configurations requires inspection of his planetary midpoints. We would expect Maybrick's Mars-Saturn and Venus-

Pluto midpoints to be heavily implicated in the horoscopes for the Ripper murders. The fact that they are not weakens the case against Maybrick. However, two of his midpoints are noticeable for the connections they formed with the Moon-Venus alignment on the night of Nichols' murder. These were his Mars-Pluto midpoint, symbolizing the possibility of confrontational violence, and his Venus-Mars midpoint, signifying sexual passion in its positive form and assault in its negative.

At Nichols' murder *the Moon had just passed over Maybrick's Mars-Pluto midpoint,* indicating confrontational violence, *while Venus had just passed over his Venus-Mars midpoint,* indicating the potential for sexual assault. The alignments we find are perfectly clear:

- Maybrick's Mars-Pluto midpoint = 20 degrees in Gemini
- Nichols' murder Moon = 25 degrees in Gemini
- Maybrick's Venus-Mars Midpoint = 20 degrees in Virgo
- Nichols' murder Venus = 22 degrees in Virgo

Astrology cannot prove that Maybrick was the Ripper, but it can demonstrate conclusively that his "personal mythology" corresponded closely with the images of profound sexual violence which lie at the heart of the Ripper myth. When we enter the realm of myth, we begin to encounter a field of consciousness which operates independently of the usual limitations of biological time. Therefore, in order to take the mythological investigation further, we need to move away from an astrology based on actual planetary measurements to a metaphysical astrology reliant on symbolic measures.

Secondary Progressions

If we want to ascertain Maybrick's deeper state of consciousness, or perhaps unconsciousness in 1888, his fiftieth year, we should examine his planetary configurations for the fiftieth day of his life. Astonishingly, we find that on December 13, 1838, symbolically the fiftieth year of Maybrick's life, it was his potentially violent Venus-Mars and Mars-Pluto (so striking on the night of Nichols' murder) which were most powerfully aligned. These midpoints were located at 20 degrees Gemini and Virgo. It so happens that the most powerful planetary alignment on the fiftieth "day" of Maybrick's life, corresponding to his deepest psychological cycles in this fiftieth year, were as follows:

- Sun 21 degrees in Sagittarius
- Venus 21 degrees in Sagittarius
- Mars 19 degrees in Virgo

Each of these progressed planets closely aligned Maybrick's potentially violent midpoints. Once again we find Mars and Venus, the planets of sexual power, closely connected.

The Yorkshire Ripper

Whether Maybrick was the Ripper or not, his horoscope repeatedly describes psychological complexes *appropriate to the Ripper.* The strangest coincidences though, occur when we enter the realms of metaphysical speculation, for it's here that we begin to come closest to the undying mythology of the Ripper, the ultimate male murderer of women. From a twentieth-century perspective, the Ripper is no longer a flesh and blood man, but a larger than life character, a being of demonic myth, still capable of inspiring fascination and fear.

The important question then, is does Maybrick's horoscope (page 56) still possess an archetypal resonance, and can this be ascertained by examination of more recent crimes? The final bizarre twist occurs when we take Maybrick's horoscope forward to October 30, 1975, the date of the first murder committed by Peter Sutcliffe, the notorious "Yorkshire Ripper." In a perverse sense, Sutcliffe was the Ripper's spiritual heir. He terrorized Yorkshire, in the north of England, in the late 1970s, committing savage murders on women who either were, or whom he thought might as well have been prostitutes.

First we find a number of planetary coincidences. For example, transiting Venus had returned to the same degree of the zodiac as at Nichols' murder, 20 degrees in Virgo. However, most astonishing is the repetition seen in Maybrick's progressions. When Sutcliffe committed *his* first murder, Maybrick's positions (see page 62) had reached exact and close alignments with those measurements for the first Ripper's murder:

- Sun 20 degrees in Pisces, in a 90 degrees separation from the progressed Sun at Nichols' murder.

- Mars 22 degrees in Virgo, within 3 degrees of progressed Mars at Nichols' murder.

This is a truly astonishing coincidence, as if Maybrick's horoscope was not only appropriate for the first Ripper but for the second as well! It's almost as if the spirit of the Ripper were alive and well in Peter Sutcliffe when *he* savaged *his* victims. Perhaps, to take a different approach, both Sutcliffe and Maybrick *had locked into the same psychological archetype via common astrological configurations*. Maybrick's horoscope confirms that he may reasonably be considered a prime suspect. Either that or the very fact that he has been accused, even though innocent, tells us something about the nature of sexual crime.

Conclusion

I have discussed my theories concerning history, myth and rectification throughout this essay, so I do not wish to repeat myself here. It is clear though, that horoscopes can be set for moments defined not by external events, but by the imagination. It is equally clear that the rules of astrology, tied to the measurable motions of celestial phenomena, can apply equally to such moments as to such objective moments as birth. It is absolutely necessary to distinguish judicial astrology, in which the astrologer's judgment is the main focus, from natural astrology, in which we are concerned with natural cycles, physical phenomena and the question of celestial "influences" or "effects." The two forms of astrology overlap, for they use the same language, but we must be clear that judicial astrology, relying on the astrologer's interpretative skills, is largely a function of the imagination. After all, the astrologer is being called upon to impart meaning to past events, predict future ones and empathise with the clients' situation. What do these acts require if not imagination? Here we must assume that we are moving away from a world in which all is certain to one in which all is bizarre and uncertain. The curious fact about astrology is that it functions as well in the realm of the subjective as in the objective.

The rectification of history, the chronicling of events according to how they should have happened rather than how they actually happened is a central feature of the great classical histories which were written at a time when astrology was widely accepted. Modern history is written, not always successfully, from a different perspective, attempting to comment on and record the past as it actually happened. Modern astrology is the product of both traditions, having been influenced by the modern trend, but remaining devoted to the second. The confusion between the two is what has given rise to the modern belief that natal horoscopes can be routinely rectified to discover a more objectively accurate time of birth. This is a thought that would never have occurred to one of the great astrologers of the Islamic world. They understood the gap between the horoscope and event, so that, for example, Masha Allah was not concerned with Mohammed's natal chart. Instead he examined the horoscope for the Sun's entry into Aries prior to the Jupiter-Saturn conjunction which preceded the prophet's birth. In other words, *he used the most appropriate horoscope.*

Therefore astrological rectification is a quest not for the objectively accurate but for the appropriate and meaningful. The question when rectifying horoscopes is not "can I find the true time at which an event occurred?" but "can I find a horoscope from which I can extract meaning?" The astrologer who pursues this line of inquiry can not avoid imposing his or her own preconceptions on the process, but should also attempt to stand back and let the universe speak for itself. There is something very big and very weird lurking out there, and, at present, only astrology presents us with an adequate means of describing it. One thing *is* certain, though: if we rely on an astrology which we imagine to be real, objective, external, and having nothing to do with our internal imaginative processes, we will miss the point.

Data for the Ripper Murders:

Mary Ann Nichols, 3:00 A.M., 31 August 1888
Annie Chapman, 5–6:00 A.M., 8 September 1888
Elizabeth Stride, 12:35–12:55 A.M., 30 September 1888
Catherine Eddowes, 1:30–1:45 A.M., 30 September 1888
Mary Kelly, 3:30–4:00 A.M., 9 November 1888

All murders took place in Whitechapel in the East End of London. All data supplied to Nick Campion by Shirley Harrison from official records.

Maurice McCann

Maurice McCann was born in Ireland. He is a member of the Irish Astrological Association and the Astrological Lodge of London, for which he has served as Chairman and Treasurer. He is also a member of the Astrological Association, NCGR, and the AFA in the United States.

Maurice (pronounced "Morris") has a BA (Hons) in the history of Astrology and has been co-principal of the Meonen School with Derek Appleby, with whom he co-wrote *Eclipses—The Power Points of Astrology.* The Meonen School is a correspondence course in horary astrology. His articles have appeared in *Réalta,* the magazine of the Irish Astrological Association; *Stjernerne,* the Danish astrological magazine; *Astrology Quarterly* and *The Astrological Journal,* the English magazines; and the American *Aspects, The Mercury Hour,* and *The Horary Review.*

Maurice has lectured, taught, and held seminars in England, Denmark, Ireland, Italy, and the United States. At present, he is devising a computer program for horary astrology and is also in the process of writing a book on timing in horary astrology.

Maurice McCann

Shakespeare's Time to Be

 Almost nothing is known about the personality of William Shakespeare, history's most celebrated poet and playwright. He left no private papers, no diaries, no letters revealing his inner thoughts or supplying us with clues to his true character. No trace of his original manuscripts has ever been uncovered. Until recently, evidence of Shakespeare the man was tied to six signatures on perfunctory legal documents, each signature differing from the other! For over three centuries, dedicated scholars around the world have searched in vain to unearth any fragments of paper—literally!—that would unveil the character and personality of this extraordinary man. No fresh material has yet appeared and the mystery surrounding his life continues.

Tradition has it that Shakespeare was born on Sunday the 23rd of April, 1564. However the birth could easily have been a day or two earlier than the 23rd, or indeed later. The parish registrar did record Shakespeare's baptism on the 26th of April, 1564. The Prayer Book's recommended interval for a child born on a Friday, Saturday, or Sunday to be baptized was the following Wednesday. It was the normal custom for babies to be baptized within three days of their birth, as infant mortality was high. The baptism date of the 26th established the tradition of birth on the 23rd. Furthermore, there were two romantic reasons for deciding on the 23rd of April: the first that it was the feast of St. George, the patron saint of England, and the second that it was on that date that Shakespeare died in 1616.

Needless to say, the task of calculating and delineating Shakespeare's horoscope was a complex challenge because of the lack of personal details.

Many tales and myths have been created about Shakespeare, and many still persist today.

John Aubrey (1626–97), while gathering information in Stratford sixty-five years after Shakespeare's death, was under the impression that Shakespeare's father was a butcher. He wrote that "his father was a butcher, and I have been told heretofore by some of the neighbours that when he was a boy he exercised his father's trade, but when he killed a calf he would do it in a high style and make a speech."

In fact, Shakespeare's father was a glover and dealer in wool. Research has since shown that the calf referred to by Aubrey was nothing more than part of local tradition. It seems that on public holidays a pasteboard head of a calf was thrust out between the curtains of the local theatre while behind it somebody mooed and bellowed and insulted the audience. Some spirited lad would then confront this calf with a wooden sword and enter into a contest of wit and abuse and finally cut off its head. It may well have been that young Shakespeare defended the audience in this theatrical entertainment and earned himself a reputation as something of a speech maker and wit.

Aubrey was notoriously unreliable and very often recorded local gossip and rumours as fact without checking their authenticity. Anthony Wood (b. December 17, 1632, Oxford; d. November 29, 1695) called Aubrey a "pretender to antiquities, roving, magotie-headed and sometimes little better than crased." Wood added that, "being exceedingly credulous," Aubrey would fill his letters with "folliries and misinformations." Aubrey's references to Shakespeare should therefore not be taken too seriously.

Another story surrounding the life of young Shakespeare states that he had to leave Stratford because he ran afoul of the local Justice of the Peace. It said that he and some local lads had stolen deer from Sir Thomas Lucy's park at Charlecote. However, there was no deer park at Charlecote at that time.

One other tale which did gain credibility was that Shakespeare's first employment on reaching London was to take care of the horses outside the playhouse while their owners attended the play. He became so popular with these theatre goers that he took on the responsibility of holding the reins of more and more horses. Eventually he had to employ several lads when his business became more than he could handle. Shakespearean scholars today tend to dismiss this story as a piece of unproven hearsay.

According to Aubrey, Shakespeare started his career in London as a member of Strange's men, an acting company which employed Christopher Beeston. Beeston became friendly with Shakespeare and acted with him in a number of plays and would have been familiar with the facts concerning Shakespeare's early career. It was Beeston's son, William, who later furnished Aubrey with tales of Shakespeare's early days in the theatre. It is true that Shakespeare and Beeston the elder appeared on stage together in Ben Jonson's play, *Everyman in His Humour*, in 1595. Beeston might well have had reliable information about Shakespeare's early career and eventual success.

Aubrey wrote that Beeston the elder claimed that Shakespeare had been a teacher for some time before becoming an actor. Although there was no hard evidence to support this view, since it was a second-hand account, it did not stop Aubrey from believing that Shakespeare had for some time been a schoolmaster. He wrote "though as Ben Jonson says of him, that he had but little Latin and less Greek"; and Aubrey added, "he understood Latin pretty well, for he had been in his younger years a schoolmaster in the country."

Another story concerning Shakespeare was discovered in a diary kept by John Mannington, a law student at the Middle Temple who heard it from another student named Edward Curle. Mannington reported that while acting in "Richard III" with Burbage in the title role, Shakespeare overheard Burbage and a pretty woman arrange a liaison. Burbage was to go to her house after the performance and knock three times on the door saying "It is I, Richard the Third." Shakespeare quickly left the theatre and followed her home and, using Burbage's signal, gained access, and, although she was surprised to see him and not Burbage, the woman made him welcome. Later when Burbage arrived and gave the pre-arranged signal, Shakespeare "with some relish returned word that William the Conqueror preceded

Richard the Third!" It would be unwise to attempt to gain an understanding of Shakespeare's character from this piece of gossip, but it does in some small way serve to show the interest that theatre lovers took in the lives of their actor heroes.

The first real evidence that Shakespeare was beginning to make a name for himself in the London theatre was in a censure made on him by a fellow playwright in September 1592. Robert Greene (1560–1592) warned his fellow dramatists against "those Puppets ... that spake from our mouths." He was seriously ill and in great poverty when he wrote a pamphlet entitled *A Groatsworth of Wit*, in which he railed against several playwrights, though his reasons for doing so were never very clear.

> ... yet trust them not: for there is an upstart Crow, beautified with our feathers, that with his Tiger's heart wrapped in a player's hide supposes he is as well able to bombast out a blank verse as the best of you: and being an absolute Johannes factotum, is in his own conceit the only Shake-scene in a country.

This quotation was a parody of one of Shakespeare's lines from *King Henry VI:*

O tiger's heart, wrapp'd in a woman's hide![1]

The reference to Shake-scene can only mean Shakespeare, who obviously was beginning to emerge as an important and popular figure in the theatre world at that time. These angry allusions are important as they affirm that Shakespeare had a number of works to his credit by September 1592 (at age 28). By June of that year, the theatres had been closed by an outbreak of plague, so *Henry VI*, Part 3 must have been on stage for some time before that date. Furthermore, since it is the third and final part of a trilogy, parts 1 and 2 must have been written in 1591, perhaps begun in 1590. He had already written one tragedy, *Titus Andronicus* which was every bit as popular as the Henry plays, two histories, *King John* and *Richard III*, three comedies, *The Comedy of Errors, The Taming of the Shrew,* and *The Two Gentlemen of Verona.*

---

1 *King Henry VI,* part III I, iv.

Thomas Nashe (b. 1567, Lowestoft, Suffolk, England; d. ?1601, Yarmouth, Norfolk.), a fellow playwright, described Greene's diatribe as a "scald, trivial, lying pamphlet."

A month or two after Greene's death, his publisher, Henry Chettle, was obliged to issue an apology to Shakespeare for having printed the *Groats-worth*. Chettle wrote in the epistle to *Kind-Heart's Dreame* (1593): "I am as sorry as if the original fault had been my fault, because myself have seen his demeanour no less civil than be excellent in the quality he professes: Besides, divers of worship have reported his uprightness of dealing which argues his honesty, and his facetious grace in writing, that approves his art." A great amount of information could possibly be deduced about Shakespeare's personal reputation from the above comments. Although, it should be made clear that Chettle had come under pressure from a number of powerful people, "divers of worship," and may have only said what he did in order to please them and redeem himself.

On a number of occasions Ben Jonson (1573–1637), the celebrated English dramatist and poet, paid tribute to Shakespeare. "I loved the man and do honour his memory on this side idolatry." He referred to him as the "Sweet Swan of Avon" and commented that "he was not of an age but for all time."

It was also said that his contemporaries spoke of Shakespeare as being a well-mannered, good-tempered man, open and reliable in his relationships with acquaintances, friends and colleagues, at ease in all the varied social groups into which his professional and his personal activities took him.

Heminge and Condell, in the foreword to the First Folio which contained thirty-six of Shakespeare's plays and was published after his death, announced that "His hand and mind went together: And what he thought, he uttered with that easiness that we have scarce received from him a blot in his papers."

Ben Jonson also wrote that a number of players had mentioned that Shakespeare never blotted out a line. "Would he had blotted a thousand," added Jonson, perhaps jokingly, and not intended in the hostile manner in which it was first believed to have been expressed. Jonson made several remarks that could be interpreted today as disparaging toward Shakespeare, but it seems that Shakespeare rarely took offense at anything Jonson had tc say.

Shakespeare's Attitude to Astrology

It is said that there are over one hundred references to astrology in Shakespeare's works. This has led many people to assume wrongly that Shakespeare was a practising astrologer, or that he had more than just a passing interest in the subject. The truth is that, in Shakespeare's day, the general public had a very good understanding of the basics of astrology, and the majority of literate people could read technical astrological judgments with ease. The seventeenth-century English astrologer William Lilly made this clear when he continually published several horoscope judgments annually in his almanacs which sold in the thousands, knowing that his readers would fully understand what was written.

The late astrologer, John Addey, was convinced that Shakespeare believed in the probity of astrology and that he had demonstrated his belief through two sets of characters throughout his plays. First there were those who supported astrology and the universal order and were on the side of righteousness, and second, there were those who believed that man is the sole arbiter of his destiny and could do as he pleased, whatever the consequences.

In *Troilus and Cressida*, Ulysses asks Agamemnon to "hear what Ulysses speaks," in a speech which demonstrates Shakespeare's steadfast belief in a divinely established order:

> The heavens themselves, the planets and this centre,
> Observe degree, priority and place,
> Insisture, course, proportion, season, form,
> Office and custom, in all line of order:
> And therefore is the glorious planet Sol
> In noble eminence enthroned and sphered
> Amidst the other; whose medicinable eye
> Corrects the ill aspects of planets evil,
> And posts like the commandment of a king,
> Sans check, to good and bad: but when the planets
> In evil mixture to disorder wander,
> What plagues and what portents, what mutiny,
> What raging of the sea, shaking of earth,
> Commotion in the winds, frights, changes, horrors,
> Divert and crack, rend and deracinate
> The unity and married calm of states
> Quite from their fixture! O, when degree is shaked,

Which is the ladder to all high designs,
The enterprise is sick! How could communities,
Degrees in schools and brotherhoods in cities,
Peaceful commerce from dividable shores,
The primogenitive and due of birth,
Prerogative of age, crowns, sceptres, laurels,
but by degree, stand in authentic place?
Take but degree away, untune that string,
And, hark, what discord follows ... [2]

Throughout the plays, many of the most admirable and sympathetic characters promote this view and often use astrological terms to declare their belief in cosmic harmony and order.

On the other hand, the opposite opinion, that everyone has unrestricted freedom to do as one pleases and a duty to further one's own selfish interests, was expounded by Edmund, Gloucester's illegitimate son in *King Lear* (Act 1, scene ii). As in most of his plays, Shakespeare used an old theatrical trick to present his characters. When characters first appeared on stage, usually alone, they would pronounce about their own nature by way of introducing themselves to the audience:

This is the excellent foppery of the world, that when
we are sick in fortune, Often the surfeit of our own
behaviour, we make guilty of our disasters the sun, the
moon and the stars: as if we were villains by necessity,
fools by heavenly compulsion; knaves, thieves and
treachers, by spherical predominance;
drunkards, liars and adulterers, by an enforced
obedience of planetary influence; and all that we are
evil in, by a divine thrusting on: an admirable evasion
of whoremaster man, to lay his goatish disposition to
the charge of a star! My father compounded with my
mother under the dragon's tail, and my nativity was
under Ursa major; so that it follows I am rough and
lecherous. Tut, I should have been that I am, had the
maidenliest star in the firmament twinkled on my
bastardizing.[3]

---

2 *Troilus and Cressida*, Act 1, scene iii.

3 King Lear, Act 1, scene ii.

Addey's summation was that:

> The movements of the Great Cosmos are real symbols
> of the Divine Order and Harmony; from time immemo-
> rial they have been seen by the wise as manifestations
> of the decrees of Heaven. These decrees in their inner
> and spiritual aspect are called Providence, and in their
> outward and manifest aspect, Fate. Therefore what
> Shakespeare's villains are saying is that the decrees of
> Providence and Fate, which are in truth the workings of
> the Divine Justice and which are written upon the face
> of the heavens, can be set ruthlessly aside by the man
> who aspires to make himself this or that.[4]

Family Background and Early Years

Shakespeare's father, John, was probably born around 1530,
in Snittersfield, a small village close to Stratford. His father,
Richard, was a tenant farmer who rented land locally and seemed
to have made an adequate living. He had the reputation of being
an honest man, though the records show that Richard was fined
on a number of occasions for minor offenses such as putting too
many cattle to graze on common land and turning them loose on
parish meadows. He acted as an appraiser and helped to value
property belonging to several people in the parish. Only someone
of good character would be considered qualified for such a
responsibility.

John Shakespeare began a seven-year apprenticeship as a
glover at the age of fourteen and, by the time he had finished, he
was master of a respectable trade, one in which he made rapid
progress. In 1556, he was chosen as one of Stratford's two ale
tasters. Only able and discreet persons were chosen for this
unpaid position. It was his duty to check the ale and bread sold in
the town each week and either to impose warnings or decide if
much sterner action needed to be taken against anyone whose
standards were unacceptable. This was his first step up the ladder
toward higher civic office.

John's business prospered and he bought a house in Green-
hill Street together with land, also buying the workshop part of

---

4 Shakespeare's "attitude to Astrology." *Astrological Journal*, Vol. V, no 4. p. 13.

the Henley Street house which until then had only been rented. He now owned the whole building, a part-family and part-business house.

By the time he married in late 1557, he already occupied the Henley Street house where all his children were born and raised. His wife was Mary Arden, the youngest of eight sisters who lived in the nearby hamlet of Wilmcote, close to Snitterfield. Her father, Robert Arden, owned a large farm and land in Wilmcote, as well as land in Snitterfield and two other farmhouses. He was Richard Shakespeare's landlord as he owned the farmhouse in which the Shakespeare family lived. Mary brought with her a good dowry and also the Wilmcote estate and part of the Snitterfield land. This had been left to her by her father who had died shortly before the marriage took place. He had obviously looked favourably upon the marriage as he had appointed Mary to be one of his two executors.

William was the third child of John and Mary Shakespeare to be baptized in Holy Trinity Church, Stratford. Both Joan, born in 1558 and Margaret, born in 1562, died in infancy. Indeed William was lucky to have escaped the plague that visited Stratford in July 1564; around two hundred people are said to have died of the disease locally. Father John's various businesses were flourishing and when John's father died in 1561, he carried on running the farm until he was able to dispose of it by passing on the lease to his brother-in-law, Alexander Webbe, who had married Mary's sister, Margaret Arden.

In the years following his term as ale taster, John Shakespeare steadily advanced in civic life. He became one of Stratford's four constables and was responsible for organising and supervising the watchmen. It was the duty of these watchmen to keep the peace and enforce fire precautions. When on several occasions armed street fights or drunken brawls erupted, the constables and watchmen had the dangerous task of disarming and arresting the culprits.

Five years before William's birth, John Shakespeare had received rapid promotion and was elected a burgess. He supervised the income vested in the town council and the management of property such as the Guild of the Holy Cross, which had formerly been a Catholic institution. He then became senior Chamberlain and was so successful in carrying out his duties that he was asked to continue in the office when his term expired. With Protestantism now on the rise, changes were in the air and fresh opportunities awaiting to be eagerly seized. There was much to do as council meetings were frequently held in the guildhall and extra duties were undertaken.

In 1565, John was installed as an alderman as a result of one of that number being expelled the previous year. He was now addressed as Master Shakespeare and was allowed to wear the alderman's thumb ring and on public occasions, at church and in the guildhall, the black gown faced with fur. Three years later, he became bailiff, Stratford's most prominent citizen representing the town's interests in all important negotiations. He was now a Justice of the Peace, issuing warrants for anyone who broke the corporation's bylaws or those unfortunates who fell into debt. He presided over the Court of Record, which ranked as a Crown Court, and was also Stratford's coroner and almoner.

John could now wear the bailiff's scarlet robe and, on official appearances and outings, he was attended by the corporation's uniformed and mace-bearing sergeants. He entertained various dignitaries and visiting preachers, and when companies of players from London came on tour to Stratford, it was John Shakespeare who granted the licences to perform and sat in the best seats with his wife and family. Strangely there is much more information available about the life and character of John Shakespeare than there is about his illustrious son.

Young William grew up in this secure and prosperous atmosphere with an imposing and remarkable father to admire and emulate, feeling safe and happy, perhaps believing it would always be so.

Eventually everything began to go wrong. William was thirteen years old when his father's success abruptly came to an end. Having been formerly regarded as the most prominent and respected subject in Stratford, John Shakespeare was now forced to hide behind closed doors fearing he would be arrested for debt if he ventured out of his home. This disgrace had come about because of John's overstretched business affairs, and especially his involvement in illegal wool transactions.

John Shakespeare had been mixed up in wool trading for a number of years. It was unlawful for anyone other than "merchants of the staple" to deal in wool, and according to Tudor law, a serious offence to infringe their monopoly. John Shakespeare was certainly not a merchant of the staple. His undertakings therefore were highly illegal. This was proven when the floorboards of the Henley Street house were taken up in the nineteenth century during restoration and large quantities of wool combings were found there. Further proof of his illegal wool dealings has since been found in the Exchequer Court records.

It has now been suggested by E. A. J. Honigmann that Shakespeare, upon leaving school, became a tutor in the household of Alexander Hoghton, a wealthy Lancashire landowner. It is possible that he then entered the service of another Lancashire magnate, Sir Thomas Hesketh. He may have become a member of Strange's Men while in the employment of Hesketh and gone to London with them after they had completed their tour of Lancashire.

Honigmann based his deductions on a number of facts. In 1579, a Lancashire man named John Cottam, who was a friend of Alexander Hoghton, became the master of the Stratford school. The Cottam family owned an estate ten miles from where Hoghton lived and they knew each other well. In Stratford, he would soon have become aware of the Shakespeare family's problems and, wishing to help a former pupil of the school, recommended William to Hoghton.

In his will, Hoghton had asked Sir Thomas Hesketh "to be friendly unto Fulk Gillom and William Shakeshafte now dwelling with me and either to take them into his service or else to help to some good master." Hesketh adored the theatre and had his own band of players, acrobats, jugglers, and musicians. It is possible, argues Honington, that William Shakeshafte was in fact William Shakespeare and that he first entered the acting profession while in Hesketh's employment. He would also have learned about life among the gentry and something about the ways of the Court, a subject upon which he later wrote with great knowledge in so many of his plays.

This is a fascinating hypothesis and, if it could be proven to be true, would explain how Shakespeare became an actor and learned so much about the theatre. It would also explain how he became so familiar with life and manners among the aristocracy. However, it still remains to be proven. There is no evidence to show that William Shakeshafte was indeed William Shakespeare.

In fact, there were a number of people by the name of Shakeshafte known to be living in that area at that time, and any one of them could have been the person mentioned in the will.

One other reason for casting doubt on this theory is the fact that Hoghton's will was dated 1581, when Shakespeare was only seventeen years of age. The tone of Hoghton's request in the will suggests that he had known Shakeshafte for some time, so Shakespeare would have been at least sixteen when he became employed as a tutor.

If Shakespeare had entered the service of Sir Thomas Hesketh directly after the death of Hoghton in 1581, and then joined Strange's Men, how did he come to be living in Stratford throughout the last nine months of 1582? As the records have proven, Shakespeare was in Stratford courting and marrying Anne Hathaway during this period. His daughter Susanna was born in May 1583 and the twins were christened on February 2, 1585 in the church at Stratford, so he must have been with his wife nine months before the birth of his daughter, in the summer of 1582. The Lancashire theory has not been proven, and it is more likely that he first left Stratford after the birth of the twins.

Another theory has stated that he remained in Stratford learning his father's trade and that he became involved with the theatre when traveling companies visited Stratford in 1583–4 and 1586–7.

Shakespeare's Marriage—At the age of eighteen, William applied for a license to marry Anne Hathaway, who had become pregnant by him. She was twenty-six years of age, somewhat older than most girls marrying at that time. Their first daughter, Susanna, was baptized six months later on May 26, 1583. It has been thought that Shakespeare was trapped into a marriage by an older woman afraid of being left on the shelf, and that their marriage was unhappy as a result. The fact that he bequeathed his second-best bed to his wife has been interpreted as a sign that he did not love her. Since nothing positive by way of proof has yet emerged to support or contradict this assertion, it is foolish to speculate upon the truth of the matter. The fact is that we do not know what kind of feelings they held for each other.

Anne Hathaway lived in Shottery, a hamlet within a mile of Stratford. Her father was Richard Hathaway, a farmer, and she was his eldest daughter. Richard Hathaway died a year before Anne's wedding, but left her a small sum of money which she received on the day of her marriage. Since William had no money of his own and was not likely to be able to support his wife and expected child, this money could not have lasted long. It is believed that his father disapproved of the courtship and was against the marriage for this very reason. Since William was under age it was within his father's power to stop the marriage. No doubt since he and his wife did not wish to condemn their unborn grandchild, he consented.

The marriage license has never been found, but the license bond has been preserved in the archives at Worcester. It says that the Bishop of Worcester had given permission to William Shakespeare and Anne Hathaway to be married after one publishing of the banns. Normally, the banns had to be published in church on three successive Sundays, but a speedier method available to couples was to obtain a license from the bishop's court. This was not unusual, and couples with friends or relatives who were willing to act as sureties often took this quicker way to the altar.

The license records that Fulk Sandells and John Rychardson were willing to stand as the two sureties, understanding that they would forfeit £40.00 if the marriage later proved to be illegal. Much speculation has surrounded this license as the clerk made a thoughtless mistake when recording Anne's surname. He called her Anne Whateley and because of this blunder, many scholars and others have speculated that Shakespeare was in love with someone else and was trying to renege on his obligation to his future wife. It is inconceivable that such a story could be true. In the first place, no proof exists that there ever was such a person as Anne Whateley. In the second place, Shakespeare, being a minor, would have found it impossible to obtain a marriage license himself. In the third place, the marriage bond itself shows that John Shakespeare gave permission for his son to marry Anne Hatheway and not Anne Whateley, and that the two sureties would not have risked their money had they suspected William of duplicity.

It is not known where or when the wedding took place; unfortunately, the date appears never to have been recorded, so the transits for that event are speculative. This is typical of the life of Shakespeare; most dates are rather vague and not exact enough for detailed astrological investigation. He was probably married within the week, otherwise what would be the point of arranging a hasty marriage?

In 1585, William's money problems began to pressure him into looking for some means of supporting his growing family, since twins had been born at the end of January. This meant that he had to seriously consider leaving his wife and family in order to seek his fortune in London.

Seven years passed before Greene's *Groatsworth of Wit* appeared, demonstrating that Shakespeare had indeed become someone of consequence in the theatre. He had already written a number of plays which had been performed on stage and had earned enough money within a few years to settle his father's affairs.

Shakespeare's Son Dies—Shakespeare's growing fame and wealth was overshadowed in the summer of 1596 when his only son Hamnet died. Neither the date nor the cause of death is known and, since William left no records of any kind, we know nothing of the grief felt at the loss of his only heir. It is evident that he wished to create a family dynasty as he had encouraged his father to apply once again for a coat of arms. The first unsuccessful application had been twenty years earlier just before the start of the family financial problems. The Shakespeare family received their coat of arms with the motto *"Non Sanz Droict,"* two months after the death of Hamnet.

The grant itself is now missing, but two drafts with notes remain that explain the reasons why the applicant was eligible: there were vague references to Shakespeares who were said to have served Henry VII, and to John Shakespeare having been a justice of the peace and bailiff of Stratford as well as a Queen's officer. He possessed lands and tenements and was of good wealth and substance. The application was accepted and the fee paid and the Garter King-of-Arms declared that "it shall be lawful for the said John Shakespeare gentleman and for his children, issue and posterity to bear and make demonstrations of that same Blazon or Achievement (coat of arms) ... without let or hindrance ..."

Seven months after the granting of arms, early in 1597, Shakespeare bought New Place, a large Stratford mansion built around 1475 by Sir Hugh Clopton. Clopton was a Stratford man who became Lord Mayor of London in 1492. Unfortunately, the house was demolished in 1759 by Francis Gastrell, a foul-tempered and silly parson who was in dispute with the corporation about the rates. The previous year he had cut down a mulberry tree that had stood in the garden from before Shakespeare's time.

New Place was three storeys high, sixty feet wide and seventy feet deep, and it overlooked the Guild Chapel, the Guildhall and the school. It is recorded that Shakespeare paid "sixty pounds in silver" but, in all probability, he paid more than this amount since the documents did not always register the correct amount for tax reasons. Shakespeare paid cash down and had no need to borrow from anyone to meet the cost, showing that he was quite wealthy at this time, spring 1597, aged thirty-three.

The purchase of New Place strengthened his links with Stratford and, although he had become a prominent figure in London, he was more often to be seen in Stratford. It would have been easier to purchase a house in London within reach of his work and bring his family there to stay with him. Certainly it would have been more convenient, but Shakespeare's heart always belonged to Stratford where he returned at every opportunity.

Francis Meres's book *Palladis Tamia* was first published in 1598, praising Shakespeare and his poetry and mentioning twelve of Shakespeare's plays.

"... the sweet, witty soul of Ovid lives in the mellifluous and honey-tongued Shakespeare, witness his Venus and Adonis, his Lucrece, his sugared Sonnets among his private friends."

Shakespeare's Father Dies—John Shakespeare died in September 1601 at the family home in Henley Street and, since he had not left a will, the house was inherited by William. His mother continued to live there after her husband's death and was joined by her daughter Judith and her husband William Hart and the first of their four children. It seems to have been a agreeable decision for everyone. John's workshop which was attached to the house is now a museum.

Shakespeare's Daughter Marries—On the 5th of June, 1607, Shakespeare's eldest daughter Susanna (born 1583) married John Hall, a doctor who had set up practice in Stratford in 1600. Hall was eight years older than his bride; he was a serious- minded man of impeccable character who was respected by everyone. He had inherited property from his father, a doctor who had lived in Bedfordshire. Dr. Hall was ahead of his time, he was interested in treating each patient as an individual human being to be studied and understood. He deduced that the diet of the time, too much meat and little or no fresh vegetables, was responsible for many of the illnesses. Scurvy was prevalent and most of his patients displayed symptoms of that malaise. He had created a medicine of his own from a blend of plant and vegetable juices, which evidently worked successfully, curing many of his patients. He was more interested in helping the sick than in worldly honours, as he rejected the office of burgess on two occasions. When he reluctantly accepted on the third occasion and was fined several times for non-attendance at the committee meetings because of attending his patients, he was finally allowed to resign. In 1626, much to his credit, he rejected an honour from Charles I and paid a large fine for the privilege of refusing it. His daughter Elizabeth was born in 1608, the only grandchild that Shakespeare lived to see.

Shakespeare's Mother Dies—Shakespeare's mother died in September 1608 in the Henley Street house where she had lived for over fifty years. Her grave is in the Holy Trinity churchyard and the record of her death in the register simply states "Mayry Shaxspere, wydowe."

The schoolmaster turned astrologer Simon Forman (1552–1611) on a visit to London in 1611 wrote a kind of diary of his visits to the theatre. Forman, a Wiltshireman, practiced medicine on and off in London from about 1583 until his death. He had gained a notorious reputation as a magician, alchemist, and astrologer. His private papers and astrological works, written in shorthand, are housed at the Ashmolean Museum in Oxford. He was meticulous in recording his astrological work and kept detailed notes. They also contain explicit details of his sexual involvements with several famous lady clients. After his death, during the investigation in 1615 into the poisoning of Sir Thomas Overbury, it became public knowledge that he had been involved with the Countess of Essex.

Forman had attended the theatre on several occasions and saw performances of Shakespeare's *Macbeth, Cymberline,* and *The Winter's Tale.* The last one he saw was on the 5th of May, 1611. By September, he was dead, drowned in the Thames.

We know that Shakespeare was in London in May, 1612, engaged on a curious piece of legal business involving his friend and former landlord, Christopher Mountjoy. Mountjoy's daughter, Mary, had married Stephen Belott, who was now claiming that money promised to the young couple had never been paid. Shakespeare was asked to make a deposition as to what had been promised. He deposed that Stephen had been "a very good and industrious servant" and that Mountjoy had often said of him that he was "a very honest fellow." Unfortunately for Belott, Shakespeare contended that he could not remember anything concerning the financial arrangements that had been made seven years previously. One of the positive results produced by this episode was that one of the six signatures, in fact the earliest of the six known to be Shakespeare's, was attached to this deposition.

The Globe Fire—On the afternoon of the 29th of June, 1613, when Shakespeare was forty-nine, during a performance of *King Henry VIII*, the Globe theatre was destroyed by fire. It has been said that, in the scene portraying King Henry's arrival at Cardinal Wolsey's house, a small canon used to fire a royal salute started the blaze. Some of the lighted paper or other flammable material had fallen upon the thatch above the stage, caught fire , and spread quickly to destroy the theatre completely.

Fortunately, no one was injured, and all the costumes and properties were saved, the manuscripts apparently being stored elsewhere. It is not known if Shakespeare was in the theatre when the disaster occurred. Almost immediately, the shareholders set about re-building the Globe and successfully achieved their aim by the spring of 1614. The Globe was even better than it was before; it was re-built as an octagonal building with a tile roof.

Second Daughter's Marriage—In the Holy Trinity Church, on the 10th of February, 1616, Shakespeare's daughter, Judith (born 1585, the twin of Hamnet), now thirty-one years of age, married Thomas Quiney. Trouble began almost immediately. It was Lent and they had married without first obtaining a license from the Bishop of Worcester and were therefore in breach of church regulations. They were summoned to the bishop's court, but Quiney failed to turn up and was briefly excommunicated. Furthermore, unknown to both Quiney's family and to his bride's, a local girl by the name of Margaret Wheeler had become pregnant by him the previous summer. Both she and her baby tragically died on the 15th of March, a month after Quiney's marriage to Judith Shakespeare.

We can surmise that Shakespeare was a moral man and was deeply distressed by the scandal. His health had been weak from the beginning of the year, and the shock only caused him more tension and further anxiety. He promptly set about revising his will in order to safeguard daughter Judith's interests. He was determined that Quiney would not get his hands on any of Judith's inheritance. The sum of 100 pounds which had been in her husband's name was transferred to her, along with a further fifty pounds, provided she made no claim to the ownership of the cottage in Chapel Lane. Furthermore, another 150 pounds would go to her three years after his death, provided her husband settled land on her to the same value. If Quiney failed to do so, Shakespeare's executers were to retain control of the money and give Judith the interest on it for the rest of her life. Her children were to share the money on her death, in this way Shakespeare guaranteed that Quiney would never benefit from his estate. It had been his intention to leave all his plate to daughter Judith, but he changed his mind and stipulated that his *granddaughter*, Susanna, would receive it instead.

Susanna inherited New Place, the Henley Street house, as well as the one next door, the Chapel Lane cottage, the Gatehouse at Blackfriars, also land and tithes in old Stratford and Welcombe. Shakespeare also created an entail and left it to her: "... for and during the natural term of her life, and after her decease to the first son of her body lawfully ensuing; and for default of such issue, to the second son of her body ... to the right heirs of me the said William Shakespeare for ever." Unfortunately, less than sixty years after his death, his direct line came to an end with the death of Susanna's daughter, Elizabeth Hall. His four grandchildren had all died childless, the entail was broken, and all the worldly goods that he had left to his heirs were dispersed.

The will was signed on the 25th of March, 1616, the day before Quiney was due to appear before the court in the Holy Trinity Church. Quiney confessed to his crimes, and his punishment was to endure public penance on three successive Sundays before the townspeople while wearing a white sheet symbolizing his remorse.

Curiously, Shakespeare's last will and testament is a very stark and plain document bereft of poetic phrases, not at all the kind of document expected from history's greatest playwright. Charles Hamilton has claimed that it was written by Shakespeare himself, and not by his lawyer, Francis Collins, or by Collins's scrivener. Was it possible that, after a lifetime as a poet and playwright, that the great bard could so easily cut short his poetic expression as not a trace of it appears in this will?

Shakespeare died on the month and day that have been considered to mark his birthdate, the 23rd of April, 1616, his fifty-second birthday, the true cause of death unknown. One of the tales surrounding his life records that he died as a result of a drinking bout with some literary friends. This story was written by a Stratford vicar fifty years after the death: "Shakespeare, Drayton and Ben Jonson had a merry meeting, and it seems drank too hard, for Shakespeare died of a fever there contracted."

This story does not accord with what others had said about Shakespeare's drinking habits: he had a reputation for abstinence! It was said that he drank very little and would often use illness as an excuse to avoid parties and merrymaking. It was quite common for actors to drink to excess, and many promising careers were quickly ended as a result, but Shakespeare had more sense.

Two days after his death, he was buried in Holy Trinity Church and on his gravestone four lines of doggerel were carved.

> Good friend for Jesus sake forbeare,
> To dig the dust enclosed here.
> Blest be the man that spares these stones,
> And cursed be he that moves my bones.

Tradition has it that Shakespeare composed these lines himself, and, to this day, his grave has been undisturbed and is now a place of pilgrimage.

His wife, Anne, died in August 1623, having witnessed the setting-up of an elaborate monument to the memory of her husband some time earlier, on the north chancel wall close to his grave. Placed in a rounded niche is a bust of Shakespeare and beneath the bust are two inscriptions. One is in Latin which praises him as a Nestor, for wisdom, as a Socrates, for genius, and as a Virgil, for poetry. It says that the earth covers him and the people mourn him, and that he now resides with the gods in Olympus. Probably the inscription was composed by his son-in-law, Dr. John Hall.

The second inscription in English says "Stay Passenger ... Read If Thou Canst." It invites the pilgrim to ponder on the greatness of Shakespeare. The plaque records that he died in his fifty-third year. It was the usual practice for the piety and exceptional qualities of the deceased to be inscribed on tombs, but whoever recorded the dedication went against the convention of the time and considered it of greater importance to celebrate him as a writer. The family must have agreed to this since their permission had to be obtained before the arrangements could be made.

The effigy was commissioned by Hall from a well-known monument sculptor named Gerard Johnson, whose workshop was situated near the Globe. Shakespeare is depicted standing with a pen in his right hand and a piece of paper under his left. The work is generally agreed to be of poor craftsmanship in the sense that it is inanimate and contrived and does not convey in any way the essence of the man. It is believed that the features were worked from a death mask which would account for the smooth well-rounded appearance of the face.

Martin Droeshout's famous portrait was painted seven years after Shakespeare's death, when the artist was twenty-two. It is a very unskilled piece of work, and the reason the printers commissioned Droeshout to do the portrait was because the artist's fee was very low. This portrait has been thoroughly examined by Lillian Schwartz, a New Jersey computer artist, who claims that it is a made-up face *based on Queen Elizabeth's portrait from the same period*. Schwartz used scanning, digitizing and scaling computer techniques and discovered that the Droeshout portrait contained several identical features in common with the Elizabeth portrait. Her conclusion was that "it was not the bloke from Stratford ... Here they made a picture for the Folio, and even at that time Shakespeare was mysterious." As to the real reason for such a deception, the answer to that mystery may never be answered.[5]

John Heminge and Henry Condell, who were friends and fellow actors of Shakespeare's, published the *First Folio* in 1623. In their "Address" to the readers they wrote that they had passed the plays on "as he conceived them," and that his works were "truly set forth according to their original." Without this publication of the *First Folio*, the world may well have been deprived of Shakespeare's literary works. Since then, his plays and sonnets have never been out of print, and have now been translated into almost every language in the world.

---

5   *The Washington Post.* May 17, 1994,. p. C5.

The Astrology

Before examining the movement of the planets as they occurred around the time of Shakespeare's birth, it is important to understand some of the techniques that astrologers practiced at that time.

It was always the perception of astrologers, at least from the time of the Arab writer Al Biruni in the eleventh century until the end of the nineteenth century, *that each individual planet had its own orbs.* The English astrologer Alan Leo overturned this precept when he decided to revolutionize astrology in 1895. As part of that revolution he introduced the concept that *aspects* had orbs. This concept has spread throughout the western astrological world and is now erroneously accepted as standard. The older astrologers would certainly have been mystified by this innovation since it was their understanding that the *planets* had power and not the aspects. To them it would be comparable to rearranging the order of the signs of the zodiac!

Al Biruni first stated that the Sun's orb was 15 degrees, the Moon had 12 degrees, Mercury and Venus had 7 degrees each, Mars had 8 degrees, and Jupiter and Saturn each had 10 degrees. Some astrologers may have added an extra degree here and there to the orbs of certain planets but, in general, all agreed with Al Biruni's list.[6] Major aspects between planets were calculated *by adding the orbs of the two planets in question and dividing the total by two.* Therefore a sextile between the Sun and Mars was known to have an 11-1/2 degree orb. The Sun had a 15 degree orb and, when added to Mars' orb of 8 degrees, resulted in 23 degrees. This was then divided by 2, resulting in an orb of 11-1/2 degrees. It was also the practice of astrologers in the sixteenth and seventeenth centuries only to use the major aspects.

Of course Uranus, Neptune, and Pluto, which were unknown in Shakespeare's day, did not have any degrees of orb. At present the exact figures within that scheme have not been decided, and the true answer to that problem has yet to be solved.

Before beginning the search for the best possible day of Shakespeare's birth, let's take what few facts we know about his

---

6 *The Book of Instruction in the Elements of the Art of Astrology,.* p. 255.

character and construct a personality file that may then be fitted to a speculative horoscope.

The most obvious fact is that he was/is the greatest playwright in world history, which means that we are searching for a horoscope with truly outstanding dimensions. The problem with this objective is that a truly outstanding horoscope will differ in the mind of each individual astrologer, and the question as to what constitutes such a horoscope is debatable.

We also know that he was a prolific writer with an extremely large vocabulary at his command; he worked long hours under pressure in order to meet his commitments. He was reported to be mild-mannered with a kindly disposition, honest and straight-dealing, and was well-loved by his friends and associates. He did not seem to harbour grudges but forgave easily, especially on those occasions when he was criticised by Greene and Jonson. There was his love for his family and home in Stratford where he returned at every opportunity. He traveled extensively because of his career, although it would seem that he never went abroad. In his professional life, he associated with groups of actors and was in business with several partners. His health was good; at least there are no reports to the contrary. With these few facts, it may be possible to construct a speculative horoscope.

In mid-sixteenth-century England, it would have been highly unlikely that parents with a baby born on the 21st or 22nd of April would have waited four or five days before having it baptised. Nevertheless it *is* worth studying the astrology for each of the following days to see if the planetary alignments promised the birth of an outstanding genius.

The 21st of April Chart

The positions of the planets at midday on Friday, the 21st of April, are not indicative of a literary genius. The Sun was in a separating square to Jupiter within a prescribed 12-degree orb, separating from a sextile to Mars and applying by sextile to Pluto. The Sun's aspects alone are not particularly outstanding; more likely they suggest a tough, assertive person, rather than a creative artist. For centuries, rumours persisted that Shakespeare was the son of a butcher and had served as a soldier in the Netherlands. Both of these occupations are ruled by Mars, a planet whose nature has nothing to do with literature.

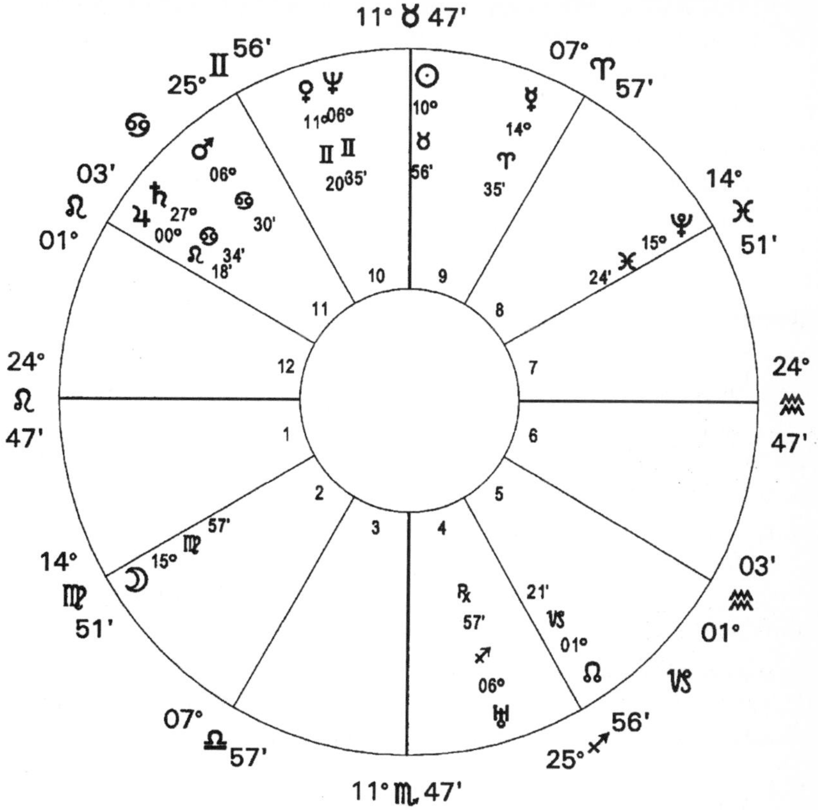

SHAKESPEARE APR 21, 1564

Midpoint Sort: 90° Dial											
☽/☿	000°16'	☽/☉	013°26'	☉/☿	027°46'	☽/♂	041°14'	☿/♄	066°05'	☽/♇	075°41'
☊	001°21'	♄/☊	014°28'	♀/♇	028°22'	☿/♀	042°58'	☉/☊	066°09'	☽	075°57'
♄/♆	002°05'	☿	014°35'	☽/♀	028°39'	♄/♇	051°29'	♆	066°35'	♆/☊	078°58'
♄/♅	002°16'	♃/☊	015°50'	♃/♄	028°56'	☽/♄	051°46'	♅/♆	066°46'	♅/☊	079°09'
♃/♆	003°27'	♂/♄	017°02'	♃	030°18'	♃/♇	052°51'	♅	066°57'	☉/♄	079°15'
♃/♅	003°38'	♂/♃	018°24'	♇/☊	038°23'	☿/☊	052°58'	☿/♃	067°27'	☉/♃	080°37'
♂/☊	003°56'	♆/♇	026°00'	☽/☊	038°39'	☽/♃	053°08'	☉/♂	068°43'	♀/☊	081°21'
♀/♄	004°27'	♅/♇	026°11'	☿/♆	040°35'	☉/♆	053°45'	♀/♆	068°57'	♂/♆	081°33'
♀/♃	005°49'	☽/♆	026°16'	☿/♅	040°46'	☉/♅	053°56'	♀/♅	069°09'	♂/♅	081°44'
♂	006°30'	☽/♅	026°27'	☉	040°56'	☿/♂	055°33'	♀	071°20'	♀/♂	083°55'
☉/♇	013°10'	♄	027°34'	♂/♇	040°57'	☉/♀	056°08'	♇	075°24'	☿/♇	090°00'

William Shakespeare
April 21, 1564 12:00 P.M. LMT
Stratford upon Avon, England
01W41 52N12
Regiomontanus

The sextiles between the Sun and Mars and between the Sun and Pluto continued throughout that weekend, influencing everyone born on those days. Astrologers in the mid-sixteenth century would not have been aware of the Sun's aspect to Pluto or the existence of the outer planets Uranus and Neptune, of course.

At midday, the Moon was placed at 15.57 Virgo, trine the Sun, square Venus, sextile Mars and in opposition to Pluto. The aspect to Venus would bestow some artistic ability but the aspects to the Sun, Mars, and Pluto only serve to reinforce those tough, assertive qualities mentioned earlier. Later in the day, the Moon began to sextile Saturn, making this a most unlikely day for the birth of someone of Shakespeare's qualities.

Mercury's aspects on the 21st looked favourable. There was a sextile to Venus as well as a wide separating sextile to Neptune and a trine to Uranus. These benefic aspects would bestow extrasensory and intuitional gifts of a high quality.

Venus was opposite Uranus, conjunct Neptune and square Pluto during the weekend, while the only applying major aspect that Mars could make was a trine to Pluto, beginning on the 23rd.

The conjunction between Venus and Neptune would endow those born with it with great artistic sensitivity and a love of beauty. There would also be an interest in mysticism, especially when in aspect to one or other of the lights.

Venus in opposition to Uranus brings difficulties and separations in marriage and relationships as there is an exaggerated idea of self will and independence. Sometimes it can lead to an uncongenial marriage or the couple will live an unconventional lifestyle. When involved with an opposition to the Venus-Neptune conjunction, Uranus could well describe the kind of marriage that Shakespeare and Anne experienced.

Shakespeare spent very long periods away from home, either living in London involved in the theatre or touring the country with a company of actors. The danger of divorce or total separation would have been a real possibility with the Moon in Virgo in square to Uranus (ruling the 7th) and Neptune, which occurred sometime before noon on the 21st. In Virgo, the sign of the Virgin, the Moon would have been less inclined to marriage, especially when in hard aspect to the erratic and divisive Uranus. Since we know that Shakespeare remained in his marriage and that he returned to his family in Stratford at every opportunity, it seems very unlikely that his horoscope would have contained these aspects.

Midpoints: Only those midpoints involving the Sun, Mercury, and Venus in major aspects with other planets will be evaluated since these three planets deal with creativity, writing and art. Because of the difficulties presented by the unknown time of birth on any of the days under investigation, midpoints involving the Moon, Ascendant, and Midheaven will not be taken into consideration.

Sun square Mercury/Uranus [Sun = Mercury/Uranus; see 40°56'/46' in the Midpoint Sort, i.e., 10°56'/46' of a Fixed Sign. — Ed.]: According to Ebertin the German astrologer who has been long accepted as the expert authority on midpoints, this midpoint gives the ability to grasp a situation quickly and the inclination to do one's work rapidly, and indicates the brilliant or inventive man. This could well apply to Shakespeare as it has been said that he worked quickly and wrote with haste, rarely making mistakes or corrections. The kind of professions listed under this midpoint are hardly likely to apply to him, i.e., mathematics, technology, and physics. This group of planetary midpoints lasted the entire weekend and into the next Monday.

The Sun square Mercury/Neptune [see 40°35']: This midpoint is said to symbolise actors, deceitful people and liars. With the Sun conjunct this point, it describes a sensitive person with a rich imagination gifted with intellectual creativity.

Sun conjunct Mars/Pluto [see 40°57']: Tremendous personal power and the ability to work hard in order to achieve ambitions; additionally, danger from accidents.

Mercury opposite Saturn/node [see 14°28']: The person born with this combination would have many sound reasonable and technical opinions to convey to others, but nothing of a poetical nature.

Mars conjunct Venus/Jupiter: This combination of planets occurred on each of the four days under examination. Mars conjunct the Venus/Jupiter midpoint gives a harmonious sex life, with decisions being made through the joy of love. Whether this was true of Shakespeare is difficult to say and may never be known.

Saturn square Sun/Mercury: This blend makes people inhibited in thinking, with a pessimistic attitude to life. There would also be a serious outlook on life, with thoughts of separation and estrangement.

Saturn square Venus/Pluto: Here is a combination that indicates a denial of love having a powerful psychological effect on anyone with these midpoints in their chart. As far as we can deduce from some of the brief statements made by his contemporaries, Shakespeare did not suffer from such discomfort.

Uranus opposite Sun/Mars: This synthesis of planets denotes hastiness and impulsive behaviour, and the tendency to work in a state of excitement overtaxing one's strength. Sudden events and adjustments to new conditions or circumstances are likely to take place: there can be a change of vocation and the likelihood of military call-up.

Uranus opposite Mercury/Jupiter: This group is said to manifest in businessmen, scientists, and orators, and while in opposition to Uranus gives qualities that Shakespeare had in full: a gift for repartee and the ability to answer questions with eloquence when challenged, making a resourceful orator.

Uranus opposite Venus/Neptune: Artists, musicians, mystics, dreamers and visionaries, according to Ebertin, have this midpoint activated in their horoscopes, but when in opposition to Uranus it is said to give a strong need for love. It confers impressionability or an easy susceptibility to external impressions, whether through other people or the environment, and makes the person with this midpoint vulnerable to seductive influences. There was also the tendency towards a sudden separation in love, with possible perversions.

Neptune square Sun/node: Neptune in hard aspect produces the inability to adapt easily so that people with this midpoint have the tendency to be easily annoyed or of being disappointed by others. There is usually disappointment in associations.

Neptune conjunct Mercury/Saturn: Those with the Mercury Saturn midpoint are said to be thinkers and philosophers but slow, dull, distrustful and possibly dishonest people. Neptune conjunct this midpoint can correlate with a state of depression, someone who is distrustful, with emotional inhibitions who plans without any prospect of realising personal goals.

In several of these midpoints there are a number of indications that someone of Shakespeare's talents may have been born on this day. They describe the actor, dreamer, and visionary, and the brilliantly inventive man skilled in repartee. Yet there are a number of difficult traits that do not conform to the descriptions of Shakespeare that have been handed down to us. They describe a person who could have been pessimistic, slow, dull, easily annoyed, and impulsive, and who lived in a state of excitement, and was fated to be disappointed in others.

Logically it is most unlikely that this was the day on which Shakespeare was born, because as already stated his baptism took place *five days later*. It would have been too long a period for his parents to wait, according to custom in light of the infant mortality rate.

The 22nd of April Chart

On this day the Sun remained just within orb of the square to Jupiter but continued to aspect Mars and Pluto (see page 92).

The Moon perfected its sextile to Saturn just before midday and then changed signs later that evening and applied to a sextile of Jupiter. Later that night the Moon would then apply by trine to Neptune and a sextile to Uranus, the first instance over that weekend when one of the lights began to positively contact the outer planets. Nevertheless it is true that the Moon will aspect these outer planets at least eight or nine times each month, indicating that a higher number of gifted people would be born, though perhaps not geniuses.

Midpoints: Mercury opposite Jupiter/Node [see 15°41'/51']: This group gives the inclination to cultivate an exchange of thoughts with others, which certainly applied to Shakespeare. There are also joint or shared successes and good cooperation between people. This describes the kind of partnership that he formed with his fellow actors in their various enterprises.

Nodes square Mercury/Pluto: The Mercury Pluto midpoint in various combinations is said to occur among various types of writers. People with this midpoint are usually described as convincing speakers who have the power to influence the public or the masses. It can also characterize a plagiarist or a demagogue; in short, persons who are guilty of fraudulent representation or misrepresentation in speaking or writing. If indeed Shakespeare were *not* the author of the plays and sonnets as has been suggested by some scholars, then he could well have *played the role of*

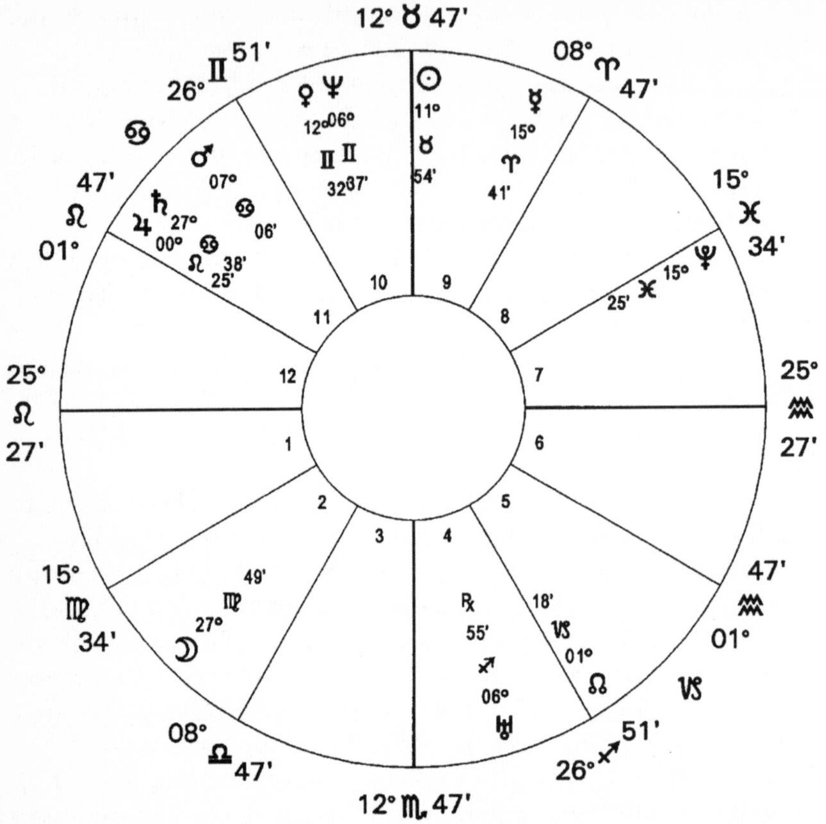

SHAKESPEARE APR 22, 1564

Midpoint Sort: 90° Dial											
☿/♇	000°33'	☉/♇	013°39'	♀/♇	028°58'	☿/♀	044°07'	☽/♃	059°07'	♇	075°25'
☊	001°18'	♄/☊	014°28'	♃/♄	029°01'	☽/☊	044°34'	☉/☊	066°36'	♆/☊	078°58'
♄/♆	002°07'	☿	015°41'	♃	030°25'	☽/♂	047°27'	♆	066°37'	♅/☊	079°07'
♄/♅	002°16'	♃/☊	015°51'	☽/♆	032°13'	♄/♇	051°31'	☿/♄	066°39'	☉/♄	079°46'
♃/♆	003°31'	♂/♄	017°22'	☽/♅	032°22'	♃/♇	052°55'	♅/♆	066°46'	☉/♃	081°09'
♃/♅	003°40'	♂/♃	018°45'	☽/♀	035°10'	☿/☊	053°30'	♅	066°55'	☽/♇	081°37'
♂/☊	004°12'	☽/☉	019°51'	♇/☊	038°22'	☉/♆	054°15'	☿/♃	068°03'	♂/♆	081°51'
♀/♄	005°05'	♆/♇	026°01'	☿/♆	041°09'	☉/♅	054°24'	☉/♂	069°30'	♀/☊	081°55'
♀/♃	006°28'	♅/♇	026°10'	♂/♇	041°15'	☿/♂	056°24'	♀/♆	069°34'	♂/♅	082°00'
☽/☿	006°45'	♄	027°38'	☿/♅	041°18'	☉/♀	057°13'	♀/♅	069°43'	♀/♂	084°49'
♂	007°06'	☉/☿	028°47'	☉	041°54'	☽/♄	057°43'	♀	072°32'	☽	087°49'

William Shakespeare
April 22, 1564 12:00 P.M. LMT
Stratford upon Avon, England
01W41 52N12
Regiomontanus

the plagiarist. Shakespeare has been depicted in the past as merely a play-patcher ["play doctor" — Ed.], but today experts have dismissed this depiction as untrue.

This Mercury/Pluto midpoint is squared by the nodes which is believed to give the desire to act as community spokesman, and to dominate others intellectually. It is improbable from the few accounts handed down to us that Shakespeare had any inclination to dominate people, intellectually or otherwise.

The following midpoints also occurred on the 22nd and were discussed in the section dealing with the 21st April. Sun square Mercury/Uranus, Sun conjunct Mars/Pluto, Mars conjunct Venus/Jupiter, Uranus opposite Mercury/Jupiter, Neptune square Sun/Node, and Neptune conjunct Mercury/Saturn.

When these midpoints are added to the list of negative traits we found on the 21st, along with the weak major aspects between the planets on the 22nd, it must be concluded that the 22nd was not the most auspicious day for Shakespeare to be born either. Besides, the serious charge of plagiarism raised by the Mercury/Pluto midpoint could be seized upon as further evidence by those who maintain that Shakespeare did not write the plays and sonnets. Whether he was the author or whether they were written by someone else has not yet been proven conclusively. For the sake of this short study, it shall be assumed that he was the author.

The 23rd of April Chart

On this day (page 94), the Sun continued to aspect Mars and Pluto and ended its square aspect to Jupiter. The Moon now in Libra began to trine Venus and oppose Mercury. These aspects reveal a very definite artistic side to the horoscope, perhaps not yet genius, but a beautiful gift of artistic and emotional expression. Here is someone who could write and speak eloquently, with a powerful mind capable of clarifying ideas and theories and presenting them in a lucid manner. These are the aspects of the actor, orator, and writer. With the Sun in Taurus and the Moon in Libra, *both signs ruled by Venus*, the artistic side is further emphasized.

Unfortunately though, the Moon was square Mars, a combative aspect which would have caused Shakespeare to be pugnacious, rebellious, and intolerant of other people. It could possibly have lead him into a life of alcohol and promiscuity and

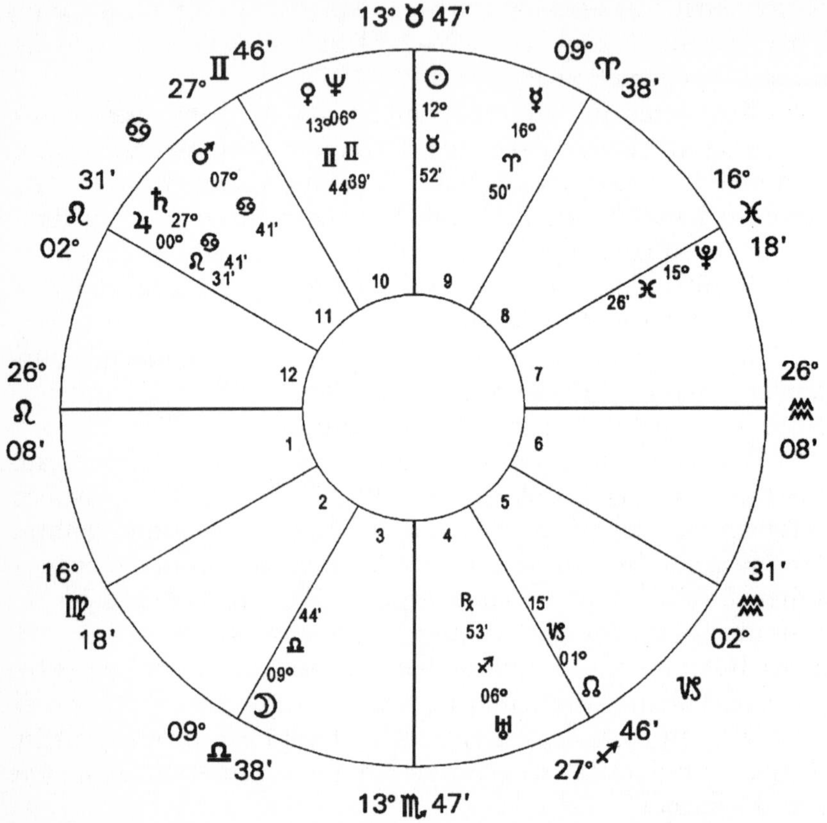

SHAKESPEARE				APR 23, 1564							
Midpoint Sort: 90° Dial											
☿/♇	001°08'	☽/☿	013°17'	♃/♄	029°06'	☉	042°52'	☽/♄	063°43'	♀	073°44'
☊	001°15'	☉/♇	014°09'	♀/♇	029°35'	☿/♀	045°17'	☽/♃	065°08'	♇	075°26'
♄/♆	002°10'	♄/☊	014°28'	☉/☿	029°51'	☽/☊	050°30'	♆	066°39'	♆/☊	078°57'
♄/♅	002°17'	♃/☊	015°53'	♃	030°31'	♄/♇	051°34'	♅/♆	066°46'	♅/☊	079°04'
♃/♆	003°35'	☿	016°50'	☽/♆	038°12'	♃/♇	052°59'	♅	066°53'	☉/♄	080°16'
♃/♅	003°42'	♂/♄	017°41'	☽/♅	038°18'	☽/♂	053°43'	☉/☊	067°03'	☉/♃	081°41'
♂/☊	004°28'	♂/♃	019°06'	♆/☊	038°21'	☿/☊	054°03'	☿/♄	067°16'	♂/♆	082°10'
♀/♄	005°43'	♆/♇	026°03'	♂/♇	041°34'	☉/♆	054°45'	☿/♃	068°41'	♂/♅	082°17'
♀/♃	007°08'	♅/♇	026°10'	☽/♀	041°44'	☉/♅	054°52'	♀/♆	070°11'	♀/☊	082°29'
♂	007°41'	☽/☉	026°18'	☿/♆	041°45'	☿/♂	057°16'	☉/♂	070°16'	♀/♂	085°43'
☽	009°44'	♄	027°41'	☿/♅	041°52'	☉/♀	058°18'	♀/♅	070°18'	☽/♇	087°35'

William Shakespeare
April 23, 1564 12:00 P.M. LMT
Stratford upon Avon, England
01W41 52N12
Regiomontanus

caused him to be quick tempered. None of this accords with what little we know of him, and it was this Moon-Mars square that first indicated that the 23rd of April, the traditional birth-date, was an unlikely date for his birth.

The mundane aspects affecting everyone born during this period are Jupiter trine Uranus and sextile Neptune with Uranus in opposition to Neptune. It would be reasonable to expect the Sun and Moon, and the Ascendant if known, to be involved with these planets in the horoscope of an outstanding public figure.

Unfortunately, the Sun was unable to contact Uranus and Neptune around the time of Shakespeare's birthday. The Moon formed a T-square with Uranus and Neptune on the 21st of April (page 87) and an easy sextile/trine on the 23rd (page 94). *Yet the Moon would have formed major aspects to the outer planets several times each month.* This alone would not have been powerful enough to explain a genius without the Sun's involvement with the outer planets. Of course, Uranus and Neptune may have been in contact with the Ascendant or MC and supplied those with this kind of horoscope with greater creative powers.

Midpoints: Mercury square Mars/Saturn [see 16°50'/17°41']: This is a potentially depressing, demoralizing combination that may create negative thoughts and dull the intellect. [This figure also may correspond to an interesting polarity of thought process-es: confused indecision or detached, life-or-death decision-mak-ing efficiency. — Ed.]

Jupiter square Sun/Mercury: This grouping of planets pre-sents the opposite qualities to the above: optimism, sound think-ing, oratorical and organizational skills. One synthesis picture tends to cancel out the other.

Jupiter square Venus/Pluto: This describes someone with abundant creative powers who wishes to create beautiful things. Here is one important midpoint that *would* support Shakespeare's high position in the literary world.

Uranus square Sun/Node: The person with this combination would be too eccentric for their own good, perhaps experiencing upsetting relationships with unusual people.

Uranus opposite Mercury/Saturn: Here we probably have great inner tension, excitability, haste, and the ability to make quick decisions.

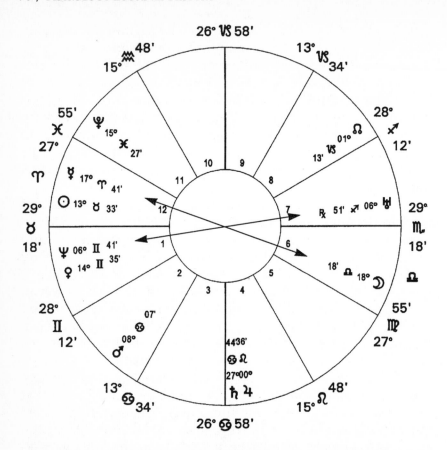

Midpoint Sort: 90° Dial														
☊	001°13'	♄/☊	014°28'	♃/♄	029°10'	☉	043°33'	☉/♀	059°04'	☉/♂	070°50'
☿/♆	001°34'	☉/♆	014°30'	♀/♆	030°01'	☿/♀	046°08'	♆	066°41'	♀	074°35'
☽/♆	001°52'	♃/☊	015°55'	☽/♆	030°36'	☽/♀	046°26'	♅/♆	066°46'	♆	075°27'
♄/♆	002°12'	♅	017°41'	☉/☿	030°37'	♄/♆	051°35'	♆	066°51'	♆/☊	078°57'
♄/♅	002°18'	♂/♄	017°55'	☽/☉	030°55'	♃/♆	053°01'	☉/☊	067°23'	♅/☊	079°02'
♃/♆	003°38'	☽/☿	017°59'	♆/☊	038°20'	☿/☊	054°27'	♄/♄	067°42'	☉/♄	080°38'
♃/♅	003°44'	☽	018°18'	♂/♆	041°47'	☽/♄	054°45'	☽/♄	068°01'	☉/♃	082°05'
♂/☊	004°40'	♂/♃	019°22'	☿/♆	042°11'	☉/♆	055°07'	♃/♄	069°08'	♂/♅	082°24'
♀/♄	006°10'	♆/♆	026°04'	♀/♅	042°16'	☉/♅	055°12'	☽/♃	069°27'	♂/♅	082°29'
♀/♃	007°36'	♅/♆	026°09'	☽/♆	042°29'	☿/♂	057°54'	♀/♆	070°38'	♀/☊	082°54'
♂	008°07'	♄	027°44'	☽/♅	042°35'	☽/♂	058°12'	♀/♅	070°43'	♀/♂	086°21'

William Shakespeare
April 24, 1564 5:08 A.M. LMT
Stratford upon Avon, England
01W41   52N12
Regiomontanus

The positive side of this birthday is that it would confer an abundance of creative powers. Conversely, there would have been conflicting mental abilities along with erratic and eccentric behavioural patterns. The square between the Moon and Mars definitely does not accord with what is known about Shakespeare. Therefore, we have astrologically sound suspicions as to whether tradition has been correct, that this day was, in fact, actually Shakespeare's birthday!

The 24th of April Chart

Around five o'clock on the morning of the 24th, the Moon finally separated from the square to Mars by the 10 degrees prescribed by traditional astrology. Upon closer examination, the planetary aspects for this day indicate that it *is* indeed the most likely birthday of all our considerations. The positions of these planets do describe what is known about Shakespeare's character in a much more positive manner than in any of the three previous days. Although the 23rd of April is the date celebrated by Shakespeare's admirers all over the world, a reasonable and strong astrological case can now be argued for the 24th.

The following midpoints which have been discussed in the previous sections also occurred on the 24th of April.

Sun=Mercury/Uranus, Mercury=Mars/Saturn, Mars= Venus/Jupiter, Jupiter=Venus/Pluto, Jupiter=Sun/Mercury, Uranus=Sun/node, Uranus=Mercury/Saturn, and the nodes= Mercury/ Pluto.

A thorough discussion of the planetary aspects for the 24th of April will be dealt with later.

The Harmogram

Kollerstrom and O'Neill (1988?) in their study "The Eureka Effect"[7] suggested that creative people would have an excess of quintile and septile aspects at birth. Taking the 23rd of April (page 96), we find only 1 quintile but 3 septiles, which was slightly below average for Kollerstrom and O'Neill's genius level. O'Neill wrote a programme to test the "harmonic power" over a specified period. When he ran this every hour for the days 21st to 25th of

---

7 Kollerstrom, N. & O'Neill, M. *The Eureka Effect.* Part 1. *The Astrological Journal.* Vol. XXX No. 2, p. 90. Part 2. Vol. XXX. No. 3. p. 136.

April, 1564, *the highest value was by far at 18:00 hours on the 21st of April.* When having tested every 6 hours for 180 days on either side of the 21st of April, *it was still the largest peak.*

Looking at the chart for this moment showed that there were 7 septiles but only 1 quintile. This again tallied with Project Eureka where only the septiles had individually reached significance.

To base anything on a study like Eureka with only 14 horoscopes and which has never been replicated would be foolish, but it is interesting that a moment within our five possible days shows so strongly in this system.

Harmogram for William Shakespeare
Central Time: April 23, 1564 at 12:00 GMT
Time Window: 360 days — Interval: 6 hours
Orb: 12/W° where W is the harmonic number (5&7) — All planets to PL

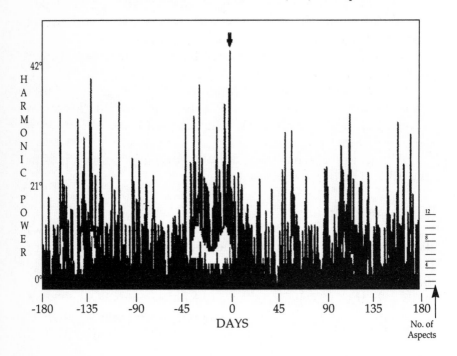

Harmogram for William Shakespeare
Central Time: April 23, 1564 at 12:00 GMT
Time Window: 5 days — Interval: 1 hour
Orb: 12/N° where N is the harmonic number (5&7) — All planets to PL

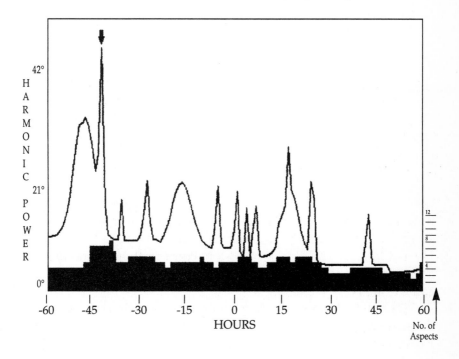

The Speculative Horoscope

Although mystery surrounds almost everything applying to Shakespeare's personality, there is still enough material available to enable us to calculate a speculative horoscope. It should be fully understood that the best that can be expected is to discover the date of his birth within a few hours. The following horoscope must not be taken as the correct time for Shakespeare's horoscope, even though it does appear to describe many of the characteristics known about him.

Apart from the obvious facts that he was a poet, playwright, and actor, we know that he married an older woman and had three children. We also know that he became wealthy and bought land and property. He loved his home town and returned there at every opportunity and he traveled extensively, usually between Stratford and London and on tour with the theatre company. It was not until around the age of twenty-eight that he first became known and established himself in his chosen career. These are just a few facts that should be verified by the speculative horoscope.

Career: His inclination for playwriting and poetry is shown by Mercury in sextile to Venus, the Ascendant ruler, with the Moon in opposition to Mercury and trine Venus (see chart, page 96). The Moon rules the 3rd House of writing and communication, and Mercury rules the 6th House of work and effort. Mercury disposes of Venus in Gemini, a sign of writing and communication, which in turn disposes of the Moon in Libra in the 6th House. The Moon is square and in mutual reception with Saturn (by exaltation), the 10th House ruler. Saturn within orbs of a sextile to the Ascendant degree and an opposition to the MC reveals that his career was his driving force. Delays would have been experienced in advancing up the ladder of success, which success did not begin until transiting Saturn had made its return. He had to learn the hard lessons that come with time and experience which are in keeping with Saturn's nature. Success did not come quickly.

The Sun, Moon, and Ascendant in Venus signs, though not in aspect, would also incline towards artistic pursuits. The Ascendant ruler conjunct Neptune within 8-1/2 degrees, is a very delicate and refined aspect giving imagination and vision. Although the correct orbs for Neptune have not yet been established, there can be little doubt that this *is* a valid aspect in Shakespeare's horoscope.

Court and Aristocracy: Saturn, the 10th House ruler in sextile to the Ascendant brought Shakespeare into contact with some of the highest and noblest people in the land. He would not have been treated as an equal since Saturn's nature would guarantee that he maintained his own place in life. Yet he would have made friends and acquaintances among the aristocracy since Saturn is the ruler of the 11th House as well. For example, Shakespeare gained the patronage of Henry Wriothesley, the Earl of Southampton, to whom *Venus and Adonis* and *The Rape of Lucrece* were dedicated, when published in April 1593 and May 1594.

Health: There is no indication that Shakespeare ever suffered from serious ill health. The 6th House ruler, Mercury, in sextile with Venus, the Ascendant ruler, is a protective influence, and with Mercury in awareness opposition to the Moon in the 6th, he would have avoided the worst of the plague and other dangerous illnesses. The Sun in the sign of the bull in sextile to Mars is an aspect that bestows strength and stamina and also enabled Shakespeare to withstand any sickness. At the same time, this Sun position and Mars aspect allowed him to endure long working hours, the prodigious work load to produce such a volume of creative excellence [along with the Moon in the 6th (the "workaholic"), ruled by Mercury and Venus. — Ed.].

Home and Family: It is well known that Shakespeare lived more often in Stratford than in London, and that he always thought of himself as a Stratford man rather than a Londoner. He preferred to reside in Stratford even though it would have been easier to move his family to London nearer to the theatres. This attitude is accounted for by the Moon, the ruler of the 4th, in trine to Venus, the Ascendant ruler. Venus in Gemini, a double-bodied sign, indicates two homes. Besides, it has long been regarded as the sign of the zodiac that rules London, so it was inevitable that he would live and work there. The Moon squaring and disposing of Saturn, which is placed in the 4th House, shows the feelings of responsibility that he held towards his parents, his wife, and children. He had a strong sense of duty. Jupiter conjoined with Saturn augments this picture clearly.

The Sun and Ascendant in Taurus made him fixed in his ways and resistant to change, so this fixity may well account for the fact that Shakespeare seemed never to have traveled abroad, but only within his own country. He loved the countryside and was never happy in the big city.

Land and Property: The Moon ruling the 4th House of land and property is trine to the Ascendant-ruler Venus and is disposed by it. The Moon is also in opposition to Mercury, the 2nd House ruler. These aspects destined Shakespeare toward the acquisition of houses and land, and Jupiter in the 4th with Saturn again amplifies this deduction.

Marriage: Shakespeare was married to an older woman from whom he separated for long periods of time. This can be ascribed to the Moon square Saturn, since Saturn is trine to the 7th cusp, representing Anne his wife; he accepted his responsibilities when she became pregnant by him. Saturn also created the hardship that he had to endure when the money began to run out early in the marriage and he had to leave for London to seek work in the theatre.

Pluto and Mars rule the 7th: Pluto is square with Venus, so important throughout our analysis. We can appreciate a decided passionate tie between Shakespeare and his wife. Mars is sextile to the Sun, a supportive marriage indicator.

Partnerships: Shakespeare worked and entered into business with a number of his fellow actors, and this can be attributed to Saturn as ruler of the 10th and 11th Houses, its aspect and those of the marriage profile listed above. Most important, perhaps, was the Sun in good aspect to Mars, the ruler of the 7th House, the house of partnerships.

Personality: The unfathomable mystery surrounding Shakespeare—the man, the authorship, the conflicts within tradition— can be attributed to Neptune in the 1st House opposing Uranus, with the Ascendant ruler Venus conjunct that Neptune. The 12th House ruler Jupiter is sextile the Ascendant degree, and the Sun is hidden in the 12th House, the house of secretiveness. Venus ruling the Ascendant in square to Pluto could profile the hidden depths of his personality. These aspects ensured that the true facts pertaining to Shakespeare's personality would remain buried.

The Moon in Libra trine Venus endowed Shakespeare with a mellow and tranquil nature. He has been characterized as someone who did not take offense when insulted and who was assured in his own abilities. He had a forgiving and loving nature.

The Libra Moon also contributed to his masterful ability to see both sides of any argument and to present them so eloquently in his plays. His principal creative theme was good and evil, which he explored in the greatest detail. The aptitude for his mental agility is suggested by the Moon's opposition to Mercury, a formidable index for a creative communicator. It was the Moon's placement in Libra, the sign of balance and fair play, and free from the square to Mars that was such a convincing argument for the 24th. Here, importantly, our time has the Moon ruling the Communication 3rd.

The puzzle as to why his personal papers, if there were any, have never been discovered could be attributed to Mercury, which generally signifies papers and manuscripts, placed in the

12th House opposed by the Moon, the ruler of his 3rd House of papers and written material. While this configuration is so strong for creative output—the inner world coming out—it could also show the hidden nature of the source and the process.

Sobriety: Saturn sextile the Ascendant degree would have made him sober, hard-working and responsible to his duties. It explains his reluctance to take part in drinking bouts with friends and why he often used excuses to decline their invitations. Shakespeare was a man with plenty of self control.

Travel: Mercury sextile Venus and in opposition to the Moon the 3rd House ruler shows a traveler, though it is believed he never traveled abroad, despite the Netherlands rumour.

Wealth: Taurus is an acquisitive sign and with the Sun and the Ascendant in Taurus, Shakespeare would have had a healthy respect for money and security. Venus sextile Mercury the 2nd House ruler, with the Moon also in aspect to both of them, profiles his ability to make money. He would have treated money seriously because of Saturn's sextile to the Ascendant degree.

Transits at His Death

The records show that Shakespeare died on the 23rd of April, 1616 when the transiting Sun had returned to within 1 degree of its natal position *in the 12th House* (see page 105).

The transiting Moon at midday that day was within one degree of an opposition to radix Neptune and a conjunction with the radix Uranus. These aspects could be linked to the continuing mystery surrounding his life and the circumstances of his death. Venus, our speculative Ascendant ruler, was also applying to an exact sextile to the birth Neptune, adding further confusion. At the same time, Venus was trine to the birth Uranus and square to the transiting Uranus.

At midday, Mercury and Mars had transited to an exact conjunction and were *also conjunct the natal Mercury in the 12th House.* More importantly, they were within a degree of an opposition to the speculative Moon.

Transiting Saturn was in trine to the fateful north node in the birth chart, and Uranus in Cancer had transited to a conjunction with the natal Mars while at the same time Pluto sextiled it. Neptune was sextile the natal Jupiter, the ruler of the 8th and 12th Houses, adding further mystery.

From a study of these transits, it is possible to argue that Charles Hamilton's assertion that *Shakespeare was murdered* was a correct one.[8] [The Solar Arc measurement (49°48') to the date of death directs the natal Uranus-Neptune opposition exactly upon McCann's deduced MC for Shakespeare, within 50' of arc! SA MC was conjunct natal Pluto; SA Ascendant was square Moon; and most telling of all, SA Mars was 1°24' from exact square to the rectified Ascendant. Bravo, Maurice! — Ed.]

Progressions at Death

The Secondary Progressed Sun was sextiled by transiting Saturn while the Progressed Moon was in opposition to both the natal and progressed Pluto and conjunct the transit south node. There is an air of finality about these aspects from both a traditional and a modern view. The Sun had reached the limit of his life span by aspecting Saturn, the planet that was once considered to be the furthest from our planet. The modern view is that Pluto is the planet furthest from earth. The progressed Moon aspecting Pluto on two counts while conjunct the south node, may well have inspired the imaginative astrologer to interpret this as an harbinger of Shakespeare's death and eventual immortality.

Progressed Venus was sextile the natal Venus; though hardly a fatal aspect, this may have acted in conjunction with the aspects formed by the progressed Sun and Moon. Since it is the Ascendant ruler, the interpretation could be that he had reached his allotted time on earth.

Mars had progressed to a conjunction with Progressed Jupiter, the 8th House and 12th House ruler, and square to transiting Pluto. Progressed Jupiter squared transiting Pluto while progressed Saturn squared transiting Saturn. Most of these aspects would have been outside the experience of 17th century astrologers but to astrologers today they would have suggested death.

A reasonable case could be claimed from the above collection of transits and progressions that the Moon's speculated natal position was somewhere around the 18th degree of Libra.

---

8 *In Search of Shakespeare*, Chapter VIII.

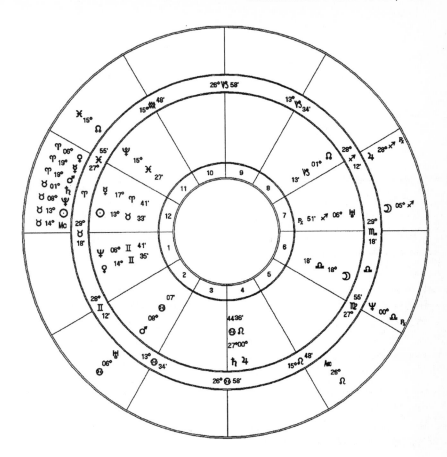

William Shakespeare
Inner Chart: Birth—April 24, 1564 5:08 A.M. O.S.
Outer chart: Death—April 23, 1616 O.S.
Stratford upon Avon, England
01W41 52N12

NOTE: Shakespeare died on April 23, 1616 Old Style. Computer programs are uniformly created to change to New Style Calendar at 00 hours, Oct. 5, 1582, which becomes/became Oct. 15, 1582, with the deletion of ten days for calendar adjustment.

Most countries of the world made this shift in calendar uniformly on Oct. 5, 1582. England did not. England changed over at noon, September 2, 1752 [the same time and date that the American Colonies did.] In effect, to most computers, Shakespeare died in England on May 3, 1616. — Ed.

Conclusion

The speculative horoscope for the 24th of April, 1564 is the only one that accords with most of the facts known at present about Shakespeare's life. It does not, however, appear to be the horoscope of a genius.

It is most unlikely that astrologers would all agree on which planets, signs, or houses *do* suggest genius. They could offer their opinion but still not be able to supply astrological proof. Most astrologers *would* probably agree, however, that the Sun, Moon, and Mercury, as well as the Ascendant and MC in a combination of major aspects to Uranus and Neptune are most likely to contribute to genius. There are no such strong astrological indications of genius in the horoscope for the 24th of April.

Neither does this horoscope conform to the Gauquelin results which proved that writers of exceptional talent are more likely to be born with the Moon in either the 9th or 12th House. When rectified in order to place the Moon in either of these houses, the horoscope did not respond as clearly as does the speculative chart. If the Moon were placed in the 9th House on the 23rd it would still square Mars, and this aspect has been considered to be inappropriate to Shakespeare. If the Moon were in the 12th House on the 24th, it would have already separated from the trine to Venus, and if in the 9th House later in the same day, it would also lose the opposition to Mercury.

The Eureka Effect experiment, though not replicated and as yet unproven, found that a high number of quintiles and especially septiles should be present in the horoscope of a genius. There were no quintiles and only one septile in this horoscope.

According to the historian and novelist, Peter Berresford Ellis, "What people tend to forget about the plays of Shakespeare is that a large percentage of them were not original works but rewrites. They were marvellous and poetic rewrites, without doubt, but rewrites nonetheless. *Macbeth*, for example, was rewritten from a play with the same title, popular in English theatres from the 1570s onwards. The historical plays were also rewritten from popular productions, such as the first and second parts of *Henry IV*."

Romeo and Juliet owes not a little genuflection to Boccaccio. This is not to accuse Shakespeare of plagiarism. Rewriting plays by actor-managers of the day was an accepted practice. What I am saying is that when one bears in mind that Shakespeare, in a great many of his works was being fed plot lines, characters and even entire scenes, his "genius" falls into perspective and he becomes a practical writer like many another.

The conclusion therefore must be that Shakespeare was born on the 24th of April, 1564, and was perhaps murdered—but as to whether he was a great literary genius and was indeed the author of the plays and sonnets cannot be proven by this horoscope.

Bibliography

Burton, S. H. *Shakespeare's Life and Stage.* Edinburgh: W. & R. Chambers Ltd., 1989.

Ebertin, R. *The Combination of Stellar Influences.* American Federation of Astrologers, Inc., 1972.

Encyclopedia Britannica.

Gauquelin, Michel and Francoise. Birth & Planetary Data gathered since 1949, Profession - Hereditary Results of Series A & B. Series C. Vol .1. Paris, France, 1972.

Hamilton, Charles. *In Search of Shakespeare.* London: Robert Hale,1986.

Honigmann, E. A. J. *Shakespeare: the "Lost Years."* Manchester, England: Manchester University Press, 1985.

Kollerstrom, N. and M. O'Neill. "The Eureka Effect." *The Astrological Journal*, Vol. XXX. 2, 90. and Vol. XXX. 3, 136.

_____. *The Harmogram, How it works and Some Case-studies.* Privately published by the authors, 1991.

MacArdle, Dorothy. *Shakespeare Man and Boy.* London: Faber & Faber, 1961.

O'Connor, Garry. *William Shakespeare: A Life.* Kent, England: Hodder & Stoughton, Sevenoaks, 1991.

Basil T. Fearrington

Basil Fearrington is a man of many talents: a full-time astrologer, full-time musician, student and teacher of the martial art Tae Kwon Do, and builder of computer programs for small business applications. Basil has done many radio shows on astrology in Philadelphia, which have attracted a large clientele and many serious astrology students.

As a musician, Basil has recorded or toured with many of the top names in music today, including Grover Washington, Stevie Wonder, George Benson, and Roberta Flack. In 1980, he was part of a production and writing team that won a Grammy award for the best R&B Song of the Year. At the present time, he is part of the team that is producing music for "New York Undercover," a television show broadcasting on the Fox Network.

Basil and his family reside in Broomall, Pennsylvania. He thanks his brother Norman, an astrologer now living in Denmark, for introducing him to astrology. Basil has written articles for *American Astrology* magazine and others.

Basil T. Fearrington

Niccoló Machiavelli: The Princely Warlord

 Fortune is a woman, and it is necessary, wanting to hold her underneath and master her, that she must be jogged and beaten. And it may be observed that she submits more readily to boldness than to caution. Therefore, like a woman, she'll always favor young men because they are much inclined to caution as to aggressiveness and daring in mastering her.

Princes should exterminate the families of the rulers who have dominion over territory that they hope to take rulership of.

Princes should murder their opponents as opposed to a simple confiscation of their property since those that are robbed can get revenge on you and those that are dead cannot. In time, men will forget the death of their father sooner than they will forget loss of patrimony.

To be truly benevolent you must be stingy with your own property and generous with what belongs to others.

It is not so important that one is virtuous. One should rather learn to utilize the appearance of being virtuous as this results in happiness.

Since a Prince is required to know how to assume a beastlike nature, he must adopt that of the fox and that of the lion; for a lion is defenseless against wolves. Hence a prince ought to be a fox in recognizing snares and a lion in driving off wolves. Those who assume

109

the bearing of a lion alone lack understanding. It follows, then, that a wise prince cannot and should not keep his pledge when it is against his interest to do so and when his reasons for making the pledge are no longer operative. If all men were good, this would be a bad precept, but since they are evil and would not pledge to you, then you need not keep yours to them. Nor did a prince ever lack legitimate reasons by which to color his bad faith. Men are so simple and so much inclined to obey immediate needs that a deceiver will never lack victims for his deceptions.

Niccoló Machiavelli, from *The Prince*

Machiavelli has been dead for over 400 years, yet his spirit, perspectives, and insights are alive in our political, military, and corporate realities today. The very mention of his name conjures up thoughts of the devil, secret murders, treachery, hypocrisy, and all that is unethical. Although he was not a powerful individual in his own right,[1] his ideas and concepts about human nature had a powerfully strong effect on others; and they still breed controversy today. With a very highly developed sense of realism, Machiavelli wrote ideas that were based on what a person is *likely* to do in certain circumstances, not on what they *should* do. His many words and the philosophy behind them were shocking to say the least, as evidenced above in the sampling of his insights. Though he wrote many books, poems, and plays, the words, ideas, and concepts of his book, *The Prince*, are the grounding for his reputation.

When Noel Tyl called me with the idea for this book, I was asked to pick a notable person in history whom I could focus on through rectification. I looked through my records and my books, and when I saw his name, Niccoló Machiavelli, my search came to a screeching halt. I had been introduced to Machiavelli's work by a former co-worker in the music business, who was, on a smaller scale, very much like any of the role models Niccoló depicts in *The Prince*; my associate did what he had to do to achieve an end result and he ignored the aesthetics of human relationships, as well as ethics, in the process.

---

1 Everything that Niccoló Machiavelli ever attempted failed.

I was a part of a very successful writing and production team that fell apart because of greed and dishonesty. Although there were hard feelings among some of the team members, there was and is still a great deal of respect for the person who formed the team. There were two authors that he used as his inspiration in the way he conducted himself in the world. One was Balthasar Gracian[2] and his *Art of Worldly Wisdom,* and the other was Niccoló Machiavelli and his shocking book on political strategy, *The Prince.*

As I began to read and understand Machiavelli's works,[3] it became easier to relate to my co-worker's insights on almost any competitive situation centered upon money, power, and acquisition—and, in parallel, I learned more about the corporate structure in the United States. With Niccoló's work as my co-worker's Bible of inspiration, it was crystal clear why he operated as he did, and it was this experience that served as the catalyst to my early interest in Niccoló Machiavelli; it is what led to my selection of writing about him for this chapter. I've *lived* it

All of the insights that Machiavelli addressed, which center upon matters connected with the condition of the State, parallel our modern-day large corporate structures and are equally applicable there. States employ power and resources through a governmental board in order to maintain and increase the financial status of the landowners, provide safety, and hopefully provide conditions that lead to a prosperous life for its citizens. A corporation also employs power and resources through a governing board to maintain and increase the financial status of its shareholders while providing a prosperous environment for its employees. Obviously, there is a clear sameness between the "State"of Niccoló's time and the large corporation of the present time. Niccoló's advice in *The Prince* is as applicable to a Chief Executive Officer as it is to a national President, King, Prime Minister, etc. Whether or not it's *advisable* is a topic that has been the focus of entire texts.

---

2   Born January 8, 1601 in the Kingdom of Aragon, Balthasar was a wise Jesuit priest and author. His *Art of Worldly Wisdom* is a book of maxims on the conduct of life and the achievement of true culture.

3   Machiavelli's reputation is founded upon *The Prince,* but he authored three other books that were clearly superior: *The Florentine History, The Art of War,* and *The Discourses Upon The First Ten Books of Titus Livy.*

An apt cinematic example of Machiavelli's observations, replete with Machiavellian symbolisms, can be seen in the 1976 movie release called *Network*. It starred Faye Dunaway, the late William Holden, the late Peter Finch, Robert Duvall, and a cast of top-flight actors including Ned Beatty. *Network* was a serious, satirical view of the world of television; it was/is also a powerfully demonstrative symbolism of corporate reality that reflects some of the insights Machiavelli talked about throughout his works. In many cases, all one needs to do is substitute the word "corporation" for Prince (in *The Prince*) to see many of the things in this movie and modern corporate life that Machiavelli observed during his lifetime in politics.

The "prince" of *Network* was the corporate structure of the "UBS" television network. Howard Beel (the character played by Peter Finch) was a senior, near-retirement-aged newscaster who had been given his two-weeks notice at the television station. Because of terrible ratings, management set out to restructure the network, starting with the evening news. Beel was singled out as being a large reason for the bad ratings of the newscast, and he was given notice. As Beel announced his (forced) retirement, he said that he was going to blow his brains out on live television, which was his way of throwing a one-two verbal punch of sarcasm to the whole ratings philosophy: if it's a question of low ratings, why not go out with a bang and get the highest of ratings with an on-the-air suicide. Although network management was very upset with his announcement, immediately terminating him, the attention that it drew made things happen and created excitement.

Beel was eventually killed by the corporate structure that he led to the top. They simply did what they had to do to quiet him and, in Machiavelli's life, *it was his observation of this kind of activity that led him to say the things he said.* My observations of *Network* don't reflect the ideals that I live by. Niccoló's observations of political and military activities that were used in writing *The Prince* do not necessarily reflect his ideals either. Machiavelli simply wrote what he saw (it can be argued that he interpreted what he saw) and delivered a simple message: if you want to be a leader of government, a leader of State, a military leader (and in modern terms, a successful CEO), please accept this book (*The Prince*), read it, and use this analysis of history and experiences in government as a guide and pathway to success. Within the realm of his experiences, he had seen many examples of successful leadership, and all he did was write about it.

Although this posture is far, far away from spiritual health, in the reality of corporate and political life in the world, *it is practical gospel.* Sometimes, I'm not so sure that it isn't a major reality in the real world, period. When Machiavelli cries out that men are bad, it sounds so reprehensible. Yet, the reason why we lock our car at night or don't leave the doors to our home open when we go away on vacation is essentially because we don't trust people, and we believe that they will steal from us if the opportunity presents itself. Locking our car door is admittedly a far cry from murdering a family, but the idea here in this study is simply to look at these ideas that make people so uncomfortable. The point is that Machiavelli is not entirely wrong in his insights of human behavior. Yet, many authors through the years have written huge texts in criticism of his supposed personal wickedness.

For many, the bottom line is a profit-versus-loss concern, not profit versus ethics. In matters of the State, elections, etc., the bottom line is winning, not honesty or the display of ethics. Niccoló is credited for being the first one to bring to light the *separation* of ethics and morals from politics. It's a testament to his insight that he not only observed these qualities so long ago but expressed these ideas so brilliantly throughout his many texts, letters, reports, and plays. Let it be noted that Niccoló Machiavelli didn't *create* the separation of ethics and morals from politics. He simply observed that separation to be useful and advantageous.

In *The Prince*, Machiavelli's basic premise is that men are selfish, greedy, cowardly, treacherous, gullible, and stupid; if you hope to have any kind of power base, if you hope to keep that power base, you must not only be willing but eager to destroy thoroughly the liberties of those whom you rule; you must know what virtue is so that you can project virtuous qualities without actually being a person of virtue; you must be willing to employ hypocrisy and deceit, and to trust no one since no one will be honest or virtuous with you. Machiavelli sees the world of politics as a place where there is no other relevant reality aside from raw, brute strength and power; the power coming as a reward for being ruthless. When I saw *Network*, I was reminded over and over again of the Machiavellian viewpoint, just as with many other movies such as *The Godfather*, *Wall Street*, and *The Firm*.

Having spent so many years in the music business and having been victimized by unethical people, it is very easy to identify firsthand with the perspective that led to the writing of *The Prince*. The financial gain from "points" and publishing[4] in the business is so massive that almost anything is apt to be said, promised, or done for that gain. Ethics and morals are totally submerged and sacrificed for financial gain, control, and power, and this is almost always the case when such gains are possible, no matter what the nature of the endeavor is. Yet, there is always the charade of the appearance of virtue. It's found in politics, in the military, in corporate life, and even in religion.

The Historical Backdrop To Niccoló's Life— Come with Me into the Treachery of the Renaissance

Much of what Machiavelli says in *The Prince* is downright cruel, harsh, and immoral. What he wrote can not be understood at all without reference to the life circumstances under which it was written. The condition of Italy (and perhaps Niccoló's own dire circumstances at the time of the writing of *The Prince*) had everything to do with his perspective and philosophy because of the constant victimization of Italy by foreign powers. Before we look at the astrology of Niccoló Machiavelli, it's important to know a little about what life was like during that period of history in Italy, and about his life in particular. There were certain individuals— the Medici, the Popes, the Borgias—and events—regional feuds, foreign invasions—that served as powerful forces in the development of his overall philosophy and perspective about politics, war, and religion.

---

4   The foundation of the music business, where fortunes are made, comes from two sources: points and publishing. The term "points" is a synonym for the percentage of the total sale on an album, compact disk, or tape. The term "publishing" refers to the ownership of a song. Writing a song does not at all guarantee ownership of that song, and there is more made from ownership than creation. When an artist owns the publishing on a song and has negotiated with the record label for a high amount of points, the potential to make millions is great. Because of that, you are apt to see the employment of many tactics that are Machiavellian in nature.

Machiavelli was born on May 3, 1469, in Florence, Italy. During this second half of the fifteenth century, the power areas of Europe consisted of Spain, France, and the Holy Roman Empire. Italy was divided into five powers. In addition to Florence, central to Tuscany, there were Venice, Naples, Milan, and the Papal States.[5] Milan was a duchy under the control of the Sforza family.[6] Venice and Florence were nominal Republics. The Papal States extended from the Tyrrhenian Sea in the west to the Adriatic Sea in the east, and were subjected to the authority of the Pope. Naples lay immediately south of the Papal states. Each of these areas was interested in preserving its own power but was just as interested in preserving a balance of power on the Italian peninsula. Each area of power could count on the others to oppose any one of them that decided to become ambitious and attempt an extension of territorial boundaries.

The Medici

As a commercial center of importance in Europe, the political and military capital of Tuscany, the Republic of Florence, exerted a tremendous amount of control over its regional cities, including Prato, Pistoia, Pisa, Volterra, Cortona, and Arezzo. Most of the political power, if not all of it, was manipulated by a group of very rich merchants, led by a powerful and influential family named Medici.[7] The family controlled all elections and handled the city tax structure. More importantly, they inherited all of Florence's wealth from trading interactions with the rest of Europe. The Medici were seemingly perpetual leaders in Florence in terms of intellectual pursuits, artistic endeavors, and style of government. The contribution that they made to art during this

---

5   A group of states or chieftains under the jurisdiction of the pope in Rome.

6   Muzio Sforza (1369–1424) was one of the strongest Italian generals of the time. His son, Francesco Sforza (1401–1466) led the Sforza mercenary troops in 1424 after the death of his father. He became Duke of Milan in 1450. Ludovico Sforza (1451–1508) was the second son of Francesco and became Duke of Milan in 1494. Caterina Sforza (1463–1509) was the illegitimate daughter of Galeazzo Maria Sforza and although she was female, she was clearly the most ruthless Sforza. After the assassination of her husband, Girolamo Riario, in 1488, she succeeded the power of Imola and was quite tyrannical. Massimiliano Sforza (1493–1530) was the eldest son of Ludovico and was Duke of Milan from 1512–1515.

7   The other wealthy families included the Soderini, Strozzi, Rucellai, Pitti, Ricci, Ridolfi, Albizzi, Capponi, and Valori. Politics in Florence revolved around the political machinations of these families to gain control of government.

period can not be overemphasized as they used a great deal of their wealth in support of it.

The members of this family were powerful: they became popes, kings, queens; they left great artistic legacies and greatly contributed to Florence's years of splendor during the Renaissance. It was under the Medici that the humanists were able to captivate Italy with philosophy, art, and scholarship. There was the architecture of Filippo Brunelleschi, the sculptured works of Lorenzo Ghiberti and Luca della Robbia, the paintings of Donatello and Masaccio, the philosophy and paintings of Fra Angelico, the genius of Michelangelo, the early Leonardo, and many more, all of whom flourished under the Medici.

Three generations of Medici ruled over Florence: Cosimo de' Medici, Piero de' Medici, and Lorenzo ("The Great") de' Medici. Although representative republican government was in place, the Medici family totally dominated the Florentine government during the fifteenth century and during most of Machiavelli's life. Their dominance in affairs of the state, which started around 1434, came about as a result of their prowess in banking throughout Italy and Europe as well as the extensive agricultural and mining enterprises that they controlled in the Province of Tuscany.

The Medici family goes back to the year 1201. At that time, Chiarissimo de' Medici founded the family fortune and was chosen "gonfalonier" in 1314 (he who bears or provides the regional flag or crest; the leader of government). His grandnephew was Salvestro de' Medici. He was chosen gonfalonier in 1378 and it was he who established the family reputation of looking out or the poor. His grandnephew was Giovanni di Bicci de' Medici, the first millionaire of the family. He was particularly skilled with banking and built his business to the point of having between ten and twenty banks spread out among various European capitals. Giovanni stayed away from politics, electing to spend most of his money on the construction of churches, supporting the development of art, and various philanthropic endeavors. When summoned by the Florentine government, he supported tax reform laws that were very good for the poor and very bad for the wealthy. Because of this, he was sadly mourned by the Florentine blue collar population when he died in 1429.

---

3 See my book *Grimmelshausen* (New York: Twayne, 1974), pp. 73–82.

Cosimo de' Medici (coh'-zee-mo day may'-di-chee)—perhaps the first Medici of major historical importance was next in line to exert influence in Florence and the first of the Medici to be actively involved in politics. Because he took over immediately after Giovanni, the tax situation was still fresh in the minds of the wealthy. Four years went by before Cosimo ran into problems. In 1433, a rival family called the Albizzi conspired to uproot the Medici. They impressed the Signory (the governing body) to press charges on Cosimo for being too opulent, a danger to the state because of the wealth and ambition of the family. Key to these charges was a mansion that Cosimo was building that was looked upon as too much a display of wealth for a private citizen. Evidence was accumulated, and he was eventually imprisoned and sentenced to death. However, he was able to arrange a bribe from his jail to the gonfalonier, and the sentence was changed *to banishment of the Medici family for ten years.* But even this sentence was terminated after one year, and the Medici returned to Florence in full force!

Cosimo was much like his father in that he used his money to build churches, support the arts (some of the great architects of Italy flourished under Cosimo). He died in 1464, and was succeeded by his son Piero de' Medici, who took over upon his death. Piero (pee-ay'-ro) was an extremely unhealthy person, a chronic invalid suffering with gout, with too mild a disposition for his office. He served as head of state for five years and, in 1469—the year of Machiavelli's birth—Piero's son Lorenzo took over, to become the most heralded Medici in literature.

Lorenzo was a revered statesman, a man of letters and, in general, a much admired and respected ruler who was greatly loved by the Florentines. He came into office at the age of twenty-one and brought much energy and ambition with him. Lorenzo was an accomplished poet; he entertained Florence with all matter of social festivities and pageants, and he selected the best artists of the day to design masks, floats, decorations, etc., for all his festive endeavors. Florence prospered under his rulership and, in acknowledgment of all his merits, Lorenzo became known as Lorenzo "The Magnificent."

Things were absolutely blissful in Florence with Lorenzo for nine years, until the Pazzi conspiracy. The Pazzis were a family of bankers who rivaled the Medici in their splendor. They were heavily supported by the Pope. Wealthy, aristocratic, and very proud, they were never happy with the power of the Medici and therefore set out to concoct and act upon a plan to overthrow them by killing Lorenzo and his third son Giuliano in the cathedral church of Santa Reparata so as to take them by surprise—do we sense the strategy Machiavelli was to observe so closely?

On the way to the Duomo, the grand cathedral in Florence, the Pazzi and Medici laughed in a way that would have led anyone to believe that they were old friends. At just the right time, Giuliano was stabbed in the chest with a dagger and died instantly. One of the Pazzi became so overwhelmed that he jumped atop Giuliano's body, fiercely stabbing at it and even stabbed himself in the leg, rendering himself useless in the skirmish. In the meantime, Lorenzo was stabbed in the throat, but his wound was very slight and he was able to defend himself with his own weapon.

In the Palazzo della Signoria,[8] there was yet another plot going on! A fellow Pazzi conspirator was trying to take over the Palazzo. The Archbishop of Pisa and two fellow conspirators were captured and left hanged and dangling outside the Palazzo window. Francesco Pazzi was hanged alongside the others. Over the course of the following fifteen years, Machiavelli would see many reminders of the Pazzi conspiracy on the walls of the Captain's Palace situated adjacent to the Palazzo.

This event, the treachery involved, and the way that the city bonded with the Medici in support and sympathy had a powerful impact on young Niccoló. As a result of the Pazzi conspiracy, there was a military action against Florence by the Pope and the army of Naples. Lorenzo was succeeded in 1494 by his incompetent son Piero, who was the leader of Florence when it began its downward journey of existence. The Medici were exiled from Florence in 1494 and returned to power in 1512 but, yet again, they were forced out of Florence in 1527.

The Borgia Family

This family is not only important in the development of Niccoló's various political and wartime philosophies, but they are important in the overall scheme of Italian history as well. Up until

---

8 The building that housed the seat of government in Florence.

the death of Lorenzo de' Medici in 1492, Florence had held its own and competed successfully in the Italian political world because of its leader's particular gift in diplomacy. Conditions had been pretty stable with very few major wars, but, eventually, the Italian peninsula lost much of its political unity. Though there were many contributing factors to this loss of political unity, one of the important factors came about as a result of the activities of a family known as the Borgias.

Alexander VI—The Borgia family was of mixed Spanish and Catalonian ancestry and were noble people in their home of Aragon. The first of the Borgias to make a name in politics was Alonso de Borja, who became Pope Calixtus III in 1455. Calixtus died in 1458, leaving behind his nephew, Rodrigo Lanzol y Borja.[9] Rodrigo was born on January 1, 1431 in Xativa, Spain. With the Sun in Capricorn as part of a cardinal grand cross involving the Mars-Uranus axis squared by Pluto opposed Mercury-Saturn, he was a powerful, driven man indeed. He became a Cardinal at the age of twenty-five (Solar Arc Sun opposed Neptune, SA Uranus square Neptune, SA Mars square Neptune, SA Pluto square Jupiter) and, at twenty-six, became the highest ranking official in the church, head of the powerful Curia. His name had been Italianized to Borgia and, in 1492, at age sixty-one (with SA Neptune square Saturn), after having *purchased* the votes of many Cardinals, was himself elected to the Papacy for a period of eleven years as Alexander VI (see horoscope, page 274).

Despite the fact that he was a first-rate administrator with a driving will and endless supplies of energy, there is simply no other way to describe Alexander than as *corrupt*. Incest, murder—you name it—history purported he did it. He was thoroughly addicted to acquiring wealth, was a dedicated womanizer, and totally abused his position. Papal gossip was very much in vogue during those days and much of the gossip about Alexander was true. The stories of his parties in the Vatican are legendary. He even had a portrait of one of his mistresses, robed as the Virgin Mary, painted over the door of his bedchamber. There were many, many mistresses, but the one that he was with the longest, Vannozza Cattanei, bore him four children. Their names were Cesare

---

9   Borja was Italianized to Borgia.

(born in 1476), Giovanni (born in 1474), Lucrezia (born in 1480), and Goffredo (born in 1481). Cesare holds a special place of infamy in the history of the Italian Renaissance years.

Alexander VI came into the Papal office with much fanfare and celebration, and his beginning was a good one. Between the time of the death of the previous Pope (Innocent) and the coronation of Alexander, there had been over 200 murders in Rome. After Alexander took office and the first murderer was captured, he made an example of him by hanging him and his brother while burning down their house. The statement was heard loud and

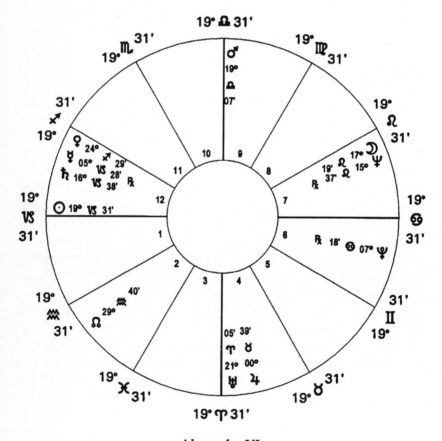

Alexander VI
Jan. 1, 1431 07:30 A.M. LMT
Xativa, Spain
03W47 40N39
Solar Houses

clear throughout Rome. Peace was restored, and respect was gained. All were glad that a strong man was on top of things as the head of the Church.

But there were soon problems to be dealt with. The Papal states were under siege by their local dictators, creating big problems for Naples and Milan. Alexander gave this job, the centralization of the Papal States, to his son Cesare.

Cesare (chay'-zah-ray) Borgia was reputed to be a very strong, athletic man who once decapitated a bull with one stroke in a bullbaiting contest. During another bullfight, he "entertained" not one, but two ferocious bulls for an extended period of time and then left the arena unharmed. He was admired by men and women, but was quite a character! He wore a ring that bore the inscription, *Fays ce que dois, advien que pourra*—which means "do what you gotta do!" I mention him here because of the colossal part he played in the development of the political philosophy of Niccoló Machiavelli, as we shall see.

Although Cesare was far from being a man of the spirit or of the Church, he was destined to be in the Church purely from heredity. In 1492, his father (Pope Alexander VI, remember) made him the archbishop of Valencia and the following year made him a cardinal. This lasted a few years until 1497, when Cesare begged his father to relieve him of the position. On August 16, 1498, the title of cardinal was removed and politics, Cesare's real passion, took over all his energies.

Alexander had high hopes that the King of Naples, Federigo III, would allow Cesare to marry his daughter Carlotta. When Federigo refused, Alexander turned his allegiance to France in order to get its help in re-securing the Papal States. The opportunity to do so came when Louis XII needed the Pope's permission for the annulment of a marriage that had been forced upon him. Alexander sent Cesare to France with the divorce papers and 200,000 ducats "for the bride." He was also granted permission to marry Anne of Brittany, widow of Charles VIII. So pleased was Louis with this that he made Cesare the Duke of Valentino and Diois in May of 1499. This gave Alexander a legal claim to two French territories. Cesare married the sister of the king of Navarre, Charlotte d'Albert. This marriage *joined the papacy with a kingdom* that was openly planning to invade Italy and take Milan and Naples—the intrigue and collusion are epic.

In Cesare, Alexander had the leader he needed in order to regain the Papal States. Alexander let it be known that Caterina Sforza and her son Ottaviano were in charge of Imola and Forli, that Pandolfo Malatesta was in charge of Rimini, that Giulio Varano was in charge of Camerino, that Astorre Manfredi was in charge of Faenza, that Guibobaldo was in charge of Urbino, and that Giovanni Sforza was in charge of Pesaro, and *that they had come into power by raping the Church!* It was Alexander's plan to reclaim these areas *by expelling all these leaders forcibly,* and eventually to have Cesare unite the whole of Italy under Alexander's rulership.

Needless to say, Cesare did conquer all of these areas throughout 1500 and 1501. Cesare had a new title now, he was the Duke of Romagna.

We will see that Machiavelli was sent by Florence to make an appeal to Cesare, to contain his glut for land and power. This was Niccoló's first time in Cesare's presence. Machiavelli was very impressed. The letter he wrote back to the Signory said, "This lord is splendid and magnificent and is so bold that there is no enterprise so great that it does not seem small to him. To gain glory and dominions he robs himself of repose, and knows neither danger or fatigue. He comes to a place before his intentions are understood. He makes himself well-liked among his soldiers, and has chosen the best men in Italy. These things make him victorious and formidable, with the aid of perpetual good fortune." Cesare went on to seize Camerino.

As a result of his conquests, Italy became insecure, and various other rulers wondered how long it would be before they lost *their* states. Paolo Orsini and Francesco Orsini, in particular, feared that Cesare would ruin their family. Vitelli, who wasn't very happy at having to give up Arezzo, formed an alliance with the Orsini, Oliverotto of Fermo, and Pandolfo Petrucci of Siena, as well as representatives of Guidobaldo. They all agreed *to turn their troops against Cesare* for the purpose of capturing and killing him.

For a period of time the conspiracy worked, especially in Urbino and Camerino. Guidobaldo even returned to power. All of the fallen rulers were now anticipating their return to their thrones. In the meantime, Cesare's lieutenants wouldn't obey him and his forces had dwindled down to a considerably low number. Then fortune reared its head: Cardinal Ferrari died and Alexander was able to use 50,000 ducats left by him to get a new army for Cesare. He also negotiated with the conspirators and won back their peace with Cesare.

The lieutenants of Cesare seized Senigallia, located on the Adriatic. Although the town itself yielded, the governor of the castle would only surrender to Cesare himself. When Cesare arrived at Senigallia, he was very kind to the four leaders of the conspiracy against him, Vitelli, Paolo, and the Orsini brothers. He lured them into a conference at the governor's palace and had Vitelli and Oliverotto strangled! The Orsini brothers were imprisoned and then killed, also on January 18, 1502. It was like the scene in *The Godfather* when Michael Corleone gets rid of the heads of the five families. Niccoló witnessed all of this and it fascinated him. He applauded it. In fact, he wrote a paper on it entitled, "The Murder of Vitellozzo Vitelli, Oliverotto Da Fermo, The Signor Pagolo, and the Duke Di Gravina Orsini." Cesare was quoted saying to Niccoló, "It is proper to snare those who are proving themselves past masters in the art of snaring others."

Niccoló thought that Cesare Borgia was the epitome of a Prince. After having seen the way France operated, he imagined Italy having a strong ruler like Cesare to unite and defend it. In chapter 8 of *The Prince*, Niccoló writes:

> When all the actions of the duke are recalled, I do not know how to blame him, but rather it appears to me, as I have said, that I ought to offer him for imitation to all those who, by the fortune or the arms of others, are raised to government. Because he, having a lofty spirit and far-reaching aims, could not have regulated his conduct otherwise, and only the shortness of the life of Alexander and his own sickness frustrated his designs. Therefore, he who considers it necessary to secure himself in his new principality, to win friends, to overcome by force or fraud, to make himself beloved and feared by the people, to be followed by the soldiers, to exterminate those who have power or reason to hurt him, to change the old order of things for the new, to be severe and gracious, magnanimous and liberal, to destroy a disloyal soldiery and to create new, to maintain friendships with kings and princes in such a way that they must help him with zeal and offend with caution, cannot find a more lively example than the actions of this man.

(It may be of interest to note here that Leonardo da' Vinci was Cesare's chief engineer and that he used many of the artist/inventor's machines.)

Cesare did not beat around the bush. He went directly to the heart of the matter. No fudging around here. The tales of the exploits of Alexander and Cesare are extensive. One story has it that the two of them used to arrest wealthy cardinals on trumped up charges and then make them pay kings' ransoms to be released. There are also many stories that suggest that they frequently poisoned wealthy cardinals in order to accelerate the reversion of their estates to the Church. As an entertainment device, Cesare would practice his skill with a bow and arrow by practicing on men who were sentenced to die. Cesare was even accused of killing his brother, the Duke of Gandia, and poor Lucrezia is reputed to have been the object of his sexual passions as well as her father's.

In August of 1503, Alexander and Cesare were attacked by serious fevers, probably malaria. On August 18th, Alexander died, and this proved to be the end of Cesare Borgia's reign as well. In May of 1504, Cesare fled to Naples where he was arrested and sent to Spain for imprisonment. In 1506, he escaped and was killed by Navarrese rebels in a battle in March of 1507.

To Niccoló, Cesare's style of leadership was the right way to lead, and he was very impressed by it, especially when compared with the likes of the Florentine leadership during the last decade of the fifteenth century. This was his perspective, and certainly one of the contributing factors towards his overall reputation as a messenger of the devil. Through the years, many have criticized Niccoló's viewpoint on Cesare as two-faced: on the one hand, he had great admiration for Cesare's ability to do whatever was necessary to achieve his goals and maintain his power base. On the other, Cesare's quick demise after his father's death was a clear indication that he was really nothing without his father. Niccoló was quick to observe this fact after Alexander's death and became most critical of Cesare. However, years later when he wrote about him in *The Prince*, he seemingly "forgot" about the fall of Cesare, choosing instead to glorify his more despicable character traits at the height of his power.

As a result of Alexander's efforts on behalf of Cesare, the balance of power in Italy was left in a very fragile and unstable state.

Ludovico Sforza,[10] the Duke of Milan, usurped power from his nephew in fear that the King of Naples would try and dethrone him. He was also afraid that Piero de' Medici, who succeeded Lorenzo, might support the King of Naples. This is why he called in the French, under Charles VIII, to invade Italy. It was the beginning of major changes throughout Italy, especially in Niccoló's Florence.

Charles VIII was so easily successful with his invasion that the Spanish King Ferdinand II of Aragon and the German Emperor Maximilian I formed a coalition with other Italian states to drive the French out of Naples. They were successful in their efforts, forcing Charles VIII out and back to France, but even though he was quickly forced out, the manner in which he easily attacked Italy had been eye-opening to other European powers.

Although there were many Peninsular wars during those days, the invasion by Charles VIII really "hit home" in Florence and had a profound political impact. Lorenzo de' Medici was succeeded by Piero de' Medici, the eldest of his three sons, generally incompetent, possessing none of Lorenzo's diplomatic skills; lacking character, far from being the statesman and administrator of public affairs that Lorenzo was. It was his general weakness and lack of leadership skills that resulted in Florence being easily taken over by Charles VIII. It has been said that it was so easy for Charles to take over that all he had to do was mark a house with chalk to seize it for billeting. The French came into Florence unopposed!

After taking over Florence, the French marched all the way down the Italian peninsula until they reached and invaded Naples in 1495.

Savonarola—Despite the uproar about the Medici and Charles VIII in Florence, not everyone was against what had happened, nor were all opposed to Charles VIII. Those who were supporters of Charles rallied around the leadership of Girolamo Savonarola,[11] a fanatical Dominican friar.

---

10 Known as "The Moor" because one of his Christian names was Mauro and he had a very dark complexion, Sforza was the ruler or Duke of Milan. By encouraging Charles VIII to invade Italy, he hoped to gain control over some of the Venetian territory. He lost power when Louis XII invaded Lombardy in September, 1499.

11 Please see Noel Tyl's wonderful analysis of Savonarola's horoscope in Tyl: *Synthesis & Counseling in Astrology*, pp. 178–181.

Savonarola, an older contemporary of Niccoló, was famous for his prophetic, apocalyptic sermons in which he predicted the death of Lorenzo de' Medici, denounced the lack of morals and worldliness in Florence and the evil ways of the papal court. After Piero de' Medici was driven out of Florence (through his surrender to Charles), Savonarola became the most influential man in Florence; he preached the strictest dogma that had Florence asong with hymns, loud with prayers, and burning with incense. His perspective of the French monarch's invasion was that it was an instrument of Divine Will that would lead Florence, as well as the rest of Italy, to restore itself to Christianity.

In the immediate period following Piero's expulsion from Florence, Savonarola made a great deal of progress in "cooling down" the Florentine anger and restoring moral decency, but he was not successful in restoring the Roman Catholic Church to purity and ridding it of corruption. His constant efforts to purge the Church of evil led *to his excommunication in 1497!* By and large, his new strict ways were highly resented and caused much hostility, particularly with Alexander VI, who would not and did not tolerate the way the Church[12] was being criticized. Savonarola was hanged and burned in the Palazzo della Signoria in Florence. His death signaled a change in governmental policies, and Florence returned to its Republican form of government for the next fourteen years.

Machiavelli certainly had his share of problems with the Papacy, focusing on two major complaints: first, the Papacy consistently provided the most horrendous example of moral behavior one could imagine, amply shown through the activities of Alexander VI. Second, the Papacy contributed greatly to the lack of unity among Italians because they were unable to occupy Italy completely, and did not allow anyone else to occupy it either. He speaks at great length about this problem in his *Discourses on Titus*

---

12 The power of the Pope was extreme during Machiavelli's lifetime, and there is a great deal of focus on the Papacy in *The Prince*. There were eight primary Popes during Niccoló's lifetime: Sixtus IV (Francesco della Rovere, Pope from 1492–1503), Pius III (Francesco Todeschini-Piccolomini, Pope for eight weeks in 1503), Julius II (Giuliano della Rovere, nephew of Sixtus IV, and Pope from 1503–1513), Leo X (Giovanni de; Medici, Pope from 1513–1521), Adrian VI (Adrian Dedel, Pope from 1622–1523), and Clement VII, the son of Giulio de' Medici and cousin of Leo X (Giulio de' Medici, Pope from 1523–1534).

Livy. Chapter 12, Book 1 is titled, "The Importance of Giving Religion a Prominent Influence In A State, And How Italy Was Ruined Because She Failed In This Respect Through The Conduct Of The Church Of Rome." In this chapter Niccoló talks about the unifying powers of the church when leaders of state keep corruption out of it and how that preserves the principles of religion because "having done this, they will find it an easy matter to keep the state devout, obedient, and united. They should seek to favor and strengthen every circumstance that tends to enhance religion, even if they themselves judge it to be false."

Shortly after Savonarola's death, Italy was invaded by another French King, Louis XII. Louis succeeded the throne that was vacated by the death of Charles VIII in 1498. He disposed of Lodovico Sforza and asserted his rights to the duchy of Milan, and partitioned Naples with the King of Spain, thus introducing another power into the Italian peninsula.

By now, with the death of Savonarola and a clearing out of the Medician influence, the Florentine government had been restored to a system of elected magistrates but was still dependent for its defense on foreign mercenary troops, a group that was totally incapable of providing any kind of a formidable defense against strong powers. The years 1498 through 1512 were a time of many continued wars and many shifts of alliances throughout Europe. They were also the best-documented years of the life of Niccoló Machiavelli.

The Life of Niccoló Machiavelli

First things first. Niccoló is pronounced as "nih-ko-ló." The final "o" in Niccoló is heavily emphasized, voiced more strongly than the rest of the name. The "i" is short as in the word "knit." In the preface of his book, *The Art of War*, his name appears in the Tuscan style, the way he preferred it and the way in which I will use it from time to time; it is Niccoló Machiavegli (pronounced almost the same, rolling the "gl" off the roof of the mouth).

The Machiavegli family had occupied the Tuscan region for approximately two centuries prior to the birth of Niccoló, playing a great role in the political goings-on of Florence for more than two centuries. His birthright included ancestry that was rich in experiences relating to real estate and politics. As many as fifteen members of the Machiavegli family served as Gonfalonier, the title given to the head of city council, loosely equating to a modern-day mayor. There were also a fair number of them that served as Republican Magistrates. Girolamo Machiavelli was a rebel who was exiled from Florence for his political stance opposing the "Regime of The Few." He was exiled to Avignon some ten years prior to the birth of Niccoló, and finally put to death in prison.

During the waning hours of his life, Niccoló's paternal grandfather, Niccoló di Buoninsegna, ostensibly a lifelong bachelor, confessed to having fathered a son named Bernardo. Bernardo was raised by his uncle, the brother of the elder Niccoló. When Bernardo came of age, he married Bartolomea Nelli, and our Niccoló was born from their union. He was named after that grandfather.

Niccoló's family was an average middle-class group without financial prowess, certainly of modest means. The greater part of his father's income was derived from his control of properties that were passed down to him through the Machiavegli ancestry. Although his father was a lawyer, he chose to live off farm and rental properties. In truth, he didn't practice much law at all and when he did, he accepted barter payments in gifts or goods. He was also constantly deluged with tax indebtedness.

There was a house that he owned on Via Guicciardini, south of the Arno, on the way to the Pitti Palace over the Ponte Vecchio. Father Bernardo also owned a house and some land in the country at a place called Sant' Andrea in Percussina, some six miles to the south of Florence, near Casciano. However, he did not own enough property to turn any real profit and was not the kind of man who was motivated enough to deal with any of the usual commercial or financial enterprises undertaken in Florence by men with considerable resources. He was quite content to make a meager living off of his ancestral properties, never providing any extra special advantages for Niccoló or his brother.[13] From the onset of his life, Niccoló was burdened with financial problems that persisted throughout his life—this is a telling dimension to guide our rectification.

---

13 Niccoló's brother was six years his junior, and became a priest.

Niccoló lived in an area of Florence called Machiavegli Court. The house he was born in was located on Via di Piaza, across the river in definite proximity to the political center of the city. I'm sure that the spirit of Niccoló planned it that way prior to birth!

Though he was a very bright youngster, the family financial status did not afford Niccoló the kind of education that his intellectual potential deserved, which undoubtedly would have placed him in a law career. His father, a cheap and frugal man, simply could not afford otherwise. From the onset, Niccoló was debilitated, economically and professionally.

Niccoló was sent to his first teacher at the age of seven; by the age of twelve he was deeply into Latin. Among the more well-known books or authors that were favorites of his were Ptolemy's *Cosmography*, anything by Petrarch, Aristotle's *Ethics*, Cicero's *Phillipic de Officils* and the author who made the grandest impression on him, Titus Livy. He was especially fond of Roman History, focusing on Livy. It was Livy who was the obvious subject of his book, *Discourses on the First Decade of Titus Livy*. By studying Roman history, Niccoló felt that he could gain answers to present-day political problems. As literature, his *Discourses* is far superior to *The Prince*. In the former, he discusses the concept of the Republic, whereas in the latter he places emphasis on the principality; on the city/state that is led by a Prince such as Cesare Borgia.

Although he was a precocious youngster, working hard at his studies and reading everything in sight, Niccoló's real education came from Florence itself. He lived very close to the center of Florence, where people who were involved in the silk business and in the manufacturing of wool gathered. Men grouped together to discuss politics, Latin poetry, literature, and all kinds of diverse opinions on many subjects; the activities in the world. Niccoló would sit and observe these conversations, listen to these concepts, and even gossip a little. Even at an early age, he was very interested in human nature and in wisdom, wondering why men did what they did and said what they said. Little did anyone know that he would grow up to become *the* voice of Renaissance politics, or better yet, the interpreter, the definer of Italian Renaissance politics. Appreciate him or not, the work of Niccoló Machiavelli helped to establish the politics of an age.

An interesting entry in a notebook that was kept by his father shows Niccoló, at age seven, being entrusted to take five *soldi* (the fee of his teacher, Maestro Matteo) to his teacher. The teacher lived on the south side of the Arno. This required Niccoló, twice a day, to go through the center of town. You can well imagine a child of seven years old making this half-mile excursion twice a day, money tightly in hand. His sense of responsibility and organization was developed even at that age. Even before we discuss the astrology of Niccoló in detail, with the emphasis on *politics*, the sense of *responsibility*, the kind of *old soul in a young body* way that he had about him, the precocious maturity, the developing sense of *responsibility*, the serious interest in *ancient tradition,* the eventual interest in *politics, strategy,* etc; all this in the mind of an astrologer automatically translates to Saturn/Capricorn. Already we sense their symbolic inclusion as a possible strength factor in the horoscope.

Niccolo's mother died in May of 1496, just after his twenty-sixth birthday. In light of his eventual disdain for the Papacy, it is interesting to note that his mother was a staunch Catholic, a very conventional, church-going woman. Aside from his early education and the death of his mother, there is no documentation available of what his life was like prior to the age of twenty-nine when his career began. (This was a major challenge, of course, for rectification).

As we have seen, after the death of Savonarola, Florence returned to the republican style of government that it enjoyed most. There was a complete turnover of personnel within the Florentine city government and, on June 19, 1498, at age twenty-nine, Niccoló was elected to the position of Secretary of the Second Chancellor, the second-highest-paid governmental position in Florence, with an annual salary of 200 sealed florins.[14] The position was confirmed on January 27, 1500 and Niccoló was re-elected every year thereafter through 1511.

The Florentine government was internal, operating independently of Italy and making its own decisions about laws and policies. It ruled the entire Tuscan empire and dealt directly with the most powerful of monarchs. As Secretary, Niccoló shared in all

---

14 Florentine currency.

international decisions, as well as important domestic issues in the developing business of Florence, *but he had no authority to make major decisions on his own.* It is not known whether or not it was because he wasn't trusted or if that was a limitation of his job description.

In Florence, the governing officials were elected for terms that lasted only *two months!* That meant a change of administration six times per year (with the exception of the chief official). Consequently, politics were a constant preoccupation on the minds of the Florentine citizens (Niccoló's obsession with politics is understandable in light of these environmental influences and the predisposition of his family history). It's interesting here to note that the reason for such short terms were twofold: the quickly changing administrations quelled the fear of dynastic control within government; second, and on a more practical note, these governing officials were required to spend the entire two months working at the Palazzo. To "go home" was the same thing as announcing your resignation. So, while you were serving the city for two months, you had no personal life; obviously it was asking too much of anyone, especially a family man, to expect more than two months of this kind of service. It was like enlistment in the military for eight weeks! Although Niccoló was a dedicated public servant, the demands on him were somewhat reduced; but he loved his work and loved politics so obsessively that it didn't make a difference to him.

On July 14, 1498 (one month after becoming Secretary of the Second Chancellor), he was made secretary to the main foreign relations committee known as "Dieci di Balia," or The Ten of Liberty and Peace, The Council of Ten, or The Ten of War. Although Niccoló's position was as Secretary, it was clear that he had more to offer, thus his selection into the Council of Ten. As Secretary of the Ten, Niccoló carried out many important missions, his specialty being foreign affairs, primarily in France, other parts of Italy, and Germany. This required spending a lot of time on horseback as an envoy to other countries and he absolutely loved it. His enthusiasm and love for his position brought him continued recognition and he was well respected by those with whom he consorted in other countries. In November of 1498, he was sent on his very first mission to the ruler of Piombino, the first of many diplomatic missions on behalf of The Ten.

Niccoló was quite *dependable, solid, reliable, trusted,*[15] and *hard-working.* In him, others felt a sense of competence and trust-worthiness that allowed them to feel comfortable that Niccoló would be taken at least respectably, if not seriously, by Princes such as Cesare Borgia. Nevertheless, he was not given the power to make important decisions on his own. Niccoló should have been given the official title of Ambassador, but his modest family position kept him from the title. Nevertheless, that is the function that he fulfilled. Almost every document and any kind of corre-spondence coming from the Republic found its way onto Nic-coló's desk.

Niccoló was married during August of 1501 (age thirty-two) to Marietta di Ludovico Corsini. In a life that seemed to be have constant obstacles, she was a blessing and remained loyal to Nic-coló until the day he died. They had six children: one died short-ly after birth, the youngest was born when Niccoló was fifty-five years old!

Prior to 1502, there had been restrictions placed on the length of time that the Chief Executive Official could spend in office. This Chief Executive was called "the Gonfalonier." In 1502, it was decided that this position would be filled for life by Piero di Tom-maso Soderini. Soderini had been instrumental in bringing about the downfall of the Medici and was a key component in the restoration of the Florentine Republic. Niccoló was chosen as his right-hand man, incurring much jealousy among his peers.

With the exile of the Medici, the hanging of Savonarola and those life-changing events that took place late in the fifteenth cen-tury, the chief preoccupation in Florence was with war. Niccoló's perspective was profoundly influenced by all of this. The vulnera-bility of Florence deeply troubled him. He saw a floundering gov-ernment that was not at all based on the good will of the people.

---

15 An interesting sideline here is that while Niccoló has garnered a reputation for being very unsavory and promoting unethical behavior, he was a very steadfast, honest, pub-lic servant to the Florentine government for fourteen years. Dishonesty was rampant in city government, but Niccoló never once exhibited anything less than perfect civil-servant behavior. While he encouraged and promoted the ruthless behavior that he saw in others, he did not practice this in his daily life. It is amazing that his reputation is so tarnished when you consider that he never stole, cheated, lied, or mishandled funds. When his political career ended, he was as financially impoverished as he was on his first day in office, despite numerous opportunities to take advantage of his sec-retarial position.

Niccoló's concerns were first and foremost that Florence should be a prosperous and safe place in which to live, that there should be good will among and for the people. Yet, foreign armies were "all over" Italy, trampling over it as if they were moving children aside. The Spanish had taken over Naples; Frenchmen invaded the kingdom periodically and were chased from Milan; the Germans and the Swiss were fighting one another; in Rome Alexander VI and his son Cesare and Julius II were scuffling in the effort to unify the Papal States; and there were moments within all of this that everyone put aside their differences to deal with Italy's only independent state, Venice. Florence was trying to find a way to regain its rulership over Pisa,[16] which had been lost during the French invasion. The first Chancellor wasn't very interested in taking a leadership role with regard to Pisa *so the responsibility for it fell squarely on the shoulders of the second Chancellor, Niccoló.*

The Philosophy: Machiavellianism

During his lifetime, Niccoló was an exceptionally original thinker who opened new ways of thinking about politics and statehood. His sole concern in life was in the development of the state.

Niccoló believed in history and suggested that history taught us that men of arms, the warrior types, are produced in society *before philosophers and men of the cloth are.* Since the basic nature of men is deceitful, greedy, selfish, etc., the perfect state needs to formulate itself in a forceful way *through its army* in order to establish laws, rules, and the formation of prescribed behaviors to be followed.

Niccoló believed that the best way to tame wicked men into obeying law and order was through religion. On the other hand, he blamed religion for its failure to make good citizens of the state. He totally rejected the ethics of Christianity in terms of its conception of relating goodness to being docile, nonresistant, etc. He believed in the Roman ethic which emphasized the welfare of the country above and over anything else; *the leader was not unethical if his actions were for the good of the state.* To Niccoló, morality was a

---

16 Pisa lies directly to the west of Florence and was its only outlet to the sea, which made it very important in terms of commerce and trade with the Mediterranean world.

code of conduct to be used in society *to maintain that society.* So if, in the process of defending the state, the government allowed itself to be *restricted by a moral code* that jeopardized the welfare of the people, it would fail. Therefore, *the ends justify the means.* In this line of thinking, fraud, lies, cheating, stealing, are honorable if used to defend the country. By this logic, Niccoló says in the *Discourses,* that Romulus did right by killing his brother.

This line of thinking quite naturally encourages war. Again, Niccoló looked at the Roman state and how it kept itself ever-ready for war. Through all of this reasoning, the bottom line was that the concept of statesmanship must be kept free of traditional moral considerations for the betterment of the state. This separation of ethics and morals from politics was a new, shocking way of thought.

Italy had become such a ragged, disjointed country, and was so weak that only violence could save her. A man like Cesare Borgia was needed, someone who could turn off his private conscience for the good of the state, no matter what actions were called for. Machiavellianism calls for a "just do it" type of attitude, with the means always justifying the end result.

The period 1498-1512 was a magnificent one for our Niccoló: the prime of his life and an important time in the history of Florence and Italy in general.

With the backdrop of Renaissance intrigue and the folds of Machiavellianism, here is a timetable of events during his life, to guide our rectification of this severe genius' horoscope:

1496: Niccoló's mother dies during mid-May.

1498: Political career begins in June.

1499: Goes on a mission to Caterina Sforza-Riario Countess of some states that were very important to Florence.

1500: Niccoló's father dies in May. He goes to France to meet with Louis XII from July to December. He is negotiating cessation of the war against Pisa.

1501: Marries Marietta Corsini in August.

1502: Pier Soderini becomes Gonfalonier of Florence for life. Niccoló becomes his most trusted assistant. Cesare Borgia seizes the Duchy of Urbino in June and Niccoló goes on a mission to the court of Cesare Borgia. He is again dispatched to the court of Cesare from October through January. He follows Borgia to Romagna and watches him suppress a conspiracy by his military captains. This wins Niccoló's respect and admiration.

1503: After the death of Alexander VI, Niccoló goes to Rome to observe the election and policies of the new pope, Giuliano (Julius II). He remains there for the duration of the year, meeting several times with Cesare Borgia to discuss the political future of north-central Italy.

1504: Cesare Borgia surrenders to Romagna and is arrested and banished to Spain as a prisoner by Pope Julius. Niccoló writes and completes the First Decennial, a book of verses that chronicle a series of events in Italy during the previous ten years. Goes on second mission to the court of Louis XII in January. Goes on mission to Pandolfo Petrucci in July.

1506: From January through August, Niccoló organizes a civil militia to make Florence independent of foreign mercenary troops. In his mind, much of the reason for Florence's vulnerability to invasion by foreign powers was due to its dependence upon foreign mercenaries because the mercenaries were incapable of providing any kind of an adequate defense in a serious war. In chapter 12 of *The Prince* he says the following:

> Mercenaries and auxiliaries are useless and dangerous; and if one holds his state based on these arms, he will stand neither firm nor safe; for they are disunited, ambitious, without discipline, unfaithful, valiant before friends, cowardly before enemies; they have neither the fear of God nor fidelity to men, and destruction is deferred only so long as the attack is. The fact is, they have no other attraction or reason for keeping the field other than a trifle of stipend, which is not sufficient to make them willing to die for you. They are ready enough to be your soldiers whilst you do not make war, but if war comes they take themselves off or run from the foe; which I should have little trouble to prove, for the ruin of Italy has been caused by nothing else than by resting all her hopes for many years on mercenaries, and although they formerly made some display and appeared valiant amongst themselves, yet when the foreigners came they showed them what they were. Thus it was that Charles, King of France, was allowed to seize Italy with chalk in hand.

From August through November Niccoló serves as the Florentine representative at the court of Pope Julius who was on his military campaign to gain authority over Bologna and Perugia and to re-conquer the provinces of the church. Niccoló observes the warrior-like Pope in action and greatly respects him. In December, the Great Committee establishes the Nine of the Militia. Niccoló is elected Secretary.

1507: Cesare Borgia dies on March 12th. Niccoló is sent on a mission to Emperor Maximilian's[17] court to negotiate the payments that he demanded from Florence to meet the expenses of his coronation as emperor in Rome.

1508: Returns from Maximilian's court in June. Is placed in charge of operations against Pisa. League of Cambray is formed to attack Venice.

1509: Florentine troops, led and trained by Niccoló, enter Pisa on June 8th and regain control of Pisa.

1510: Niccoló's third mission to France in June to meet with Louis XII. Returns to work on the militia.

1511: Pope Julius forms the Holy League in order to fight French expansion. Niccoló makes his fourth trip to France.

1512: *The beginning of the end for Niccoló.* His militia is over-matched in the Battle of Prato. The Medici family is restored to power on September 14th in Florence with help from Spanish troops. The Florentine Republic is wiped out. *Niccoló is dismissed from office on November 7, 1512.*

1513: *Niccoló is imprisoned on February 12th,* accused of being a part of a conspiracy against the Medici. While in prison he is tortured on a device called the rack. He is released on March 11th. Retires to the Machiavegli villa in Sant Andrea where he composes *The Prince.*

1514: Writes but does not complete the Second Decennial, covering the years 1505-1509. Starts writing *The Art Of War,* probably his greatest work as an author.

1515: Becomes a member of the literary circle around Cosimo Rucellai at the Orti Oricellari.

1516: Niccoló presents *The Prince* to the nephew of Lorenzo de'

---

17 Elected King of Germans in 1485. In February, 1508, and with Pope Julius II's consent, he assumes the title of Roman Emperor Elect.

Medici, who has by now replaced the unsuitable Giuliano as the governor of Florence. It is ignored.

1517: Writes a fable called *Belfagor*, an unfinished fantasy called *The Golden Ass* and a comedy called *Andria*.

1518: Niccoló's comedy, *The Mandragola,* is published.

1519: Lorenzo de' Medici dies prematurely and is succeeded by Cardinal Giulio de' Medici. Niccoló is commissioned by Giulio to write *The Florentine Histories* and is given minor missions to carry out. Leo X comes to Niccoló for political advice.

1520: Writes *The Life of Castruccio Castracani,* a short biography.

1521: *The Art of War* is published. Makes the first mission to Tuscany since his exile and is commissioned in May to go to a conclave of Franciscan Friars in Carpi. Pope Leo dies and is succeeded by Hadrian VI. The tumultuous period of 1512-1517 finally shows signs of turning around and picking up.

1522: Has a scandalous, disastrous love affair.

1525: In mid-January, his comedy play *Clizia* is performed publicly in Florence. Travels to Rome to present *The Florentine History* to Pope Clement. Discusses the formation of a civil militia to defend Florence and Romagna with the Pope.

1526: Niccoló's idea of a commission, the Curators of the Walls (overseeing the fortification of the Florentine walls), is approved by Pope Clement during April and in May (18th) he is elected Secretary and Quartermaster of the commission.

1527: Clement's diplomatic mistakes lead to a sacking of Rome in May (16) by mercenaries under Charles V. The Florentines seize the opportunity and expel the Medici to re-establish the Republic. Niccoló has high hopes of being reinstated to his position but is rejected (June 10) because of his association with the previous regime. *He dies as a result of violent stomach problems on June 21, 1527.*

1531: The *Discourses Upon The Books of Titus Livy* are published.

1532: *The Prince* is published.

The Astrology of Niccoló Machiavelli— The Rectification Process

In his book, *The Golden Ass*, Niccoló states the following about his birth information: "Born 1469, May, day three, hour four, minute unknown." We have a starting point of 5/3/69 at 4:30 A.M.[18] Local Mean Time in Florence. With my first look at this horoscope, I thought to myself, "Yes! This makes sense already." The Aquarian Moon in the 10th House suggests social or humanitarian needs expressed through the career in a public way; Capricorn on the Midheaven certainly fits for a political career; Mercury, as final dispositor of the chart is strong in the Ascendant, certainly symbolizing Niccoló's ability as thinker, observer, communicator, and writer. Jupiter in the 4th would show the hope for rewards in terms of security in his homeland. My thinking at the time was ecstatic. "I can't be far off now!" *But I was way off:* there is a passage in the book, *Vita de Niccoló Machiavelli* (the life of Machiavelli), which states that Niccoló was born "during the fourth hour of *the night!*" On May 3, 1469, sunset was between 7 P.M. and 7:30 P.M. Of course, this changed my starting time radically, from between 4 A.M. and 5 A.M. to between 11 P.M. and 12 midnight!

Had I stopped with my first impression, which seemed valid, was sensible, and *felt* very good, I would have been way off track. It's best *not* to start the rectification process by fitting the Ascendant and planetary placements to one's idea of what "should be" or what "seems" correct according to the way we see the individual in question. Every horoscope embodies all twelve Signs, so we have to be careful with quick assumptions. If, for example, we have a choice between a Leo Moon and a Virgo Moon, we can not make a decision based on the fact that the person may be analytical when there are so many people with the Moon in Leo who *are* hyperanalytical, because of other planetary considerations. Nor do we settle on a Taurus Ascendant because the neck is thick. It isn't that these aren't valid ways of thinking; we all use this kind of logic instinctively, but when it comes to thorough rectification it can be shaky ground for deductions. A crisp event orientation is the secure way to rectification. At the

---

18 When the time of birth is narrowed down to within an hour, it's wise to start at the halfway point of the hour in question.

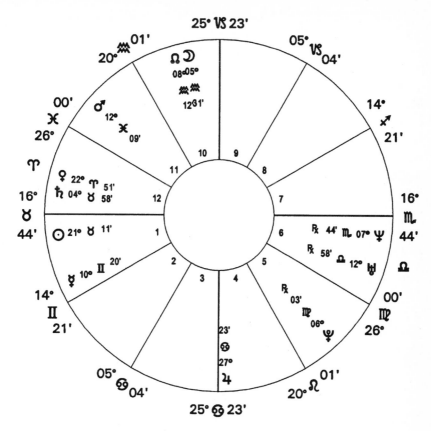

Orientation Chart
Niccoló Machiavelli
May 3, 1469 04:30 A.M. LMT
Florence, Italy
11E15 43N46
Placidus Houses

risk of exposing my 9th House Saturn, I must say in reference to the rectification process, "just the facts please."

There are many techniques that can be employed in rectification, just as for astrological analysis in general. These techniques include transits, Solar/Lunar/planetary arcs,[19] Secondary Pro-

---

19 With Solar and planetary arcs we are taking the Secondary Progressed position of the Sun, Moon, or planet in question. From it, we subtract the natal position of the Sun for a Solar Arc, Moon for Lunar, etc., and then add the arc to all natal positions.

gressions; Tertiary Progressions, Naibod arcs, Quotidians (for the siderealists), and there are converse methods of progressions too. The techniques that one uses are dependent upon personal style and usually upon what has successfully worked with consistency in the past in one's practical way of measuring astrological life time. In the majority of cases, I prefer to use transits, Solar Arcs and Secondary Progressions, fitting all measurements into the Lunation Cycle,[20] not just in rectification but for projecting forward in time, as well as going back in time with my clients. When I'm really looking for additional corroboration on a point, I'll also look at the Tertiary Progressions,[21] and I have recently started to experiment with *converse* Tertiary Progressions.

Overall, I've found that the techniques one uses depend on what one has to work with. If someone gives you a birth time as "between 2 A.M. and 10 P.M.," the methodology has to change a bit from a birth time span given as "1 P.M.–1:20 P.M.," because you don't have as many factors to consider when the span of time is short.

I must pause here to make a comment about the use of computers with astrology. If you are a serious student or seasoned astrologer and are not using a computer for your calculations, you are doing a serious injustice to yourself. The computer will not, by any means, allow you to analyze a horoscope any better than the same horoscope done manually. Just because you have a laser printer that prints twenty quadzillion pages per minute at ninety billion dots per inch and a computer that operates faster than the speed of light doesn't mean anything when it comes to doing a horoscope. The same degree of difficulty exists whether the chart is neatly printed or sloppily handwritten. I happen to be the owner of a sophisticated computer/printer setup with three professional programs and speak from personal experience. However, there is just no comparison when it comes to the speed at which you can *prepare* your work and more importantly, its accuracy.

---

20 The Lunation Cycle represents the aspect relationship between the Secondary Progressed Sun and Secondary Progressed Moon. As they form aspects with one another, there is a symbolic representation of the turning points in an individual's life. The cycle lasts approximately twenty-nine years.

21 In this type of progression, one day in the ephemeris is equal to one lunar month. In other words, if you are doing Tertiary Progressions for the tenth year of life, multiply ten by thirteen (there are thirteen lunar returns per year) to get the number of days after birth, which, in this case, is equal to 130. Computer programs do the work, thank goodness!

For example, it took me less than five minutes to print out a list of transits, Solar Arcs, Secondary Progressions, Tertiary Progressions and the Lunation Cycle for Niccoló's *entire life,* all in chronological order and timed to seconds of clock time accuracy! I'd still be working with those details if I had computed all that manually with pencil and paper—only a monk could have taken on that task! Have you ever tried to construct a 90 or 45 degree midpoint sort manually with pencil and paper? A root canal without an anesthetic might be less painful! After you've gone blind and your hands are dripping blood three hours later, you'll finally have a sort, but with a fifteen percent error count. Also, if you are research-oriented at all and need to work with data prior to the twentieth century, especially regarding eclipses, the computer gives you a significant advantage because the ephemeris is built in. Most good programs, including the Matrix Blue★Star professional version that I own, are automatically configured to give planetary positions well into the B.C. dates, and up through and beyond the year 2300. Not only are they included in the program, you can print hard copy of them and even customize your own ephemeris.

When it comes to rectification in particular, computers are indispensable, as is a good program, because you get the benefit of seeing the chart on-screen and you can make instant changes to the angles with the press of a key. The best program for rectification that I have used is called Star Trax 8000. It was designed by astrologer Alphee Lavoie. Unlike other programs that simply re-calculate an Ascendant or Midheaven that you've selected, Star Trax computes angles based on compiled events in the life of the person in question.

The first step toward successful rectification of the horoscope is to compile a list of as many factual events in the life as you can get. We have done this for Machiavelli (pages 288–291), against the backdrop of his times of intrigue. Then, we want to look especially at outer planet transits to the angles, Arcs to the *angles* (focusing on the Solar Arc), and the movement of the Secondary Progressed Moon over the angles. Although I use them as a last resort, eclipses can also be used very helpfully to rectify a horoscope.

One of the most important facts of Niccoló's life is that *he always had a financial struggle.* In fact, it is said that his family was left quite impoverished upon his death. During his career years between 1498–1512 (a semi-Saturn Cycle?), he threatened to step down from his position several times because of a lack of funds.

Having referred back to the important facts, we want to compile a list of character and personality traits:

1. Steadfast.
2. Reliable.
3. Administrative.
4. An organizer.
5. Liked the shock effect, doing and saying things that surprised people.
6. Patriotic (just before his death Niccoló proclaimed that he loved his native city—more than he loved his own soul).
7. Trustworthy.
8. Energetic.
9. Great respect for tradition and history.
10. Practical and doesn't believe in wasting time.
11. Loves strategy.
12. An effective communicator/writer.
13. Cynical.
14. At the age of forty-four, Niccoló wrote that politics was the passion of his life.
15. Doesn't like half measures. Prefers a clean sweep or nothing at all.
16. A trusted advisor, counselor and teacher.
17. Inspired by powerful people and grandiose concepts.

When we look at this list and go to the planetary positions in the ephemeris, *we shouldn't be surprised by what we find.* In other words, if we have someone with a dominant character trait of being oppressively emotional, we aren't going to expect to see forty-nine planets in Aquarius! Although some of the qualities listed above for Machiavelli require an investigation into deeper parameters than just a planet in its Sign, for the most part we can see the reflection of *Taurean* qualities, we can feel his love of shocking people in the Aquarian Moon, the strength of Mercury as a communicator, etc. We can get comfortable with what we see and can move forward without questioning the birthdate.

We know that the birth took place between 11 P.M. and 11:59 P.M. Any horoscope that is constructed for that time period in Florence will have a Capricorn Ascendant, a Scorpio Midheaven, and the Moon in Aquarius. All of this fits our deepening impression of Machiavelli. Much of the work is done already. Now we need to deduce and prove the degrees of the Midheaven and Ascendant.

Because there is nothing factual written anywhere about Niccoló prior to the age of twenty-nine—except his early schooling and the death of his mother just after his twenty-sixth birthday—some 30 degrees of arc, progression, and transit activity within the first orbit of Saturn, for example, are barren. If you look at my orientation horoscope (page 293), there is a lot of Solar Arc activity involving angles that takes place prior to the age of twenty-nine. [Saturn=ASC, Neptune=ASC, Uranus=ASC, Venus conj ASC, MC=Moon, etc. — Ed.] Our lack of *early* facts limits the process of rectification to the events that took place after the age of twenty-nine, along with the death of his mother just after his twenty-sixth birthday.

The "first try" rectification horoscope was cast for 11:30 P.M. LMT (page 298). I am immediately comfortable with the 4th House Sun as a symbol of Niccoló's entire purpose; all his words, all his thoughts, were centered around and through the organization of a structure (Taurus), both politically and militarily, for the benefit of Florence, his homeland (4th House). His deathbed statement was, "I love my native city more than my own soul."

An Aquarian Moon in the 1st House is the quintessence of individualism. The Moon in any Sign in the 1st House is given to strong individualistic expression of highly individual needs, the moreso when it is in Aquarius. The Aquarian Moon is an active one, reaching out, trying to get things done for others. In this case, it is working overtime to fulfill the heart's focus and love for the city of Florence (the basic life energy of the Sun in the 4th focused individualistically through the Moon). Niccoló's every action is based upon making Florentine society a better place for all of its inhabitants. So we feel comfortable with this position and we know that it's accurate because our time span between 11 P.M. and 11:59 P.M. will not place the Moon in any other house.

Mercury in Gemini in the creative 5th House and the fortified 3rd House "feel" good and corroborate Niccoló's authorship and the playwright dimensions. In *The Encyclopedia of Medical Astrology,* H. L. Cornell says that a person who is fond of a political life is "born under the strong influence of the tropical signs Cancer and Capricorn." In that politics was the passion of Niccoló's life, along with his strategic nature, his systematic nature, the seriousness of purpose, the organizational ability, and the dark way of interpreting people, places, and things, Capricorn is highly fitting. Also, Niccoló was very cynical. Charles Carter writes in his *Encyclopedia of Psychological Astrology* that "a cynical person has the habit of sneering at harmless pleasures and a disbelief in the worth of human aims and life in general. It would probably be found

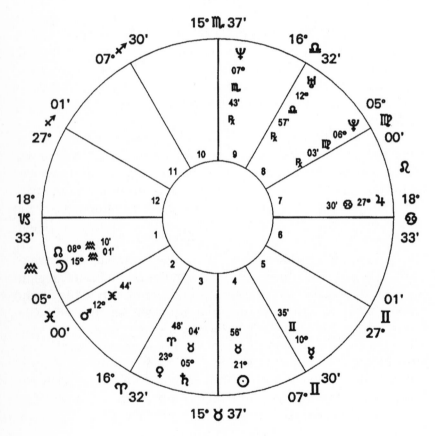

"First Try"
Niccoló Machiavelli
May 3, 1469 11:30 P.M. LMT
Florence, Italy
11E15 43N46
Placidus Houses

under Virgo, Scorpio, and Capricorn assets. Capricorn is very easily depressed by failure and non-recognition."

On top of all this, Niccoló was a person who concluded that "men are bad." In general, his way of projecting himself to the world was indeed very cynical, and everything that we know about his outlook certainly shows an attunement to Saturnian dimensions. With Scorpio strong on the Midheaven, its ruler in Virgo, we cover all three areas here. Also, as a vocational guide, the ruler of the Midheaven in Virgo would correspond to a service vocation.

Having established a first-try chart, we now want to narrow down the events to focus on those that had the most meaning to him. In this case, the job is easy and requires no value judgment. Machiavelli lived and breathed politics and strategy, so we want to look first and foremost at the career beginning and ending. In that his political career started in June of 1498, we are certainly going to look for angular activity during that time just as we would during any major event in any person's life.[22] Because of his love and passion for politics, his dismissal from office is paramount in the astrological scheme of things and should certainly be reflected in the horoscope.

On June 19, 1498, Niccoló was elected to a political career. Then on July 14, 1498 he was elected to his position with the Ten of War. He was dismissed from office on November 7, 1512. We want to look at the slower-moving planets from Jupiter through Pluto on these dates to see if there is a formation in or around a certain degree.

---

22 I am reminded as I write these words of the plight of O. J. Simpson who is in jail awaiting a trial for two murders. His confirmed birth data is 7/9/47 at 8:08 A.M. PST San Francisco. Transiting Pluto is separating from a square to his horizon and he's experiencing the mid-life Solar Arc semi-square that we all absorb around the age of forty-five. As huge an event as this is in O. J.'s life, there is absolutely nothing angular occurring in his horoscope, nothing really at all to symbolize the event. In my experiences it is one of the great mystery cases in astrology and certainly sends a message to us all that there is probably as much to learn as what we already know. It is living proof that we cannot always find "it" in the horoscope. Sometimes real life defies our measurements.

June 18, 1498	July 14, 1498	Nov. 7, 1512
Jupiter **13 Cap 13**	Jupiter **10 Cap 06**	Jupiter 23 Pis 42
Saturn **4 Tau 4**	Saturn **6 Tau 22**	Saturn **7 Sco 24**
Uranus 21 Aqu 41	Uranus 20 Aqu 55	Uranus **14 Ari 31**
Neptune **11 Cap 33**	Neptune **10 Cap 53**	Nep 11 Aqu 02
Pluto 17 Sco 43	Pluto 17 Sco 29	Pluto 22 Sag 14

What is immediately apparent from these positions is the position of Saturn at the outset and end of Niccoló's career. They are almost in exact opposition. In that Saturn embraces career matters within its symbolism, it isn't at all surprising to find that there was such a grand change for him during the Saturn Return and during Saturn's transiting in opposition to its own place.[23] This is especially so because of its natal position in a Cadent House, setting things up for a new beginning over the 4th House cusp or a career emphasis of some kind transiting the 10th House cusp. We need to dig deeper for other corroborations.

The area of the cardinal Signs between 10–14 degrees is active on all three dates. Could this mean something? In looking at my "first try" horoscope, this cardinal area didn't reveal anything in terms of angles. But what would happen if I moved the Ascendant back to, say, *13 degrees Capricorn* to coincide with Jupiter's transit of the Ascendant when he first took public office? Not the strongest of beginnings, but a beginning for sure, as we shall see.

Horoscope Try Two, timed to 11:11 P.M. for Jupiter's transit of the Ascendant, is basically the same horoscope with one exception: Uranus is now in the 9th House. Its position there almost forces the eye to become more conscious of the SA Uranus projection to the Midheaven, almost invariably an indication of a career event and/or an upheaval of some kind involving a parent. Its distance from the Midheaven would place Uranus there during the time of the career beginning. By itself, I felt more comfortable with Uranus in the 9th as opposed to its 8th House position. If you look at the 9th House in terms of the world outlook, the placement of Uranus is certainly going to suggest something unique, uncommon, eccentric, or individualistic about the outlook. In addition, Uranus in the 9th House corroborates the

---

23 Saturn's transiting relationship to itself always suggests a shifting of gears in the life.

expression of individuality and individualistic development in foreign affairs. Working with this factor alone told me that I was headed in the right direction, that I should be working toward 11:00 as opposed to midnight; i.e., to close in on the important Solar Arc, with the special Jupiter transit already accounted for.

Solar Arc Uranus would reach the Midheaven sometime in the twenty-eighth to twenty-ninth year (the distance in degrees from 12 Libra to 10 Scorpio). It certainly makes sense, but then again, maybe this Uranus is the key to timing the death of his

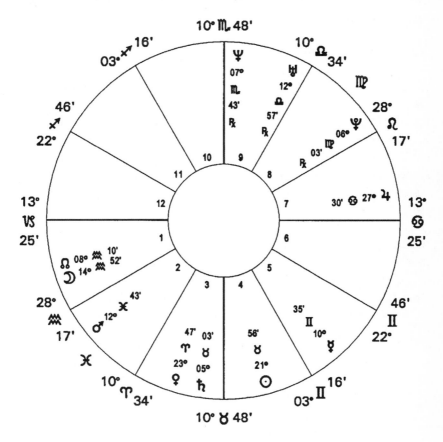

"Second Try"
Niccoló Machiavelli
May 3, 1469 11:11 P.M. LMT
Florence, Italy
11E15 43N46
Placidus Houses

mother during mid-May, just after his twenty-sixth birthday; i.e., an earlier Midheaven, a shorter arc for an earlier age. After all, there were so many other symbols *already* involved with the start of the career. What if we set up the chart this way to key the Solar Arc progression of Uranus to the Midheaven exactly when Niccoló's mother died? Transiting Pluto was squaring his Moon at the time and perhaps worked together with SA Uranus. This would require subtracting approximately 8 minutes in time to get the Midheaven to 8 degrees Scorpio. Since the death of his mother took place just weeks after his twenty-sixth birthday, we'd need to move Uranus 26 degrees from 12 Libra to 8 Scorpio. At 11:03:14 P.M. LMT, the SA of Uranus to the Midheaven becomes exact two weeks after Niccoló's twenty-sixth birthday.

And now, with a Midheaven of 8 degrees Scorpio+, we can now look forward in time to the month (November) when he was dismissed from office in 1512. Transiting Saturn would have been less than a degree away from being exactly on the 8 Scorpio Midheaven, making the somber picture Saturn=Neptune/MC (*Insecurity and uncertainty, the tendency to worry,* Ebertin; *The feeling of being wiped out; needing to correct past mistakes with open honest, clear statements and plans,* Tyl)! Natal Neptune would now be powerfully situated on the Midheaven, certainly a symbol of his involvement with the theater as a playwright and perhaps contributing somewhat to his nebulous public persona his fit with professional intrigue.

With an Ascendant adjusted to 11 degrees Capricorn, we see the June/July period in 1498, the beginning of his career, as being quite powerful through the following transiting measurements:

> Uranus square Sun on June 6th
> Saturn's return on June 23rd *conjunct the Nadir* (the new
>   beginning)
> Neptune conjunct *Ascendant* on June 24th
> Jupiter conjunct *Ascendant* on July 3rd

and we add:

> SA Moon conjunct Mars on July 4th

This establishes clearly the Ascendant and Midheaven through the transits as they parallel the career beginning and ending, the two most important events of his life. Everything seems to be approaching order, and we can move further with other refinements.

The years between late 1512 and 1517 were terrible for Niccoló: he was out of politics and forcibly exiled from his beloved Florence. In fact, he experienced a merciless string of hard times from life particularly between 1513 and 1515 (Tr. Saturn conj. MC, Tr. Saturn opp Sun, Tr. Saturn square Moon, Tr. Neptune conj. Moon, SA Uranus=Asc, SA ASC=Mars/Neptune, Tr. Saturn square Pluto, SP Moon opp Saturn) In a famous letter dated December 10, 1513, Niccoló wrote to Francesco Vettori:[24]

> I am living on my farm since I had my last bad luck.[25] I have until now been snaring thrushes[26] with my own hands. I got up with a bundle of cages on my back, prepared birdlime, went out with a bundle of cages on my back, so that I looked like Geta when he was returning from the harbor with Amphitryon's books.[27] I caught at least two thrushes and at most six. And so I did all September. Then this pastime, pitiful and strange as it is, gave out, to my displeasure. And what sort of life it is I tell you.
>
> I get up in the morning with the sun and go to a grove I am having cut down, where I remain two hours to look over the work of the past day and kill some time with the cutters, who have always some bad-luck story to tell, about either themselves or their neighbors.
>
> Leaving the grove, I go to a spring, and thence to my aviary. I have a book in my pocket, either Dante or Petrarch, or one of the lesser poets, such as Tibullus, Ovid, or Petrarch, and the like. I read of their tender passions and loves, remember mine, enjoy myself a while in that sort of dreaming. Then I go along the road to the inn; I speak with those who pass, ask news of their villages, learn various things, and note the

---

24 Niccoló worked with Vettori as an aid on various missions and was godfather to one of his children.

25 Referring to the month spent in prison.

26 Trapping birds and catching them.

27 Referring to a story founded on the Amphitru of Platus.

various tastes and different fancies of men. In the course of these things comes the hour for dinner, where with my family I eat such food as this poor farm of mine and my tiny property allow. Having eaten, I go back to the inn; there is the host, usually a butcher, a miller, two furnace tenders. With these I sink into vulgarity for the whole day playing games that bring on a thousand disputes, insults, and offensive words and usually we are fighting over a penny. So it is that in these trifles I keep my brain from growing mouldy, and satisfy the malice of this fate of mine, being glad to have her drive me along this road, to see if she will be ashamed of it. I do not dread poverty. I am not frightened by death. I give myself over to them.

I have composed a work on Princedoms, where I go as deeply as I can into considerations on the subject, debating what a princedom is, of what kinds they are, how they are gained, how they are kept, why they are lost. I am dedicating it to Giuliano de' Medici.

It's enough to make you cry, isn't it? This is a man who is severely depressed and unhappy. These excerpts from his letters typify the kind of internal pain that Niccoló experienced during this four-year period. It was one thing to lose job and position, but completely another thing to have been deprived of the "privilege" of being a Florentine citizen. This killed his spirit, deeply affecting his ideas about himself. The transit of Neptune had him in a befuddled state about his identity. This is the spirit in which *The Prince* was written. It has to be a contributing factor to the cynicism that runs rampant through so many words.

On June 10, 1514, Niccoló wrote another letter to Vettori that has the following passage:

I am staying among my lice in this village, without finding a man who remembers my service to Florence or who believes that I might be good for anything. It is impossible to stay this way. One day I will be forced out of the house and place myself as tutor or secretary to a constable, if I cannot do otherwise, or stick myself in some deserted land to teach writing to the young, and leave my family who may as well count me dead; they could do much better without me because I am an expense to them.

These letters were written as transiting Saturn was exactly opposed the Sun and widely squared his Moon with Neptune moving into conjunction with the Moon. Niccoló is totally despondent, hopelessly depressed and without value to himself or others. In *The Principles and Practices of Astrology*, Tyl observes about the transit of Saturn in opposition to the Sun, "Ambition is symbolically as far away from the core center of identity as it can get. Fulfillment of ambition can seem out of reach; enormous frustration can enter the life." Yes it can and this was a most difficult, difficult, time in Niccoló's life. However, the absence from politics and the exile from Florence gave him plenty of time to put his experiences into words and compose three wonderful books.

An Astrological Life Summary
(expansion from page 288–291)

May 1496: Mother dies.	SA Uranus=MC
June/July 1498: Elected to Office.	Tr. Uranus sq. Sun June 6 Saturn Return June 23 Tr. Neptune conj. ASC June 24 Tr. Jupiter conj. ASC July 3 SA Moon conj. Mars July 4
Jan. 1500: Confirmed into office.	SP Moon trine Jupiter
May 1500: Father's death.	Tr. Saturn conj. Sun
Aug. 1501: Marriage.	Tr. Jupiter conj. Saturn SA Pluto=Sun TP ASC conj. Venus
Mar. 1502: Becomes assistant to newly elected Gonfalonier.	Tr. Jupiter opp MC
June 1502: Spends time with Cesare as a diplomatic emissary. Important turning point in his intellectual development.	Tr. Jupiter conj. Sun
Oct. 1502: Influential Cesare Campaign.	SP Moon conj. Saturn SA Sun=MC
Dec. 1506: Elected Secy. 9 of Militia.	Tr. Pluto opp Mercury SP New Moon
June 1509: Leads army to victory over Pisa.	SA Mars=Sun Tr. Jupiter square Mars

Aug. 1512: Loses Battle of Prato.	Tr. Saturn sq. Jupiter
Nov. 1512: Career is ended.	Tr. Saturn conj. MC SA Saturn=Sun/ASC
Feb. 1513: Sent to prison.	SA Mars=Neptune/ASC
Summer 1514: Love affair.	Tr. Uranus conj. Venus
Oct. 1515: Becomes member of literary circle around Cosimo Rucellai at the Orti Oricellari.	SP Moon conj. MC
Apr. 1518: *The Mandragola* is published.	SA Venus=Mercury Tr. Uranus conj. Nadir SP Sun trine MC SA Mercury conj. Jupiter
Nov. 1519: Commission for Florentine History.	Tr. Jupiter conj. MC
May 1521: *Art of War* published. Given first mission in 9 years.	Tr. Pluto conj. ASC Tr. Uranus conj. Sun Tr. Saturn conj. Moon
1522: Scandalous love affair.	SP Moon sq. Venus Tr. Uranus conj. Sun Tr. Jupiter sq. Venus SA Sun sq. Uranus TP Venus conj. Saturn TP Venus opp Neptune TP Venus sq. Node
1525: *Clizia* performed publicly. Travels to Rome to present *Florentine Histories.* Last of his five children is born.	SA Uranus sq. Pluto Tr. Jupiter sq. ASC Tr. Jupiter conj. Venus
Apr./May 1526: Idea to create Commission to fortify Florentine walls accepted. Elected Secretary and Quarter- master. *Back into politics!*	SA Venus=Jupiter/MC Tr. Jupiter conj. Sun Tr. Saturn sq. ASC Tr. Uranus conj. Mercury Tr. Saturn opp Uranus SA Mercury=Saturn

During 1525, Francis I was defeated at Pavia and Clement VII was highly ineffective and helpless against Charles V. Niccoló sent letters to the Pope in an effort to provide or suggest options that could be used against, what appeared to be an imminent conquest of Italy by the Spanish and the Germans. When Giovanni de' Medici died, the Germans advanced upon Florence. Niccoló rushed to the city with a report that documented how best to provide Florence with protection by restoring the walls surrounding the city. The Germans bypassed Florence and instead went to Rome. Yet, as a result of key errors made by Clement, Florence was sacked on May 16, 1527, but was then returned to a Republican government.

Niccoló was ecstatic and applied for his old position as the Secretary of The Ten of War. He was turned down on June 10th, 1527 because of his former dealings with the Medici. He died eleven days later of stomach complications. Transiting Mars was exactly square the Sun (in the 4th House-the end of the matter), transiting Pluto was exactly sesquiquadrate natal Pluto (in the 8th House-matters of death), and transiting Saturn was square Jupiter (in Cancer, the stomach). The measurements are clear and the deductions are solid. The final adjustment of the angles in the horoscope was keyed by the Solar Arc measurement of Uranus to the Midheaven, symbolizing the death of Niccoló's mother. This is also corroborated by the midpoint picture, Mercury=ASC/MC, a picture that makes Mercury a central figure in the horoscope and could only have occurred within the first eleven minutes or so of the hour in which Niccoló was born. The rectified angles work with precision, and we can see the well-documented characterlogical dimensions spelled out clearly in the horoscope. The rectified horoscope of Niccoló Machiavelli is shown on page 308.

Chart Analysis

Niccoló's horoscope gives us plenty of food for thought: it is a fairly complicated, demanding chart with an Air Grand Trine among Moon, Mercury, and Uranus, and two T-squares (Saturn-Neptune (MC) squared by the Moon and Mars-Pluto squared by Mercury)! The heart and soul of any horoscope is built upon the blending of the Signs that are held by the Sun and Moon at birth. Together, they establish an ideal for the astrologer in terms of character and personality projection, which is then distributed and projected through the lens of the Ascendant. Here, with the Sun in Taurus, we know to expect a life-energy emphasis on struc-

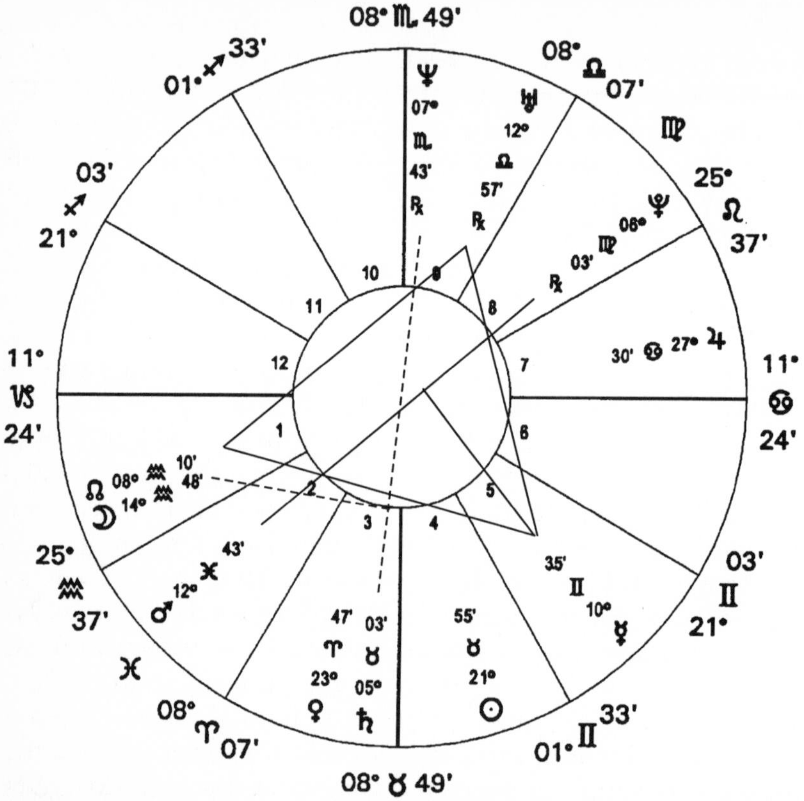

NICCOLO MACHIAVELLI MAY 03, 1469

Midpoint Sort: 45° Dial

☉/☊	000°03'	☿/☊	009°22'	♃/Asc	019°27'	☿/♂	026°39'	♄	035°03'	☿/Asc	041°00'
☉/Mc	000°22'	☿/Mc	009°42'	♃/♅	020°13'	♃	027°30'	☽/♃	036°09'	☽/♆	041°15'
♃/♇	001°46'	♂/♆	010°13'	♇	021°03'	♂	027°43'	♄/♆	036°23'	☽/☊	041°29'
☿/♀	002°11'	☽/♇	010°25'	♄/Asc	023°14'	☽/Asc	028°06'	♄/☊	036°37'	☿/♅	041°46'
♀/♂	003°15'	♂/☊	010°26'	☿/♇	023°19'	☽/♅	028°52'	♄/Mc	036°56'	☽/Mc	041°49'
☽/☉	003°22'	♂/Mc	010°46'	♀	023°47'	♀/♄	029°25'	♆	037°43'	♂/Asc	042°04'
☿/♃	004°02'	Asc	011°24'	♄/♅	024°00'	♀/♆	030°45'	☉/♀	037°51'	♂/♅	042°50'
♂/♃	005°06'	♅/Asc	012°11'	♂/♇	024°23'	♀/☊	030°58'	♆/☊	037°56'	☉/♄	043°29'
♄/♇	005°33'	☽/☿	012°41'	♆/Asc	024°33'	♃/♄	031°17'	☊	038°10'	☽	044°48'
♆/♇	006°53'	♅	012°57'	☊/Asc	024°47'	♀/Mc	031°18'	♆/Mc	038°16'	☉/♆	044°49'
☉	006°55'	☽/♂	013°45'	Mc/Asc	025°07'	☉/Asc	031°40'	☊/Mc	038°29'	♀/♇	044°55'
♇/☊	007°06'	☉/♇	013°59'	♅/♆	025°20'	☉/♅	032°26'	♇/Asc	038°43'		
♇/Mc	007°26'	☉/☿	016°15'	♅/☊	025°33'	♃/♆	032°36'	Mc	038°49'		
☿/♄	007°49'	☉/♂	017°19'	☿	025°35'	♃/☊	032°50'	♅/♇	039°30'		
♂/♄	008°53'	♀/Asc	017°35'	♀/♃	025°38'	♃/Mc	033°09'	☉/♃	039°42'		
☿/♆	009°09'	♀/♅	018°22'	♅/Mc	025°53'	☽/♀	034°17'	☽/♄	039°56'		

Niccoló Machiavelli
May 3, 1469 11:03 P.M. LMT
Florence, Italy
11E15 43N46
Placidus Houses

ture, on building things, on form, foundation, stability, and a maintenance of the status quo, whatever it might be. There will need to be a feeling of being protected within all of this that will express itself in the world through the need to be socially significant, humanitarian, unique, off-beat, and with a reaching out to do things for other people, to be of special social service or significance somehow. The life-energy form needs to have structure within the home(land) and needs to project itself independently to achieve its ends. Together, the fundamental life-energy and the personality needs combine for a strong fixity of purpose, determination, and a toughness that may express itself under pressure with extreme independence and feelings of superiority. With Sun=Saturn/Pluto and Mercury/Saturn, we know that the life energy will need to orient itself around hard work and serious thoughts to fulfill itself.

When I first started studying astrology, I thought that trines made a horoscope good and squares made a horoscope bad; I suppose that this is typical for all new students. I'd see a person with a preponderance of trines and practically bow down to them in envy (I have only two "measly" trines in my horoscope, one of them involving Mercury trine the Midheaven. Is that why I'm writing and teaching?) The horoscopes with trines were considered fortunate and the horoscopes with squares were considered "malefic" (ooh I hate that word!). Spiritually, the soul incarnating with a preponderance of trines has worked out the dynamics of the planets involved to the point where the planetary functions are now supportive and come in the form of a talent that one doesn't have to work hard for.

In a Grand Trine, we are seeing one set of needs supporting another set of needs that supports another set of needs, all flowing smoothly together. It's a huge support system, a day at the beach to the psyche of the person in question. By itself, the grand trine is a defense mechanism, speaking psychodynamically. There is an inner feeling of contentment and a high level of self-motivation or self-sufficiency in the sense of not being affected by another person; one is given over to an isolationist type of existence, motivated from within and unaffected by the environment or goings-on of other people. It can be extremely difficult dealing with such a person because the defense is impenetrable. When there is a planet within the complex making an aspect[28] to another planet in the horoscope, this planet gives an outlet to the focus on the Self by providing a release in terms of the nature of the planet, its Sign, House, etc.

For Niccoló, Mercury from within the Grand Trine squares the opposition of Mars-Pluto. The square with Mars gives an assertiveness to the thought processes and communicative facilities. The square with Pluto gives communicative power, obsessiveness in the thinking, extreme opinionation, and a thought process that has a deep sensitivity to disruption. This same Mercury is also well supported in its trines to Uranus and the Moon. In analysis of the horoscope, of this type of configuration, we don't need a "ring around the rosy" dissection of all the parts as I've done so far with Mercury. Analysis has to combine feeling with facts and, when we look at this Mercury, the way it is positioned and aspected, we can *feel* its strength without specifics. We know that *the Mercurial functions are strong*, and that's it. There's no need to talk about a quick temper and all of the cookbook things we've read ad infinitum. The idea is to cut to the chase quickly.

Niccoló was a huge believer in military strength. His book, *The Art of War*, is a brilliant book of military strategy. The need function of a Mercury in a developmentally tense relationship with Mars and Pluto certainly finds an outlet for these dynamics in the conceptualization of military strategy.

The Mars/Pluto opposition is highly energetic and powerful, but the application of this energy into the world may have trouble "finding the mark." What's suggested here is that the style of energy, in terms of the mind, is actually too much for the world to accept! Perhaps this T-square configuration is the key to the controversy that surrounds Machiavelli's work. In 1564, the Catholic church published a Tridentine Index which listed Niccoló Machiavelli as one of the authors who was banned by the church. An edict was put out that said, "if you value body and

---

28 Conjunction, semi-square, square, sesquiquadrate, and opposition only. Trines and sextiles keep things the way they are and are not motivational. I have three computer programs for astrology with approximately 1000 charts collected in each one. I took a random sample of the charts of people who have accomplished extraordinarily in their lives. I tallied all aspects and the trine came up the least amount of times *with squares being the most common aspect among the charts.*

soul, you are forbidden to read or purchase works by these authors." Going further, Mars ruling the 3rd House and disposing of Venus in the 3rd further corroborates the cerebral dimensions. Mars trines the Midheaven, taking the energies of the T-square above the horizon and out into the world through the application of diffused energies to the career.

On an outer level the Mars-Pluto opposition in the 2-8 axis is a clear symbolism of his lifelong struggle with finances and, on an inner level, we know that there would be acute self-esteem issues to talk about, surely involving parental expectations. Let us not overlook the peculiar dilution of applied energy with *Mars in Pisces*.

Parental tension symbols abound here: the Moon is conjunct the nodal axis and the Saturn-Neptune opposition falls on the parental House cusps. Additionally, the Sun and Moon are square. This certainly suggests that there were differences in personality or character between his parents or that there was some kind of upheaval in the home on or around the time that he was born. (With Saturn and Neptune so close to the angles, we know that there were parental events in the very early life which are important. Yet, we cannot verify it factually.) And it would appear that the maternal influence is powerful here, affecting the way Niccoló orients himself in relationships (Moon rules the 7th House), as well as his sense of idealism and his sense of control and ambition. In all the books that have been written about Niccoló, the many, many words, we read *nothing* of Niccoló's mother except for the fact that she was a staunch Catholic, certainly symbolized in the square of the Moon to Saturn. History doesn't tell us much in this regard, but this horoscope tells us, without factual documentation, that there were certainly harsh, demanding parental concerns in his early life, his early learning experiences. There's no doubt about it.

Mercury is very powerful here as the final dispositor of the chart and because it shares the Air Grand Trine and one of the T-squares. In addition, it opposes the ASC/MC midpoint,[29] making it a central focus to the entire horoscope and giving it a powerful strength.

---

29 There was only a ten-minute span during this hour when Mercury was opposing this midpoint. Though I didn't mention it in the rectification process, this is one of the characterological dimensions that steered me toward 11:00 as opposed to 11:59.

Any planet in hard aspect relationship to the Sun/Moon midpoint or the Ascendant/Midheaven midpoint is given powerful presence, and any such configuration should perhaps be treated with as much weight and importance as we give to planetary positions. With the Ascendant/Midheaven midpoint, we are looking at focal energy that's going to be powerfully important in a person's everyday orientation to the world.

Pluto=ASC/MC would be symbolic of intensity in the way he/she goes about doing things. The martial artist, action actor, Jean-Claude Van Damme[30] has Pluto=ASC/MC in his horoscope. A person with Venus=ASC/MC would have a preference for diplomacy, peace, or perhaps a heightened aesthetic sense in the way they do what they do. Producer, arranger, composer Quincy Jones, a musical icon, has Venus=ASC/MC in his horoscope.[31] Mars=ASC/MC gives the opposite influence, where one prefers to be a straight-shooter, disliking diplomacy and preferring a direct, aggressive approach. Mussolini had this in his horoscope, as does athlete extraordinaire, Michael Jordan.[32] If you've read any of the many books that have been published on Michael Jordan, the one common observation of him is that he is very competitive and aggressive in all of his pursuits.

Not only is a planet at this midpoint very powerful but all of the midpoint pictures involved are as well. An examination of these pictures will tell us a lot about the self-actualization process of Niccoló (Tyl, midpoint images; *Synthesis & Counseling in Astrology*):

Mercury= Mars/Pluto: the tenacious pursuit of plans
Mercury=Neptune/ASC: a great imagination
Mercury=Node/ASC: exchanging ideas with others; traveling to meetings
Mercury=Uranus/Neptune: the usage of individuation and imagination in communicating
Mercury=Uranus/Node: excited thoughts shared with others
Mercury=Venus/Jupiter: graceful communication; successful writing

---

30 Born October 8, 1960 at 6:45 A.M. CET in Berchem-Agathe, Belgium 004E17 50N42 (birth time from Lois Rodden's *Data News*).

31 Born March 14, 1933 at 8:40 P.M. CST in Chicago, Ill. (birth time, Lois Rodden).

32 Born February 17, 1963 at 10:20 A.M. EST in Brooklyn, N.Y. (birth time, Lois Rodden).

Mercury=Uranus/MC: individualistic communication with
 regard to the career

This one planetary overview tells us the story of a man who
tenaciously pursues his plans and individualistic ideas, his imagination, sharing these ideas with others. *My* imagination takes me
back to Florence and I see Niccoló giving a lecture to a highly
intellectual, scholarly group of people as he does on the *Discourses on The First Ten Books of Titus Livy*. It is Mercury operating at its
finest! With what we know of Niccoló, Mercury had to be important in the horoscope, and *it is so*.

The other T-square (much looser orbs) involves the Sat-
urn/Neptune opposition upon the parental axis squared by the
Moon. In this opposition, ideals and ambitions are at a tug of war.
There can be an idealization of ambition or a strong sense of concrete realization attached to the ideals, all focused here on the
need to project the Self uniquely somehow. There is definitely
pressure on the self-image that brings relationship concerns into
play (the Moon rules the 7th) as well as the self-esteem dimensions already discussed.

The closest aspect in a horoscope is always symbolic of an
important theme in the person's life. Here, with Mars sesquiquadrate to Jupiter, we get the sense of a person fighting for
beliefs and/or against the beliefs of others. The Mars-Jupiter relationship is important in this horoscope because of the midpoint
picture Sun = Mars/Jupiter, which makes it a focus of the way
that his central life energy orients itself in the world. If we view
Mars as applied energy and see Jupiter in the sense of the 9th
House (philosophy, religion, etc.), we see depiction of our Princely Warlord. The relationship of Mars to Jupiter (strengthening
Mars) here also inclines to a love of freedom and uninhibited
actions with unrestrained expressions of physicality and sexuality, free from rules and regulations. Applied energy is in a relationship with the symbol of expansion. One overdoes everything!

There is also a close Mars-Uranus quincunx, showing the
necessity to adjust thinking to the thoughts of others (9th House).
In fact, if we go back to the Mars-Pluto opposition, we can see the
fight with the values of other people and how so much of his perspective relates to the values of others. Although this Mars is
modestly placed in Pisces, it is extremely active. Its rulership of

the 3rd House adds to his communications prowess. All of this tells us that the man was tremendously energetic, full of ideas, and that he was an idea man.

In the book *Working With Astrology*, Charles Harvey and Michael Harding give a masterful treatment to the very difficult subject of harmonics, which is also dealt with at length by astrologer David Hamblin in his excellent text, *Harmonics In Astrology*. This is not the place for a full discussion of harmonics, but there are a few interesting points to discuss regarding Niccoló's horoscope from the harmonic perspective.

We all owe the late John Addey tremendous appreciation for his pioneering work on harmonics. Harmonic charts provide the astrologer with a way of looking at an individual from a different perspective. In looking at such charts, it is possible to gain a greater understanding or additional insights with a more rounded picture of a person than often is possible through traditional methods. The analysis of Hitler's horoscope by Harvey and Harding is a textbook example of the additional insights available from harmonic analysis.

To compute a harmonic chart, select the desired harmonic (3rd, 5th, etc.). Convert the lights, planets, node and angles into 360 degree notation. For example, a planet at 3 degrees 33 minutes Cancer would convert to 93.33 degrees. Multiply each position by the number of the desired harmonic. If the product is larger than 360, subtract 360 from the product until it is less than 360. Then reconvert the position back to zodiacal notation. Signs and Houses are meaningless in this system. *You are looking only at aspects.* Of course, your computer program should do this for you in a flash.

When we look at our horoscope traditionally, we are seeing it in the 1st harmonic. The 3rd harmonic, for example, is a chart of three-ness. It is representative of the trine (360 divided by 3=120, hence the trine). Two planets that are square in a 3rd harmonic chart are going to tell you that the person is *enjoying* the tension between the planets, while there is a difficulty trying to reach fulfillment in what the planets represent. A trine in the 3rd harmonic is going to tell you something about that which this person really loves or enjoys. The 4th harmonic chart is representative of the square (360 divided by 4=90). Planets that are in a hard aspect relationship in the 4th harmonic chart will *demand* some kind of relationship with the external environment in order to manifest some kind of resolve. A trine in the 4th harmonic suggests an enjoyment of the struggle between the planets involved and so it goes with each harmonic.

The seventh harmonic chart tells you of those things that inspire a person, that turn the person on. The closest aspect in Niccoló's seventh harmonic chart (shown on the previous page) is Jupiter square Pluto. As we know, the relationship between Jupiter and Pluto, the expansion of power, has humongous, olympic potentials. Tyl associates their relationship with a

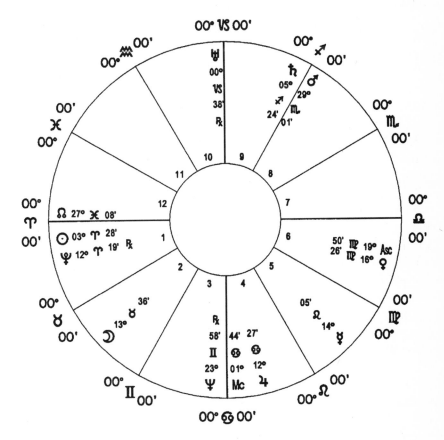

Seventh Harmonic
Niccoló Machiavelli
May 3, 1469 11:03 P.M. LMT
Florence, Italy
11E15   43N46
Equal Houses

tremendous sense of *resourcefulness* and in observation of the horoscopes of those who are extremely successful, it is uncanny how consistently active the Jupiter/Pluto midpoint is, as is the hard natal relationship between the two. Whenever I see the two planets together I start to think in terms of large, sweeping, grandiose actions, concepts, etc. This aspect in the seventh harmonic chart shows Niccoló being inspired by that which is grandiose, and we can see, from the depths of his psyche, the element of his *all-or-nothing* attitude (also shown in the natal Mars-Jupiter relationship) and his attraction to men of great, grand power. Of this aspect, Hamblin says that one is inspired by that which is "grand and noble as well as with that which involves ruthlessness!" It's perfect!

There is also a Uranus/Midheaven opposition squared by the Sun. In this aspect, we see how inspired Niccoló is with anything that's shocking, different, unique, and individuated. Of Sun square Uranus, Hamblin says that one is inspired by all that which is Uranian—individuality, originality, brilliance and "with a liking to disturb and shock other people." For Machiavelli, it is all an echo of the Aquarian Moon.

In a mini-personal analysis of my own horoscope from a harmonic perspective, astrologer Michael Harding told me that it is very common to see Sun-Moon-Mercury aspects in the fifth harmonic charts of those who are linguistically gifted because, among other things, the fifth harmonic has a lot to do with language. John Addey, as well as Charles Harvey, said that planets which come together in the 5th harmonic are indicative of the manner and style in which a person goes about imposing some kind of order on the world, and that this particularly relates to language. We don't know why this is yet, but observations tell us that it is so.

As an example, Noel Tyl has written eighteen published books, has edited a number of others, and was the editor of the great magazine, *Astrology Now.* We all know that he is a consummate communicator with a commanding style and has a vocabulary like tinsel on a Christmas tree. In *his* 5th harmonic chart we see Mercury opposed Pluto, trine Saturn (exactly) squared by a Sun/Mars conjunction! This is a man with a powerful command of language, who loves intellectual discipline and who has a commanding style about him in the way he communicates.

In Niccoló's fifth harmonic chart, we see the Sun trine Moon, with the Sun at the apex of a T-square with a Mercury-Saturn opposition. This is an echo of the natal Sun=Mercury/Saturn midpoint picture. Here, with the Mercury-Saturn opposition dominating, we see a person who is an organized, serious thinker and communicator. Hamblin says of this aspect, "adopting a style of controlled and disciplined thought and communication: having thought-systems that center around practical reality and the absence of illusion." It's uncannily descriptive. Niccoló always

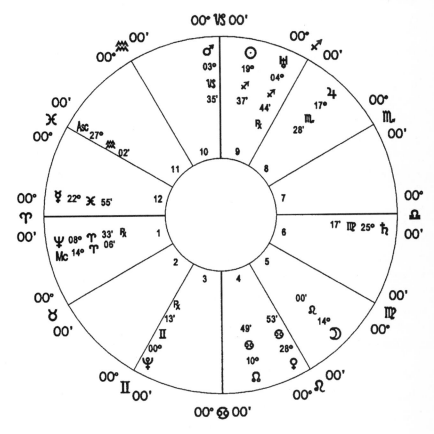

Fifth Harmonic
Niccoló Machiavelli
May 3, 1469 11:03 P.M. LMT
Florence, Italy
11E15   43N46
Equal Houses

encouraged the absence of illusion and the necessity of dealing with things the way they really are, not as you imagine them to be and this is a very important aspect of the man.

Although he was married for twenty-six years until his death (and the father of five children), Niccoló was not a saint as a husband. Throughout his marriage there were several affairs, two of which were very serious, and he was a constant visitor to various brothels in and around Florence (Venus sesquiquadrate Pluto, natal chart, page 308). Ironically, in all of his letters and all that is written about him, his wife is curiously out of the picture. With Venus in Aries we get the sense of *ego* needs operating in terms of desires as opposed to emotional needs seeking fulfillment. The Venus square to Jupiter tells us that Niccoló probably went overboard in these matters. This square between Venus and Jupiter is not connected into the rest of the chart here and seems to operate outside of everything else. Jupiter is disposed of by the very tense Moon in Aquarius. Although he was very conscientious about taking care of his family, his marriage was not his first priority.

It is interesting to note the Capricorn Ascendant working alongside the Aquarius Moon Rising and Uranus closely square the Ascendant. It is a blend of the old and the new, tradition vs. avant garde. Niccoló pushed the utilitarian conception of history to an extreme by suggesting that it was possible, by diligent study of the past, to foresee what is likely to happen in the future in any republic and to apply those remedies used by the ancients. This conceptualization of history opened new concepts in politics and is a clear display of the blending of Capricornian and Aquarian characteristics. In *The Discourses*, he wrote:

> Wise men say, not without reason, that whoever wishes to foresee the future must consult the past; for human events ever resemble those of the preceding times. This arises from the fact that they are produced by men who have been, and will ever be, animated by the same passions; and thus they must necessarily have the same results.

As I finished this chapter we are sharing, late in the night, I heard something in my bookcase fall to the floor behind it. Honest! I got up to see what it was, and it was Dane Rudhyar's book on *The Sabian Symbols*. As astrologers, we all tend to go through certain phases of development wherein we utilize certain techniques and develop certain interests over others. For example, over the past year I have been totally absorbed with mundane astrology. Some years ago, I developed an ephemeral interest in the Sabian symbols through Dane Rudhyar's well-written book on the subject. It had been years since I even opened this book. I don't know why this book fell to the floor as opposed to any of the other 200 or so books that could have. But because it did, I was led, out of curiosity, to look at the symbols and the translations for the degrees of the Ascendant and Midheaven.

The symbol for Niccoló's Ascendant degree says, *An illustrated lecture on natural science reveals little-known aspects of life.* It is linked to "the acquisition of extensive knowledge and the satisfaction of intellectual curiosity." Rudhyar says that the symbolism involving the Ascendant shows the type of experience through which one best realizes a sense of uniqueness and destiny. Here, we see an emphasis on curiosity, knowledge, etc. The symbol for Machiavelli's Midheaven degree, the public persona, says simply, *A Dentist At Work.* Here, we see teeth being used to tear down food so that it can be chewed, swallowed and utilized by the body. Symbolically speaking then, we see the teeth as representative of social and cultural patterns that cause a decay of society. We can see in these two pictures how the use of knowledge is attempting to rid society of all the social problems as Niccoló perceives them. Our rectification even fits on the deepest esoteric level! Having established the angles in correlation with the most important events in the life and with the additional corroboration of characterological and symbolic dimensions, we feel complete with the rectification and our job is finished.

The life of Niccoló was, by and large, a sad one. Denied the education he deserved because of circumstances beyond his control, unable to reach the political heights that his heart clamored for, and never able to succeed with any of his plans (beyond positions in which he served), and being very disturbed with the plight of his homeland, *his was a life of trial and tribulation.* Nevertheless, he has secured a place in history and will be remembered forever in the world of politics. He was an author, poet, playwright, ambassador, teacher, father, husband, and historian. Above all, he was a true original, our princely warlord, in a time of intrigue and change, Niccoló Machiavelli.

Bibliography

Adams, Robert M. *The Prince.* New York: W. W. Norton & Co. Inc., 1977.

Bull, George. *Machiavelli The Prince.* England: Penguin Classics, 1981.

Carter, Charles. *Encyclopedia of Psychological Astrology.* London: The Theosophical Publishing House, 1963.

Cornell, H. L. *Encyclopedia of Medical Astrology.* New York: Samuel Weiser Inc., 1972.

Donno, Daniel. *The Prince.* New York: Bantam Publications, 1981.

Durant, Will. *The Renaissance.* New York: Simon and Schuster, 1981.

Ebertin, Reinhold. *The Combination Of Stellar Influences.* Aalen, Germany: Ebertin-Verlag, 1972.

Gilbert, Allan. *The Letters of Machiavelli.* Chicago: The University of Chicago Press, 1961.

de Grazia, Sebastian. *Machiavelli In Hell.* Princeton, NJ: Princeton University Press, 1989.

Hamblin, David. *Harmonic Charts, A New Dimension In Astrology.* Northhamshire, England: Aquarian Press, 1983.

Hammerslough, Bruce. *Forecasting Backward and Forward: Modern Techniques of Timing and Rectification.* St. Paul, MN: Llewellyn Publications, 1994.

Harding, Michael. *Hymns To The Gods.* London, England: Arkana Books, 1992.

Harding, Michael/Harvey, Charles. *Working With Astrology: The Psychology of Harmonics, Midpoints and Astro*Carto*Graphy.* London: Arkana Books, 1990.

Jay, Antony. *Management & Machiavelli.* San Diego: Pfeiffer & Company 1991.

Marriot, W. K. *Niccoló Machiavelli, The Prince.* New York: Alfred A. Knopf, Inc., 1908.

Munkasey, Michael. *Midpoints Unleashing The Power Of The Planets.* San Diego: ACS Publications, 1991.

Penman, Bruce. *Niccoló Machiavelli-The Prince.* London, England & Rutland, VT: J. M. Dent & Sons Ltd. & Charles E. Tuttle Co., Inc.,1981.

Plumb, J. H. *The Italian Renaissance.* Boston: Houghton Mifflin Company, 1961.

Rudhyar, Dane. *An Astrological Mandala: The Cycle of Transformation and Its 360 Symbolic Phases.* New York: Random House, 1973.

Rudowski, Victor Anthony. *The Prince, A Historical Critique.* New York: Twayne Publications, 1982.

Skinner, Quentin. *Machiavelli—The Prince.* Cambridge, England: Cambridge Publications, 1988.

Strauss, Leo. *Thoughts On Machiavelli.* Chicago: University of Chicago Press, 1958.

Tyl, Noel. *Principles & Practice of Astrology-Volume VII—Integrated Transits.* St. Paul, MN: Llewellyn Publications, 1974.

_____. *Synthesis & Counseling In Astrology.* St. Paul, MN: Llewellyn Publications, 1994.

_____. *Teaching & Study Guide.* St. Paul, MN: Llewellyn Publications, 1976.

Tim Lyons

Born in Boston, Massachusetts in 1949, Tim Lyons holds a B.A. degree in English from Occidental College in Los Angeles and an M.A. in Creative Writing from the Johns Hopkins University. He has practiced meditation according to the teachings of the Kagyu Lineage of Tibetan Buddhism since 1978, and began his study of astrology about the same time. He has also done formal studies of stage acting and t'ai chi chuan. Author of *Astrology Beyond Ego* (Quest Books, 1986) and a columnist for *American Astrology* magazine, he teaches composition in the state college system of Colorado and maintains an active astrological counseling and teaching practice. His writings, astrological or otherwise, have appeared in *The Mountain Astrologer, Welcome to Planet Earth, Chrysalis, East-West, The Vajradhatu Sun, American Astrology,* and others.

Tim Lyons

Benjamin Franklin's Electric Spark

First, the laudatory; and at some length:

The secret of Franklin's amazing capacity for assimilating experience without being warped or discolored by it is perhaps to be found in his disposition to take life with infinite zest and yet with humorous detachment. Always immersed in affairs, he seems never completely absorbed by them; mastering easily whatever comes his way, there remain powers in reserve never wholly engaged ... He was a business man, and a good one; but having won a competence he retired. He was an inventor and a philanthropist, but not by profession; perceiving the need, he invented a stove or founded a hospital. He was a politician and a diplomat, and none more skilled; but not from choice; for the most part he accepted as a duty the offices that were thrust upon him. He was a writer, a prolific one; yet his writings were nearly all occasional, prompted by the need of the moment ... He was a literary artist of rare merit, the master of a style which for clarity, precision, and pliable adhesion to the form and pressure of the idea to be conveyed has rarely been equalled. Yet once having learned the trade he was little preoccupied with the art of writing ... In spite of his ready attention to the business at hand, there is something casual about his efficient dispatch of it; he manages somehow to remain aloof, a spectator still, with amiable curiosity watching himself functioning effectively in the world. (Carl S. Becker: "Franklin's Character," from *The Dictionary of American Biography*)[1]

Then, the decidedly non-laudatory, again at some length:

...probably I haven't got over those Poor Richard tags yet. I rankle still with them. They are thorns in young flesh.

Because, although I still believe that honesty is the best policy, I dislike policy altogether; though it is just as well not to count your chickens before they are hatched, it's still more hateful to count them with gloating when they are hatched. It has taken me many years and countless smarts to get out of that barbed wire moral enclosure that Poor Richard rigged up. Here am I now in tatters and scratched to ribbons, sitting in the middle of Benjamin's America looking at the barbed wire, and the fat sheep crawling under the fence to get fat outside, and the watchdogs yelling at the gate lest by chance anyone should get out by the proper exit. Oh, America! Oh, Benjamin! And I just utter a long loud curse against Benjamin and the American corral. (D. H. Lawrence, from *Studies in Classic American Literature*)[2]

The Franklin Coat of Many Colors

If it's true, as Benjamin Franklin should have said but (to my knowledge) didn't, that great men inspire rather diverse judgments about themselves and their actions, then Benjamin Franklin, erstwhile caller of lightning from the heavens, stovemaker, general, politician, developer of postal systems, of public fire departments, subscription libraries, philosophical societies and universities, would-be paramour to aristocratic French ladies and, it seems, non-aristocratic American ones; wit, statesman, ambassador plenipotentiary, satirist, hoaxster, rustic and non-rustic philosopher, campaigner for justice and social advancement, proclaimer of maxims on money, morality, and practical sagacity,

---

1 Brian M. Barbour, ed. *Benjamin Franklin: A Collection of Critical Essays* (Englewood Cliffs, NJ: Prentice-Hall, 1979) pp. 11-12.

2 Ibid., p. 68.

self-adulator, Freemason, inventor of batteries, lightning rods, the glass harmonica and bifocals, improver of sailing ships and ventilation-systems, America's first Horatio Alger and (according to many) general good fellow, must have been a great man indeed.

To some, this man of many activities stands as a model American, even a model human being, the paragon of civilized virtues extending from the practical to the intellectual; yet others might point out (as Charles Angoff does in his *A Literary History of the American People*[3]) that Franklin's autobiography hasn't "a word about nobility, nor a word about honor, nor a word about grandeur of the soul" and that, rather than being a father of all Yankees, Franklin might more accurately be called "the Father of all Kiwanians." Franklin has, over the years, received the adulation of practical men of business as well as scientists, while being sometimes castigated by artists and visionaries (e.g., Herman Melville, D. H. Lawrence); and yet, in his way, he was sometimes an artist and a visionary himself, though his creation was his life and his vision was more a concrete than an abstract affair.

Even Lawrence, perhaps Franklin's most eloquent detractor, admits that he admires Franklin (without, he says, "liking" him) for "his sturdy courage first of all, then his sagacity, then his glimpsing into the thunders of electricity, then his common-sense humour. All the qualities of a great man, and never more than a great citizen" (though then he adds, "Middle-sized, sturdy, snuff-colored Doctor Franklin, one of the soundest citizens that ever trod or 'used venery'").[4]

Because there's so much disagreement about Franklin's character, it might be best to begin with those matters *about which Franklin's eulogists and detractors agree.* Whatever we think of him, Franklin was certainly a man of genius, as the list offered above demonstrates. He was generally known as "the philosopher" in public, and he lived this role as few others have been able. He was instrumental in discovering the nature of electricity, contributed to the success of the American Revolution and the structure of the American Constitution, and either instituted or invented a galaxy of helpful policies, programs, and devices, as the list above only begins to demonstrate.

---

3 Quoted in Charles White, *Benjamin Franklin: A Study in Self-Mythology* (New York: Garland Publishing, 1987).

4 Barbour, op. cit., p. 67.

Franklin served as ambassador to France at a time when that country's aid was crucial to the American revolutionary effort. When younger, he had proven a capable commander of troops in the field, as well as a deft negotiator with Indians and settlers alike. Decades later, he saw to it that John Paul Jones had a ship in which to torment the British and create a myth, that the French government had a man they could trust and understand when they had money to lend (and even when they didn't), and that the English diplomats had a thorn in their side whenever necessary.

He penned essays on subjects varying from religion to politics to sailing to farting, wrote bagatelles and songs, gave us maxims that have become part of our contemporary lexicon, and was esteemed as a sage in both Europe and America. Thousands mourned him when he left Paris, and thousands more when he died, a few years later, in Philadelphia. He was a man both of action and of thought, combining them into unique and some-would-say unsurpassed accomplishments. He respected both French sophistication and Native American taciturnity, had a tolerant view of humankind's foibles wherever he encountered them (almost), yet worked indefatigably for the betterment of human society.

On the other hand, Franklin was greatly, one might even say obsessively, concerned with material gain, not only as an end in itself, but as a way to virtue. To read many of his writings is to be confronted with the assumption that *virtue and material benefit are, if not identical, at least close kin;* and though we might wish that he outgrew this assumption as he grew older, his *Autobiography* strongly suggests that he did not. He preached the virtues of thrift, discipline, abstemiousness and proper appearances to whomever would listen. Pursuing material gain became, in many of his writings, both a sign of virtue and a way to become more virtuous. Franklin was not above lauding his own virtuous industriousness:

> I mention this industry the more particularly and the more
> freely, though it seems to be talking in my own praise, that
> those of my posterity who shall read it may know the use of
> that virtue, when they see its effects in my favor throughout
> this relation.[5]

---

5   Quoted in White, op. cit., p. 60.

He was certainly one of the first and most effective spokesmen for the *capitalistic endeavor*, and was recognized as such by Max Weber, who, quoting Franklin at length to the effect that time is money, and that money is of "the prolific, generating nature," noted simply that it is surely "the spirit of capitalism which speaks here in characteristic fashion ...." He adds:

> The peculiarity of this philosophy of avarice appears to be the ideal of the honest man of credit, and above all the idea of a duty of the individual toward the increase of his capital, which is assumed as an end in itself. Truly what is here preached is not simply a means of making one's way in the world, but a peculiar ethic. The infraction of its rules is treated not as foolishness but as a forgetfulness of duty. That is the essence of the matter. It is not mere business astuteness, that sort of thing is common enough, it is an ethos. This is the quality which interests us.[6]

And:

> The earning of money within the modern economic order is, so long as it is done legally, the result and the expression of virtue and proficiency in a calling; and this virtue and proficiency are, as it is now not difficult to see, the real Alpha and Omega of Franklin's ethic, as expressed in the passages we have quoted, as well as in all his works without exception.[7]

On the other hand, we might interpret Franklin's ethic to indicate that he was a true child of the Enlightenment (a matter to which we will return):

> ... behind the *Autobiography* is the idea of Natural Progress, so cherished by the Enlightenment. Mankind was moving inevitably toward a millennium that would establish the Kingdom of Heaven on earth. It is true that all through the Christian era man strove to perfect himself, but the struggle was a purely personal one, with the sole aim of attaining one's salvation. But to the thinkers of the Enlightenment (of which Franklin is the American archetype to the point of

---

6 From Max Weber, *The Spirit of Capitalism*, in Barbour, op. cit., p. 17.
7 Ibid., p. 19.

mythic dimensions ...), moral and material struggle by an individual resulted in the improvement of the whole world.[8]

Though Franklin may have seemed, at times, to live a completely puritanical life, evidence suggests that he did not, in many cases, follow his own dictums, at least not once he had gained a level of material prosperity. In *The Temple and the Lodge*, Michael Baignet and Richard Leigh write of then-Postmaster-General-of-the-Colonies Franklin's visits to the estate of British Postmaster General (and, possibly, fellow Freemason) Sir Francis Dashwood:

> And Franklin—that "snuff-colored little man" as D. H. Lawrence called him, sanctimonious author of *Poor Richard's Almanac*, proponent of temperance, frugality, industry, moderation and cleanliness while primly exhorting his readers not to "use venery"—became a member of Dashwood's "Franciscans." A paragon of moral rectitude at home, Franklin, in England, would apparently let his wig down, and the caves under Dashwood's estate at West Wycombe would become a boudoir for the cavortings of libidinous Postmasters-General.[9]

Later, in France, he evinced a taste for decidedly non-puritanical pursuits, particularly regarding women. As one biographer puts it, he

> ... swept his memory clean of all the shrivelling maxims of Poor Richard and gathering up the thirteen Virtues of his quondam creed—including Temperance, Silence, Order, Frugality and Moderation—he dropped them through a hole in his mind and closed the lid upon them with a barely muffled thud.[10]

---

8 White op. cit., pp. 2-3.

9 Baigent, Michael and Richard Leigh, *The Temple and the Lodge* (New York: Arcade, 1989) p. 235.

10 Russell, Phillips, *Benjamin Franklin: The First Civilized American*, New York: Brentano's Publishers. 1926, p. 255.

In a similar vein, a young Franklin bucked tradition with his open support of his illegitimate son. In "Polly Baker's Speech" (an early essay), he took on the persona of a woman with an illegitimate child, coming to her defense for "following the laws of nature if not of the province."[11]

Franklin's life was so full and varied that a brief chronological sketch will help us orient ourselves. After failing, at an early age, at the chandler's trade [wax candles], he became an able printer. Between 1733 and 1744, while beginning to prosper as a printer, he became a clerk to the court of Pennsylvania, was elected to its Congress, invented the Franklin Stove, founded the Union Fire Company, planned city police, and became known for his support and organization of public philanthropies—so much so that it was said in Philadelphia that no plan could prosper lacking his *imprimatur*.

By the early 1750s, Franklin was performing experiments with electricity that catapulted him into positions of eminence among the scientific societies of Europe, receiving honors which paved the way for his later work as a diplomat. (That is, he entered those diplomatic circles with a certain degree of respect, known not as a backwoods politician but as a man of erudition.) He served as emissary to England to debate with Parliament on the issue of taxing the Proprietaries of Pennsylvania (1757–62).

Nearly a decade later (1765), again in England, he represented the colonies as a whole in their campaign against the Stamp Tax, not returning until 1775. Upon that return, he contributed to the writing of the Declaration of Independence, and then served nearly a decade (1776-85) in France as U.S. emissary and later Ambassador Plenipotentiary in the negotiations for French financial and military aid. When he finally returned to Philadelphia, he was again elected to office, first on the Philadelphia Common Council, later as president of the Supreme Executive Council of the State (i.e., governor), and later still as one of Pennsylvania's representatives to the Constitutional Convention. He retired from public life in 1788, and died in 1790 (April 17) in Philadelphia, where he was buried.

---

11. From Carl Van Doren, *Benjamin Franklin* (New York: Viking Press, 1938), p. 154.

The complexity and multifariousness of Franklin's public life might make the task before us—the rectification of his horoscope—seem a daunting task, for his significant achievements were numerous and varied, and it will be difficult to know how to weigh one against another. Most people direct their lives toward one end: Franklin directed his toward many, any of which would have been, for most, the pinnacle of a life's achievement. Adding to the problem is that we will not always know quite how to take what Franklin says about himself or his actions, for he seemed to write with an eye, not toward the whole truth, but toward the creation of a personal mythology, one he would hide behind or exploit as situations required.

This idea needs some amplification. It often seems that Franklin wrote and acted with an eye toward posterity, perhaps most evidently in his *Autobiography*. In his practical affairs he was generally willing to take on whatever role produced optimum results. Later in his life, he often found himself playing the role that harmonized most nicely with the self-created mythical Franklin that preceded him. Of course, as Charles W. White points out in *Benjamin Franklin: A Study in Self-Mythology*:[12]

> The Franklin myth, like the myths surrounding other great men, had its beginnings in fact. He did invent the Franklin stove, bifocal spectacles, the first battery, and the lightning rod. He did establish America's first subscription library, the first volunteer fire company, the first insurance company, the first street cleaning and paving corps, and our present postal system. He did found the first charity hospital in Pennsylvania, the academy that grew into the University of Pennsylvania, the American Philosophical Society, the first school of agricultural science, and a society for "Promoting the Abolition of Slavery."[13]

White goes on to point out, however, that the narrative of the *Autobiography* is not as straightforward as it seems. He asks us to consider, first, the fact that Franklin addressed his narrative to his son William:

---

12 This line of argument is drawn from White's book. The interpretation seems to me justified, and other scholars seem to accept it even if they don't work the idea out so explicitly.

13 White, op. cit., pp. 5-6.

Franklin writes as an older man would to his son who is in his teens or twenties, about the same age as Franklin was when he began his career in Philadelphia. The implication is that the son may make a similar success of his life by imitating the father's behavior. The fact is that in 1771, when the first part of the *Autobiography* was written, William Franklin was about forty years old and hardly in need of advice about how to make something of himself since he [sic] was the Royal governor of New Jersey.[14]

When the second section of the book was written, in 1784 after the Revolution

he [Franklin] had the bitter memory of his own son's loyalty as a Tory to the government of George III. During the war William had been imprisoned and, upon release, had become president of the Associated Loyalists of New York. He even had the effrontery to write Franklin a letter in 1775, urging him to retire from public life.[15]

These wounds were, apparently, never healed, the implications of the *Autobiography* notwithstanding. Franklin wrote in his will:

The part he [William] acted against me in the late war, which is of public notoriety, will account for my leaving him no more of an estate he endeavored to deprive me of.[16]

White suggests that Franklin's relationships with his brother and father were similarly mythologized:

Family relationships, particularly those involving his father and brother James, are important ingredients in the *Autobiography's* story. Both men frequently behaved badly toward the young Franklin, and one detects his dilemma in trying to give the facts of his early boyhood in Boston and, at the same time, smooth over what must have been strong resentments. Writing from the pinnacle of a success already achieved,

---

14 Ibid., p. 7-8.
15 Ibid., p. 8.
16 Ibid.

Franklin could afford to look back with forgiveness. Further-more, to love one's father and brother, in spite of differences, and, more importantly, to *have always* loved them was as nec-essary for his pose as it was to be his mother's affectionate son. But unlike his obvious love for Abiah [his mother], Franklin seems hard pressed to demonstrate the same feel-ings for Josiah [his father].[17]

The truth was that Franklin's father subjected him to harsh terms in his early apprenticeship as a printer to James, and came down hard on the young Benjamin for using his talents in any but the most practical ways. Josiah insisted on "virtues" of order and propriety very similar to those later espoused by his son.

In addition to being a self-mythologizer, Franklin was a mas-ter of literary disguises and a frequent perpetrator of literary hoaxes, often writing under pseudonyms or publishing articles about imaginary events. He began these practices in his teens, and they became important tools in his ongoing efforts to sway public opinion toward the views or causes he espoused. One of his most famous hoaxes appeared under the title, "From the Count de Schaumbergh to the Baron Hohendorf, Commanding the Hessian Troops in America" (1777; sometimes called "The Sale of the Hessians,")[18], a satire dealing with how the British pur-chased Hessian mercenaries. The speaker in the piece is The Count de Schaumbergh; he writes to the Baron Hohendorf:

> I am about to send you some new recruits. Don't economize them. Remember glory before all things. Glory is true wealth. There is nothing degrades the soldier like love of money. He must care only for honor and reputation, but this reputation must be acquired in the midst of dangers. A battle gained without costing the conqueror any blood is an inglorious suc-cess, while the conquered cover themselves with glory by perishing with their arms in their hands.[19]

---

17 Ibid., 14-15.

18 Van Doren (575) says of this piece: "While *The Sale of the Hessians* is not certainly known to be by Franklin, it can hardly have been by anybody else. In style and temper it is another Franklin hoax, and vitriol in print."

19 Quoted in Van Doren, op. cit., p. 575.

Though Schaumberg is gratified that 1,605 out of 1,970 mercenaries died, he says he would have preferred that there be no survivors at all, for if all had been killed, he was due some money.

Franklin's many hoaxes, subterfuges, and pseudonyms might seem to present obstacles to the rectification. However, as we will see, they actually aid us in the process, for they are nicely symbolized in the rectified chart. Before proceeding to that rectification, though, we might first look simply at the sign-placements and aspects for Franklin's birthday to see how these reflect some of the varied facets of Franklin's character and activities sketched above.

Signs, Planets, and Character

Franklin was born on January 17, 1706 New Style (N.S.) in Boston, Massachusetts. Confusion might arise about this date, however, because the Old Style calendar was in effect in Boston at that time. According to that calendar, the date was January 6, 1706. A person-in-the-street on the day of Franklin's birth would have told you it was the 6th, and Franklin certainly would have celebrated his birthday on that date (at least until the calendars were changed in the United States). [The American colonies were under British rule and didn't change the calendar until noon, September 2, 1752, when *England* finally caught up with change. — Ed.] The January 17 date generally in use reflects, therefore, not what people would have said at the time, but the adjustment necessary to reconcile birthdates of that period with our present calendar-system. From an astrological point of view, the adjustment is necessary if we are to ascertain the correct planetary positions for Franklin's birth. Because my computer uses the New Style calendar for all birthdates after 0 hours October 15, 1582, I have computed Franklin's birth data based on the New Style date even though the Old Style calendar was actually in effect. (This seems to be the standard practice, which is why Franklin's birthdate is generally said to be January 17, not January 6.)

The Sun was in late Capricorn, and Franklin certainly manifests many elements of the Capricorn archetype, both questionable and laudable. As an example of the former, he apparently lived according to (and certainly preached the virtues of) a series of shoulds and oughts. (Recall Kathleen Burt's *Archetypes of the*

Zodiac): "At the mundane level, the Capricorn archetype can be recognized every year in conversations about shoulds and oughts ..."[20]) Franklin was concerned with material success and the doings of the material world. Hardly a mystic, Franklin's values were by and large worldly values, and as we have seen, even virtue was virtuous because it yielded practical rewards.

Early in life, he devoted himself to finding a profession, to securing his financial stability; and he did this with a diligence and a degree of self-scrutiny that was truly remarkable. (Some of this, along with Franklin's ability to look at the workings of the mundane world and recommend technical improvements, seems to reflect not only Capricorn, but also the Virgo decanate in which his Sun is posited, as well as Pluto in the rectified 6th House and occult ruler of the rectified Ascendant—to be developed in this chapter.) As he matured, he worked increasingly within the halls of bureaucracy and government in the capacities listed above.

Capricorn has a reputation of being concerned with the relationship between means and ends. (Not that Capricorn is a less ethical sign than others, but Capricorn's ethical questions often involve the means-ends relationship.) So it was with Franklin. For example, in his early twenties, he undertook a self-designed program of moral rectification, motivated not so much by any abstract notion as by a desire to get on more effectively in the world. The program consisted of virtues which seem laudable enough in themselves, but those virtues were considered not ends-in-themselves, but means to achieve material prosperity more effectively. (This program is discussed further below.)

However, though Franklin was ambitious to get ahead in the world, a quality redolent of Capricorn, as he grew older he became less ambitious for material gain or position (both of which were already his), but for influence on the society in which he lived. While early on it often seemed that no amount of effort was too great if it helped him to advance, he later found himself in the positions that he did *not* receive because he sought them, but because he was sought out, and because it was a principle with him never to turn down a position if it was offered to him *if* accepting would

---

20 Kathleen Burt, *Archetypes of the Zodiac* (St. Paul: Llewellyn), 1988, p. 357.

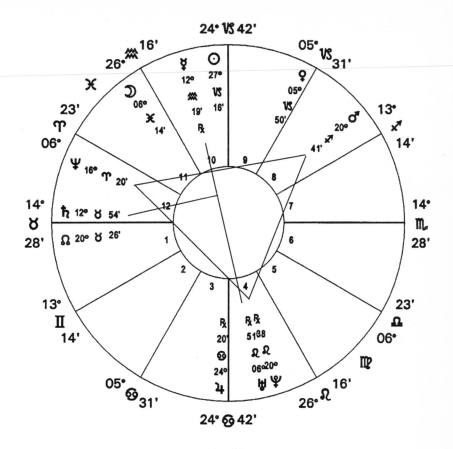

Benjamin Franklin (Noon)
Jan. 17, 1706 00:00 P.M. LMT
Boston, Massachusetts
71W04 42N22
Koch Houses

serve the benefit of his fellow man.[21] This last point will be significant to the rectification: Franklin's advance to positions of eminence later in life took place largely because of his values—and the value he placed on improving society—not because he sought personal power. If he was a man bent on accomplishment, he was

---

21 Benjamin Franklin, *Autobiography and Other Writings* (Boston: Houghton-Mifflin, 1958) p. 103-4.

increasingly bent on accomplishment that served the social good;[22] and he gave a good deal of attention to finding the best means to bring this about.

Saturn, dispositor of the Capricorn Sun, is in Taurus, at the focal point of a T-square with Mercury and Uranus, which stand in opposition to each other in Aquarius and Leo respectively. This T-square symbolizes one of the major conundrums in Franklin's life: how to reconcile two distinct yet interwoven potencies of mind, one practical, grounded and effective, the other brilliant, inventive and iconoclastic. In the war for Franklin's time, the former won out, though many of his finest achievements show the two working in a startlingly effective harmony. Still, the inventive side generally got the short end of the scheduling stick, and a part of Franklin clearly regretted the sacrifice, as we will see.

The Mercury-Saturn square manifested early in Franklin's life, as a determination to improve his mind by dint of hard work, and as a tendency, early and late, to see everything in strictly material terms. We see the former tendency in the young Franklin's self-imposed regimen for improving his writing style. He

> studied the book [Addison and Steele's *The Spectator*], made notes on the various papers, laid them by, and then tried to rewrite them in a form as good as the original. Comparison showed him his defects. He carried his practice ever further and finding his vocabulary needed enrichment, turned the tales into verse and back again into prose. These experiments apparently occupied him for a considerable period; the resulting benefit was perceptible. He at last fancied that in certain particulars, he had improved the method or the language, and this encouraged him to think he "might possibly in time come to be a tolerable English writer."[23]

The tendency to see the world in strictly material terms has already been discussed: one need only read the *Autobiography*, or "Advice to a Tradesman," or select one of a multitude of passages from *Poor Richard* to be convinced that materialism ran through Franklin like the Schuylkill through Philadelphia, providing him

---

22 Ibid., pp. 85–88.
23 Russell, op. cit., p. 17.

with what he needed to live. To borrow Liz Greene's description of Mercury-Saturn, we see in Franklin "a compensatory development of great facility at earthy matters," a tendency to be pragmatic, to resist abstract thought,[24] to retreat from imagination when it fails to produce practical benefit.

We might recall, in discussing Mercury-Saturn (particularly with Saturn in Taurus, and, as I will argue, the 2nd House), what was said above about Franklin thinking primarily in terms of loss and gain, for his truths were generally the truths of the marketplace, and his values those of the practical man of action. Money (Taurus) was central:

> Remember that money is of the prolific, generating nature. Money can beget money, and its offspring can beget more, and so on ... The more there is of it, the more it produces every turning, so that the profits rise quicker and quicker. He that kills a breeding sow, destroys all her offspring to the thousandth generation. He that murders a crown, destroys all that it might have produced, even scores of pounds.[25]

Much of this also argues for the father's strong, restrictive, ordering influence on Franklin's thinking, a matter hinted at above, and not unusual with Mercury-Saturn aspects. This influence which extended not only to Franklin's manner of thought, but also to what he thought about. While it's true that Franklin rebelled against that father (Uranus), in large part on the grounds of freedom of thought, he also seemed, at times, very much in his father's pragmatic line (Saturn). He tells us, for example, that his father was, as Franklin himself was to be later, "frequently visited by leading men who consulted him for his opinion in affairs of the town ... and showed a good deal of respect for his judgement and advice. He was also much consulted by private persons about their affairs when any difficulty occurred ...."[26]

An early incident shows how hard Franklin's father was on matters of imagination. In his teens, Benjamin was apprenticed under his brother James as a printer's assistant. Working with

---

24 Liz Greene, *Saturn* (New York: Samuel Weiser, 1976), p. 106.
25 "Advice to a Young Tradesman," in Franklin, op. cit., p. 166.
26 Ibid., p. 8.

James was by no means pleasant, for the two brothers were in constant disagreement. Benjamin read at night (as suggested above; Addison and Steele's *Spectator* seems to have been a major influence[27]) and wrote some ballads, which upon publication made "a great noise."[28] The result seems all-too-typical of many Mercury-Saturn conflicts, not so much in that Benjamin "beams with that vanity, the obtrusions of which he struggles to subdue for the rest of his life,"[29] but because of his father's reaction:

> Enter the lowering villain. It is Benjamin's father. He sets about the favorite New England pastime of killing youthful joy. Leave poetry to loafers. There's no money in it. Verse-makers are "generally beggars." Stick to business. Get on.[30]

The Mercury-Saturn square symbolizes the side of Franklin which many people (see the D. H. Lawrence quotation above) find unpleasant and objectionable. However, as Franklin matured, his shrewdness was transferred from the constant search for personal, practical gain to a constant search to find new ways to improve the world around him. His Mercury-Saturn was not mere pedantry, but part genius, for a genius is considered so not because he might have startling ideas, but because he does something with those ideas. In Franklin's case, his ideas increasingly served the well-being of the social group (Mercury in Aquarius).

One of the ways Franklin served the world, of course, was through his many inventions. We might think, at first glance, that Saturn symbolizes the pragmatic side of his mind, and Uranus the more inventive side; but this doesn't seem entirely true. What is true is that, with such a strong Mercury-Uranus connection, Franklin was quick minded, given to sudden insights. But unlike in myth where Kronos-Saturn's demands deprive Ouranos of life-giving power, in Franklin's mind *it was Saturn's demands for pragmatic use*, manifest through his close, patient, precise observation of the world around him, *that often gave birth to his inventive insights.*

---

27 Russell, op. cit., pp. 20ff.

28 Quoted. in Russell, op. cit., p. 26.

29 Russell, op. cit. p. 26.

30 Russell, op. cit., pp. 26-7.

One case might be taken as typical. Franklin, on his way to London to negotiate the taxation of the Proprietaries, still had both the presence and openness of mind to observe the way the ship settled too deeply into the water, and to write an essay on how to build and load ships so the problems were alleviated.[31] Acute observation of what came to his view seemed to be less a determination of Franklin's than an unbreakable habit and exercise in creative living. The fact that Saturn is in Taurus certainly reiterates his ability to put his thoughts to resourceful use. In Franklin's practical dealings was a flash, not of the pragmatic pedant, but of genius, of suddenly seeing entirely new possibilities (Uranus) while remaining grounded in the here-and-now demands of life (Saturn).

The Mercury-Uranus opposition forms the backbone of a yod configuration, with Uranus as the focal planet. The Moon-Venus sextile forms, along with Mercury, the base of the yod. There is obviously a lot of energy flowing down into Uranus, and it vies with Saturn for control of Franklin's mind.

A conspicuous characteristic of a yod, of course, is that the apex planet often feels like an energy one is somehow *destined to use.*[32] Yet, paradoxically, the quincunxes that form the yod often arise through concatenations of circumstances that prevent the facile use of that planet. One is, it seems, drawn by circumstances to other matters, and the potential of the apex planet incubates for some time, developing itself through experiences which, paradoxically enough, seem to restrict its use. *A person must develop the skill of the sextile through the apparent restrictions of the quincunxes.* Often the skills seem to be absorbed by the restrictions (as they incubate within them), yet the apex planet's energies often seem to appear suddenly, as if from something outside the individual's orbit of experience.[33]

In Franklin's case, the work with electricity (Uranus) did seem to come (more than literally!) "out of the blue," within the span of a few years, though it had clearly been incubating for

---

31 Van Doren, op. cit., p. 265-66.

32 My explication of the yod owes much to Bil Tierney. See his *Dynamics of Aspect Analysis* (Reno: CRCS, 1983), 145ff.

33 This characteristic was first brought to my attention in Noel Tyl's writings concerning the dynamics of "adjustment," but I can't recall the volume.

years while Franklin's genius manifested partly through patient, joyful observation of the physical world, and partly through professional service in which he acquiesced (feminine planets) and which honed (quincunx) his mind while demanding his time (also the quincunxes). The Moon-Venus sextile in water and earth suggests being at home in the physical world, a contentment that burst into prominence through flashes of brilliance that were really the result of Franklin's steady curiosity about how the world functions. As is typical with yods, Franklin's remained in abeyance until triggered into manifestation by a transit: transiting Uranus arriving to conjoin Mercury, oppose Uranus and square Saturn in 1746–7, prodding Franklin into his remarkable work in electricity.

Even after his earth-shattering work with lightning (c. 1746–52), Franklin longed to get back to his scientific studies and to his electrical apparatus, but affairs in the world drew him into other directions. The Moon is in Pisces, suggesting a felt obligation to help others, and a constant availability. Venus in Capricorn suggests that Franklin formed many professional relationships, and that he valued working in the professional world, and that he had much of value to contribute there. The very potentials of the sextile drew him away from the demands of apex Uranus. (That the work of Uranus was Franklin's one joy—not something he felt driven to by circumstances (yod), but a natural creative response to life—this is a factor in the rectification, a suggestive piece of evidence among many others, as we will see.)

I have not yet mentioned either Franklin's Sun-Jupiter opposition or his grand trine in fire signs (Mars, Neptune, Pluto). The former is reflected most obviously in the fact that Franklin lived, by anyone's standards, a rather itinerant life, much of it in foreign lands serving in various Jupiterian capacities (another important fact to be considered in the rectification, as we will see). Alan Oken titles the Sun-Jupiter opposition "The Wanderer" and writes that it often brings about physical travel and that the individual will have many opportunities, which can often lead him far afield from his starting point.[34]

---

34 Alan Oken, *Complete Astrology* (New York: Bantam, 1988), p. 404.

Oken adds that the aspect can also indicate "religious difficulties," which was true with Franklin, however well he handled them. We will return to this issue in a discussion of Franklin's life around 1730–34, a period important to the rectification.

Certainly the Sun-Jupiter opposition points in a preliminary way toward Franklin's work as a diplomat in a foreign country, and also toward his reputation as a philosopher both in the colonies and abroad. As we will see, these tendencies receive added emphasis in the rectified horoscope, being related there specifically to career and vocation (MC). Even without the aid of houses, however, we can conjecture that, as Jupiter is disposited by the Moon in Pisces, Franklin's diplomatic work and travels would be motivated by a very personal need to serve the greater good. We might also infer from the fact that Jupiter disposits Mars in Sagittarius that the Jupiter principles at work in Franklin's life (e.g., philosophy, travels, diplomacy) manifested through action instead of mere contemplation, study, or publishing, however evident these might have been.

Mars is part of the grand trine in fire signs with Neptune in Aries and Pluto in Leo. The trine between Neptune and Pluto was in effect throughout much of the eighteenth century. It moved through several signs during Franklin's life, with Neptune moving from Aries to Libra, and Pluto moving from Leo to Aquarius (thus covering all the signs of the zodiac except Pisces) before the aspect began to dissipate during the 1790s. It stands as one of the principle indicators of the historical epoch called the Enlightenment, briefly alluded to above, symbolizing as it does a creative union between inspiration (Neptune) and transformative action (Pluto): transformative activity arising from collective idealism.

Franklin's Grand Trine suggests that through action based on principle (Mars in Sagittarius) related to his life-long quest for meaning within the limits of social living (Capricorn Sun opposed Jupiter), Franklin served as a conduit for the collective potency indicated by Neptune-Pluto. (Mars in the rectified 9th House will suggest that this action took place in a foreign land; its proximity to the Sagittarius MC will point to the importance of this principled action in Franklin's vocation as diplomat.)

It would be hard to dispute that Franklin acted as a conduit for collective currents. Few people have been more focal in this regard. The trine between Neptune and Pluto might suggest a dormant spiritual power or a dormant but powerful ideal. Because these two planets were as yet undiscovered, their energy was an undercurrent percolating beneath the surface of events, or in secret among a small number of people (e.g., Freemasons).[35] With the grand trine also focusing on Franklin's Mars and (as we will see) MC, he became a conduit for human potentials just coming into collective focus (Neptune-Pluto being stimulated by Uranus into a grand trine, a matter discussed at length below). With his strong Capricorn-Saturn-Uranus influence, he was able to give these potentials a revolutionary form.

Rectification I: Finding Our General Way

In rectifying a horoscope, there are two broad areas of concern and investigation. Most obviously, one must use various time analysis techniques to arrive at the correct time of birth. However, the result of one's work—the rectified horoscope—must also resonate with what we know of the individual's character.

Of course, the judgments one makes about the individual's character (and the tendency to see facets of that character reflected in hypothetical horoscopes) may actually influence the hypotheses one makes in the rectification process. In addition, in trying to understand the meaning of various transits and progressions, one will be influenced by the hypothetical natal house placements of the planets being used, as the transiting or progressed planets will bring into manifestation events connected not only with the area of the horoscope directly affected by the transits or progressions, but also the natal placement and derived factors (e.g., the house ruled by a planet).

We know that Franklin was christened on January 17, 1706. There is no solid evidence to indicate when during that day he was born, other than that it was in the morning.[36] The christening

---

35 The energies of undiscovered planets may not be available to the collective, but they *do* seem to be available to people working in isolation. Witness the awareness, on the part of individuals (e.g., Buddhist sages) dedicating their lives to insight, compassion and transformation, or the energies we call Uranus, Neptune, and Pluto. This awareness, however, was generally not transmitted to the collective; and when it was, the nature of the message was generally altered to suit the needs of the prevailing hierarchies (Saturn), as was the case with Jesus' teachings.

would have taken place in the afternoon *in any case,* as the preacher would have been busy with the service in the morning.[37] Various times have been proposed, most of them between 9:40 A.M. and 11:00 A.M.

I do not know for certain why other writers have chosen times in this range, but it's probably at least partly because if you place the birth time much earlier than, say, 9:00 A.M., you end up with a horoscope emphasizing the northern, or lower hemisphere, and without any planets in the 10th House. The lower hemisphere emphasis would suggest that Franklin's nature was an internalized one. Planets in this hemisphere

> ... show urges that require depth of experience before the individual can utilize them openly and purposefully in his external environment. He tends to contain these urges in a self-absorbed manner for some time before he attempts to direct them towards more impersonal social concerns.[38]

The individual with an emphasized northern hemisphere

> ... grows best by assimilating his life experience and relating it to the deeper reality of his inner nature. He is conditioned to get intimately in touch with his subjective identity much more here than in any other Hemisphere.[39]

All of which is, as we have seen, precisely what did not characterize Franklin's life. He quickly turned any inner examination toward the external world, and seemed little concerned with any subjective truth that did not have evident application in the social world or promise to repay significant dividends. It seems more appropriate, then, that the rectified chart have some significant planets in the upper hemisphere. And since we are dealing with a man for whom professional work and reputation were such driving forces, and who, in professional spheres, enjoyed such enormous success and had such enormous influence, and whose

---

36 Personal communication with Leo Lemay, Professor of English at the University of Delaware, currently writing a multi-volume biography of Franklin.

37 Professor Lemay, personal communication.

38 Tierney, op. cit., p. 261.

39 Ibid.

professional work was so constant (Franklin worked steadily and effectively until he was over eighty years old), we would expect some sort of 10th House emphasis.

However, once we agree that there would most probably be an emphasized 10th House, we still must decide what sort of emphasis it should be. The 11:00 A.M. horoscope that has been suggested by some (see chart, page 344) has Capricorn on the Midheaven with Venus in the 9th House side conjoining and the Sun in the 10th House. Mars in Sagittarius is in the 9th House, while both Mercury and the Moon are in the 11th, with Uranus and Pluto in

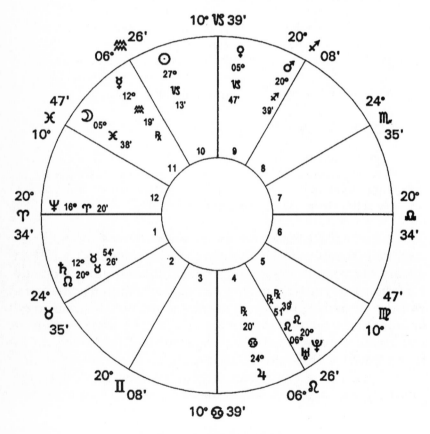

Benjamin Franklin—First Try
Jan. 17, 1706   11:00 A.M. LMT
Boston, Massachusetts
71W04   42N22
Koch Houses

the 5th and Jupiter in the 4th. Neptune hovers near the Ascendant on the 12th House side, with focal Saturn in the 1st.

Though I generally feel that, as a matter of logic or statistical likelihood, any horoscope with a time right on the hour should be regarded with suspicion, this one has some persuasive points to recommend it, so it's not surprising that some have advocated it. For example, Mars' placement in the 9th would certainly reiterate the tendency to travel, and because Mars rules the Aries Ascendant, travel would be, as it was, a central feature of Franklin's life. Besides, the importance of Franklin's being an active philosopher, already suggested by Mars in Sagittarius itself, would be strengthened by having Aries rising. The 10th House Sun would augur success, while Venus near the Midheaven might symbolize Franklin's diplomacy. Mercury in the 11th would point to Franklin's social concerns, and Uranus in the 5th would suggest (as above) that electrical interests were something Franklin needed no prodding to follow, that they constituted a natural creative flowering of his nature.

These features are attractive. The rectified horoscope will retain some of them, and will either substitute for others or restate them more precisely. It's also worth noting, however, that the 11:00 A.M. horoscope has at least two factors which seem highly questionable: the Capricorn Midheaven and the Aries Ascendant.

The Midheaven symbolizes the focus of a person's vocation or career, and tells us much about that person's reputation. In this it is distinguished from the Ascendant, for though both angles might be said to symbolize that which is projected upon a person (which is also to say how a person appears and acts)[40], the Ascendant seems to symbolize interactions (or projections!) related to the *interpersonal* sphere, while the Midheaven symbolizes the same related to *professional activities* and *reputation*.

The problem with the Capricorn Midheaven is that Franklin's reputation was *not* characterized by Capricorn, howevermuch Capricorn energy went into his work. He was generally known as "the philosopher," and the professional positions he held are related to Sagittarius: diplomat, writer, printer, publisher, philanthropist, humorist, religious leader (e.g., among the Freemasons; see below), ambassador.

Admittedly, some of these might have arisen anyway due to Jupiter's opposition to his Sun, but for Franklin they arose specifically as *vocational* endeavors, and virtually all such endeavors had that mark. While Franklin held positions of authority, he generally had those positions thrust on him. He did not seek out the positions that brought him his greatest fame and through which he had such an enormous influence on world events. (This fact—that Franklin was sought out more than he sought, that he acquiesced in positions rather than clambering after them—might also suggest Pisces rising, not Aries.) Though clearly not without ambition, his ambition focused itself on *social causes instead of personal aggrandizement*, suggesting an 11th House Sun, not the 10th House Sun of the 11:00 A.M. chart.

Certainly Franklin pursued vocational objectives diligently early on: he was, after all, a Capricorn Sun. But much of his motivation, then, was to attain financial security, suggesting not a first house Saturn dispositing that Capricorn Sun, but a *2nd House Saturn* (which would arise with many Sagittarius-rising charts). With a Capricorn Sun opposed to Jupiter, we might expect that, sooner or later, Franklin's diligence would be imbued with principle. However, as Franklin grew older, it was increasingly matters of principle that drove him into professional accomplishment, and this too suggests Sagittarius on the MC instead of Capricorn. Also, Capricorn on the MC implies Cancer on the IC, suggesting a close connection to home and roots, which Franklin did not seem to have. In turn, Sagittarius on the MC means *Gemini on the IC*, one bald interpretation of which is that he had two homes, which, by the end of his life, considering his love of France, is precisely what Franklin had.

Also, Mercury would rule a Gemini nadir. Mercury's square to Saturn more precisely symbolizes the dominance of ideas promulgated by Franklin's father than does a 4th House ruled by the Moon in Pisces.[41] As some of the material above suggests, the

---

40 This is so because people often respond to or acquiesce in what is projected upon them, to a greater or lesser degree. Thus projections make it difficult not only for the projector, but for the person projected upon. Certain energies are emphasized, often at the expense of others.

41 I take, here, the 4th House to at least partly indicate the father. I realize there is some debate on this point. It seems to me that whereas the 10th House often indicates the public influence of the father, the 4th often points to the private influences, and often to the influences of the father's unconscious or automatic behavior. Here, the 4th is connected to the father first because it's the 4th, and second because, with Gemini at the nadir, Mercury's square to Saturn becomes a 4th-House matter.

squelching of Franklin's ideas and natural intellectual effervescence is generally mentioned by Franklin's biographers as the conspicuous feature of his childhood.

The Aries Ascendant might, at first glance, seem appropriate for Franklin. He was certainly a pioneer, and was able to cut through delusion quite decisively. His connection with experience was direct and penetrating. Aries rising, however, tends to plunge into activity headfirst, often without sufficient forethought, and most reports on Franklin's diplomatic and personal style suggest that such headlong plunging was hardly his approach. He was subtly self-assertive, not impetuously so as might be suggested by Aries rising.

Aries rising with Mars elevated in Sagittarius would suggest a certain bluntness and perhaps even a devil-may-care attitude that Franklin generally did not demonstrate. Consider, for example, his response when he was warned (quite accurately) by a friend that even in his household in France (during the war) he was surrounded by spies:

> I have long observed one rule which prevents any inconvenience from such practices. It is simply this: to be concerned in no affairs that I should blush to have made public, and to do nothing but what spies may see, and welcome ... If I was sure, therefore, that my *valet de place* was a spy, as he probably is, I think I should not discharge him for that, if in other respects I liked him."[42, 43]

Franklin's basic strategy, in diplomacy as elsewhere, was characterized by indirection and subtlety, and rather than thrust himself into roles, he allowed himself to be cast into whatever role would most effectively help him gain his ends:

> It was no hardship for Franklin to assume the role he found waiting for him [in France], because it was his nature to be thoughtful, witty, benevolent, cheerful, and homely. He was not a Quaker, as the French thought, but he was willing to let

---

42 Van Doren, op. cit., p. 569.

43 A side note: In fact it was not Franklin's *valet de chambre* who was a spy, but his confidante, Edward Bancroft.

them think it. Paris admired the sect for its gentle, resolute merits and spoke of William Penn as a Lycurgus. Franklin, by no means a philosopher of the backwoods, for thirty years had lived among scholars and scientists, merchants and politicians, clergymen and men of fashion. His manners were as urbane and expert as his prose. But the French were looking for a hero who should combine the reason and wit of Voltaire with the primitive virtues celebrated by Rousseau, and they were sure they had found their hero in Franklin. He denied them nothing they expected.[44]

It hardly seems likely that one with Aries rising (especially with Mars elevated) would so readily accept the roles thrust on him by others, even if Neptune were close to the Ascendant (as it is for the 11 A.M. horoscope). Pisces is a more likely suspect here.

However, within Franklin's circumspection and willingness to accept the roles offered, there was a tremendous determination and focus, and this is suggested, as we will see, by Aries being intercepted in the 1st House (Koch Houses), with Pisces on the Ascendant suggesting the mentioned subtlety, and Taurus on the 2nd suggesting his determined pursuit of money early, and his staunchness regarding personal and social values late.

Consider, as another example of Franklin's indirection and subtlety, the incident in 1782 in which the United States and England signed a preliminary treaty ending the Revolutionary War without the knowledge of France.[45] The treaty still had to be ratified by Parliament, of course, but in signing that treaty without informing the French ministers, particularly Charles Vergennes, Franklin had broken an important promise he had made earlier to the effect that the United States would make no treaty with the English without French involvement. The situation needed delicate handling, particularly as Franklin still had to work through another loan from the French government.

His handling of it was a model of tact and indirection. He duly informed Vergennes that the preliminary articles of the treaty had

---

44 Van Doren, op. cit., pp. 569-70.

45. France being also at war with England, her interests were closely interwoven with those of the colonies.

been settled. Subsequently, he sent Vergennes a copy of the treaty, then called upon him. Vergennes offered that the signing "had not been particularly civil to the king."[46] Fortunately for Franklin, Vergennes felt the worst offense was "incivility." In the matter of the loan, however, Franklin had to press somewhat diligently for money. He wrote to Vergennes, telling him that a ship was soon to sail for America, and might he (Franklin) be able to send a letter on that ship which might inform Congress of what aid might be forthcoming, for he feared Congress would be "reduced to despair when they find nothing is yet obtained"?[47] Van Doren writes:

> Vergennes, master of the muffled language of diplomacy, knew that Franklin was not only pressing him for money but also telling him that without it Congress would probably do nothing more for France, if any unforeseen new need should arise.[48]

Vergennes became a bit more pointed in telling Franklin that he had been surprised to find out that Franklin and his colleagues were now

> about to hold out a certain hope of peace to America without even informing yourself on the state of the negotiations on our part. You are wise and discreet, Sir; you perfectly understand what is due propriety; you have all your life performed your duties. I pray you to consider how you propose to fulfill those duties which are due to the king. I am not desirous of enlarging these reflections; I commit them to your own integrity. When you shall be pleased to relieve my uncertainty I will entreat the king to enable me to answer your demands.[49]

Van Doren points out that Vergennes' remarks were "essentially a gesture" because he "could not afford to withhold the loan so long as there was any chance of further hostilities." Franklin's reply to all this again demonstrates tact and indirection:

---

46 Van Doren, op. cit., p. 695.
47 Ibid., p. 696.
48 Ibid., p. 696.
49 Quoted in Van Doren, ibid., p. 696.

He [Franklin] had thought, he said, of the American ship with its British passport as partly a convenience to Vergennes. If the American dispatches did not go promptly Congress might be left to hear of the agreement from the English first, which would surely be improper. As to the agreement itself, he again reminded Vergennes that it was only a provisional one, dependent on the French treaty of peace. As to the hurried closing of these preliminary articles, Vergennes's "observation" was "apparently just: that in not consulting you before they were signed we have been guilty of neglecting a point of bienseance [propriety]. But, as all this was not from want of respect for the king, whom we all love and honor, we hope it will be excused; and that the great work which has hitherto been so happily conducted, is so nearly brought to perfection, and is so glorious to his reign, will not be ruined by a single indiscretion of ours. And certainly the whole edifice sinks to the ground immediately if you refuse on that account to give us any further assistance."[50]

Franklin added, then, that the English "flatter themselves that they have divided us," and trusted that "this little misunderstanding will therefore be kept a secret and that they [the English] will find themselves totally mistaken."

None of this sounds like an Aries rising with Mars in Sagittarius (however much Aries was at work), for the actions in question were part of Franklin's focused pursuit of his ends. (It's also worth noting that it was not Franklin's idea to act without the French. Rather, he was apparently persuaded to accept this course of action by the convictions of the other American ambassadors. Van Doren writes, "Left to himself, he [Franklin] would probably have kept up the most courteous relations with Vergennes."[51]) We might particularly consider Franklin's remarks about the king, where Franklin is hardly being direct. He wrote, in another context, about the foolishness of hereditary titles—a piece which he did not publish because it might have seemed insulting to the French monarchy, as, no doubt, it would have, for to Franklin, hereditary titles were

---

50 Ibid., pp. 696–7.
51 Ibid., p. 694.

... not only groundless and absurd but often hurtful to that posterity [ie. who receive the hereditary titles], since it is apt to make them proud, disdaining to be employed in useful arts and thence falling into poverty and all the meannesses, servility and wretchedness attending it; which is the present case with much of what is called the noblesse in Europe.[52]

Also worth noting in this context is a matter discussed briefly above: that in general, when approaching any situation in which he would try to sway public or diplomatic opinion, he would begin by writing an essay on the subject, often under a pseudo-nym (and often as a hoax of some kind). Again and again, Franklin entered situations *veiled*, even though, in so doing, he was quite fixed on his purpose (i.e., intercepted Aries). With Pisces rising, Neptune,would rule the Ascendant from intercepted Aries, and thus be disposited by Mars in Sagittarius in the 9th. Franklin began situations with an indirection (Neptune) often based on a disguise (1st House) related to the published writing (9th House): indirection (Pisces) veiling great identification of purpose (Aries).

Rectification II: In the Ball-Park, at the Very Least

1. Planets and Houses, Again

As is evident from the foregoing, I believe that Franklin was born with Pisces rising and a Sagittarius Midheaven. More specif-ically, I feel the birth time was 10:05 A.M. This time yields a horo-scope which reflects Franklin's character quite accurately, and which responds quite accurately to transits and Solar Arc mea-surements. Before looking at those, let's examine the additional elements of character revealed by this horoscope.

The 10:05 P.M. horoscope places Uranus in the 5th, the Sun in the 11th, and Moon in the 12th. All of these seem quite appropri-ate, most obviously that of Uranus, for, as mentioned, Franklin's studies in electricity were the activity Franklin loved most deeply, and scientific inquiry was something to which he was most natu-rally drawn. Uranus in the 5th suggests that he was a natural inventor—an inventor by natural inclination and through joyful

---

52 Quoted in Van Doren, ibid., p. 707.

spontaneity. That this joyfulness manifested through practical invention is symbolized by Uranus' square to the 2nd House Saturn in Taurus. Also, with the Mercury-Uranus opposition as the focus of the yod extending from the 11th House to the 5th, we see related Franklin's inventiveness and his concern for the social welfare. The most ready example of this is that even before he drew lightning from the sky, Franklin had hit upon the idea of a lightning rod for houses. Insight began as play (5th), became practical invention (2nd), then extended to society at large (11th): Franklin's T-square.

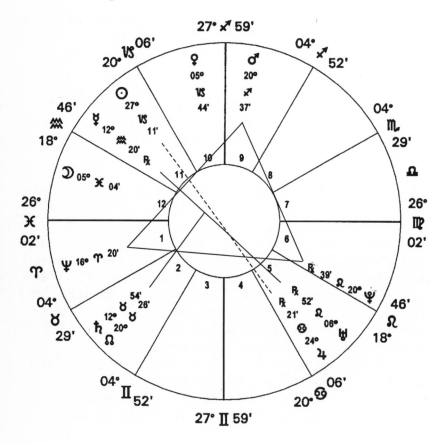

Benjamin Franklin
Jan. 17, 1706 10:05 A.M. LMT
Boston, Massachusetts
71W04 42N22
Koch Houses

The Sun in the 11th also makes sense. Franklin's guiding principle, from at least age thirty onward (that is, after the Saturn Return, which often helps people to uncover the true nature of their solar energy) was to help the society in which he found himself. The tendency is also evident in Franklin's early writings for his brother's paper: the same tendency, admixed with youthful rebellion. Social principles guided him as surely as any compass throughout the later stages of his life. Not only that, but if we accept the argument (offered below) that Freemasonry occupied a more important position in Franklin's life and activity than is generally acknowledged, then the 11th House makes sense as a symbol of societies in which Franklin held a prominent position (Sun, and in Capricorn, which rules the house) and which profoundly influenced his drive toward self-fulfillment. Freemasonry aside, Franklin always had important leadership positions within societies, most notably his own Junto, and he did much work to establish new societies or social enterprises based on principles of social justice.

As for the Moon in the 12th, it suggests not only quasi-clandestine relationships with women, but also the fact that without all that much regret he left his home and wife behind for long periods of time. Venus in the 10th also makes sense considering the number of French women with whom Franklin had dealings—sometimes quasi-romantic ones—through his professional work. It also symbolizes what was noted above: that personal relationships were vital to Franklin in his diplomatic work, for it was his ability to maintain warm professional relationships with the French that enabled him to be the successful diplomat he was.

Saturn in the 2nd also seems right, not only in itself, reflecting as it does Franklin's constant concern with material value and money (which might, after all, be sufficiently symbolized by Saturn's sign-placement), but also because with Saturn at the focal point of a T-square, the "empty leg" becomes the 8th House. We would expect that Franklin would have to take into consideration the values of others if he hoped to find any balance in the world.

Numerous incidents in Franklin's life suggest the strength of that 8th House. It was in evidence in the Proprietary dispute, when the issue was whether the Proprietaries should be taxed like any other citizen of Pennsylvania. Similarly, the Stamp Act dispute was about other people's money, as was much of his work in France, where he was constantly trying to obtain loans from the French government. Even early in his life, Franklin was much concerned with what other people valued, and saw how this was important to his own ability to get on in the world (Saturn in the 2nd):

> I began now [c. 1730] gradually to pay off the debt I was under for the printing house. In order to secure my credit and character as a tradesman, I took care not only to be in *reality* industrious and frugal, but to avoid all *appearances* of the contrary. I dressed plain and was seen at no places of idle diversion. I never went out fishing or shooting; a book, indeed, sometimes debauched me from my work, but that was seldom, snug, and gave no scandal; and to show that I was not above my business, I sometimes brought home the paper I purchased at the stores, thro' the streets on a wheel barrow. Thus being esteemed an industrious, thriving, young man, and paying duly for what I bought, the merchants who imported stationary solicited my custom; others proposed supplying me with books, and I went on swimmingly. In the meantime Keimer's [his rival's] credit and business declining daily, he was at last forced to sell his printing house to satisfy creditors. He went to Barbadoes and there lived some years in very poor circumstances.[53]

There is, finally, the curious appropriateness of the Sabian Symbols for the 10:05 A.M. Midheaven and Ascendant. The former reads, "An old bridge over a beautiful stream is still in constant use." Rudhyar's keynote seems to epitomize Franklin's work:

> The enduring elements in a society which reveal its ability to significantly link the genius of its individuals to the everyday needs of the collectivity.[54]

The symbol for the Ascendant-degree is, "The harvest moon illumines a clear autumnal sky." Rudhyar's keynote is, "The light of fulfillment that blesses work well-done,"[55] which was certainly

---

53 Franklin, op. cit., pp. 60-61.
54 Dane Rudhyar, *An Astrological Mandala* (New York: Vintage, 1974), p. 226.
55 Ibid., p. 286.

a constant feature of Franklin's life, and might also be said to be a re-statement of the *Autobiography's* theme: that virtue will be rewarded in obvious ways.

2. Transits (and Miscellaneous Remarks!)

The evidence presented so far for the 10:05 A.M. birth time is intriguing, but relies on my interpretation of Franklin's character and might on that ground be felt suspect. In addition, much of that evidence supports not only a 10:05 chart, but any chart for around that time which would suggest those elements of Franklin's character. Time analysis techniques don't eliminate the subjective element, but they do demand objective evidence for specific times in Franklin's life. Transits will indicate that 10:05 is, at the very least, pretty close; Solar Arc progressions will suggest its precision.

Transits to the MC should be particularly telling for Franklin simply because so much of his life-emphasis was on vocational matters (not surprisingly, with Saturn at the apex of his T-square, and dispositing the Sun). Saturn conjoined the MC during three periods of Franklin's life: in 1782, 1752–3, and 1723–4.

Saturn's movement to the MC will often coincide with a person's maximum success in the external world, or it can coincide with a major "fall from grace." One reaps the rewards, whatever they are, of one's work in the world. Robert Hand puts the matter quite succinctly:

> This is the time when all your past preparations for the future will have their most important consequences. This transit represents an important life pinnacle for you, but it also entails very important duties and responsibilities ...

> But if you have taken shortcuts anywhere or broken the rules of the game you are playing, you will have trouble in those areas of your life. President Nixon fell from power as a result of actions taken at this time and in the years previous. The Watergate break-in occurred within days of Saturn's transit over his Midheaven.

> The areas of your life that you have prepared carefully will become tremendously productive now. Your opportunities are at a peak for achievement and for additional responsibility and power in your work and in your personal life. This

period will continue for several years. People will look to you
for leadership, whether you want it or not. [56]

In Franklin's case, the second and third transits of Saturn
over his MC largely epitomized the tremendous productivity
Hand mentions, while the first transit epitomized the troubles.

The 1782 transits took place on February 3, June 18, andNo-
vember 3. The events that took place then can be better understood with a bit of background. In 1778, Franklin signed the treaty
for the French alliance with the United States (Saturn transiting
opposite natal Saturn; SA Saturn trine natal ASC; SA Jupiter sextile natal Uranus). In 1779, he had been appointed Ambassador
Plenipotentiary to France (SA Uranus sextile both natal Mars and
natal Pluto; therefore at their midpoint, and completing a Kite to
the Grand Trine, having opposed Neptune a few years earlier;
transiting Jupiter crosses DESC). In September 1783, he signed the
Treaty of Paris, ending the American Revolution.

This last date might make us think that the Midheaven is
wrong, that Saturn's conjunction there should coincide with the
treaty signing at least approximately. However, the signing of the
actual treaty was in many ways merely *the formalization of work
done in 1782* which closely coincides with the Saturn-MC transits.
The 1783 signing date actually coincides with Saturn's *station* at 6
Capricorn, directly conjoined Franklin's 10th House Venus, exalted ruler of the Pisces Ascendant. (This transit was the last of a
series of Saturn-Venus conjunctions; we will soon encounter the
first of that series.)

On July 9, 1782, just after Saturn's retrograde transit to the
10:05 P.M. MC, Franklin presented to English negotiator Oswald a
memorandum of what he thought the essential points of peace.
Though not an official draft of the treaty, these four points nevertheless constituted the essential points of the treaty that was
signed over a year later. Of course, Franklin may have been either
drafting or formulating that document when the precise transit
took place on June 18. In any case, on June 15, Franklin was
informed that Britain was ready to treat with the United States,
and would offer independence in the bargain. Earlier, on the 13th
of May, Franklin's spirits were lifted by the news that war prison-

---

56 Robert Hand, *Planets in Transit* (Rockport: Para Research, 1976).p. 362.

ers would be unconditionally released, a hopeful sign, opening the door to substantial negotiations. Jupiter conjoined the 10:05 MC on May 10.

On October 5, 1782, as Saturn loomed in on the 10:05 MC, the British were given the first draft, now in official form, of the terms proposed by America. Franklin was ill at the time, having become physically overtaxed. (He was, after all, seventy-six years old!). The terms were "the same as Franklin's four necessary points of July 9th ... This trial version of the treaty ... reached London on the 11th."[57] The final Saturn-MC conjunction on November 3 brought a series of intensive meetings between English and American negotiators. They met "at eleven every day and dined four times together to continue their work into the evening."[58] Articles were drawn up on November 5, and signed at the end of the month[59] as Saturn moved into Capricorn.

The first of the Saturn-Venus series took place in January, 1783. It brought the mentioned difficulties between Franklin and French minister Vergennes. As noted, Venus in Capricorn in the 10th suggests the importance of personal relationships in one's professional dealings, and here Franklin, having acted contrary to his promises (i.e., to refrain from signing without consulting France), was inviting, we might say, the wrath of Saturn. As Hand's discussion of Nixon suggests, Franklin might have endangered his mission by skipping steps, by "breaking the rules of the game." Only the delicate tact of professional idealism (Venus exalted ruler of Pisces Ascendant) brought Franklin through successfully. These strained relations certainly seem appropriate to a Saturn-Venus transit, their professional arena being connected to the 10th House.

The previous Saturn-MC conjunction on December 24, 1752 brought a significant increase in Franklin's reputation among the scientific societies of Europe. However, as in the previous case, too quick a look might suggest that there's something amiss with the 10:05 P.M. birth time. For example, on November 30, 1753, nearly a year after the proposed conjunction, he was awarded the Copley Medal of the Royal Society of London for his researches in

---

57 Van Doren, op. cit., p. 687.

58 Ibid., p. 689.

59 Ibid., p. 689.

electricity and lightning. Harvard and Yale had presented him with honorary degrees of Master of Arts in July and September of that year respectively. This period was characterized, not by Saturn but by Jupiter. First, there was the Jupiter return in early July, 1753. Then there was Jupiter's series of sesquiquadrates to both the MC and ASC beginning on September 24, 1753, and extending well into 1754. Finally, Jupiter was opposing Mercury and squaring Saturn during that period.

If we go back just a bit, however, we find the event associated with the Saturn-MC conjunction. The famous kite experiment had taken place in June, 1752, with transiting Saturn conjoining Mars and (June 20) SA ASC conjoining Saturn. (It is perhaps notable that Franklin's bringing lightning down to earth as he did was associated with Saturn!) Franklin published his findings in the October 19 issue of his *Gazette* (Saturn again conjoining natal Mars), the same issue containing "Franklin's first positive statement of How to Secure Houses, etc., from Lightning."[60] These developments took some time to reach Europe, however, and the event which seems to epitomize transiting Saturn on the MC came on December 21, 1752, as Franklin's account of the electrical kite was read at the Royal Society, an event which led to the Copley Medal being conferred a year later. The Midheaven being in Sagittarius, here as in 1782, the developments involved a foreign country and a document of some kind. (This event was not associated with a significant Jupiter transit, however, as Jupiter was back around 10 Cancer, not yet in a position to bring such recognition.)

It's also interesting, not for purposes of rectification, but for understanding Franklin's life generally, and the functioning of his yod in particular, that his initial researches into electricity (1746) took place with *Uranus conjoining his natal Mercury and opposing his natal Uranus*. This was one of his midlife transits, made particularly potent by transiting Uranus approximately coinciding conjunction to natal Mercury and square to focal Saturn. The transit set the yod into motion, the result being Franklin's shocking (!) discoveries about lightning. That this was a midlife transit suggests that after his many years of public service in Philadelphia, Franklin was ready to break out and start in a new direction. That

---

60 Ibid., p. 164.

new direction is aptly symbolized not by the Capricorn Sun or Saturn in Taurus in the 2nd House, but by Mercury in Aquarius in the 11th and Uranus in Leo in the 5th. As I have suggested, Uranus in the 5th suggests that electrical studies were a natural, creative drive for Franklin. Witness what he wrote on March 28, 1747 (with transiting Uranus precisely on his natal Mercury), of his researches:

> I never was before engaged in any study that so totally engrossed my attention and my time as this has lately done; for, what with making experiments when I can be alone, and repeating them to my friends and acquaintance who, from the novelty of the thing, come continually in crowds to see them, I have during some months past had little leisure for anything else.[61]

As his life progressed, however, Franklin's Uranus was increasingly drawn toward pursuits symbolized by Jupiter and Saturn. This is not surprising, considering the T-square and the opposition between Jupiter and his Capricorn Sun. However, again unlike in the myth, where Ouranus, in being castrated by Saturn, loses the life-giving power of his insight, in Franklin's case the demands of Saturn merely turned the insights of Uranus in a political direction more than a scientific one. There, as in the Philadelphia field, he served to bring Uranus down to earth, providing the practical grounding which turned the spark of freedom into the fire of revolution.

We might say, therefore, that Franklin entered the second half of life more Uranian than ever before, beginning to use his genius in ever more useful ways (natal square between Saturn and Uranus). The process had actually begun in the early 1730s when Franklin began to extend himself into Philadelphia society, contributing to it in some of the diverse ways suggested above. (The period was characterized by, among other factors, Franklin's Progressed New Moon on September 17, 1732, and transiting Uranus' conjunction to the 10:05 MC in 1736.) After Uranus had opposed its natal position, however, Franklin's activity became increasingly wide in scope. By 1752–3, with Saturn conjoining

---

61 Ibid., p. 155.

Franklin's MC for the second time, his reputation as a philosopher had become an international one.

It's probably worthwhile to remember how significant Franklin's work with electricity was—not for Franklin himself (for the transits of Saturn tell us that), but for the world in general. One biographer tells us:

> In 1752–3 these were not mysteries but wonders. A man in Philadelphia in America, bred a tradesman, remote from the learned world, had hit upon a secret which enabled him, and other men, to catch and tame the lightning, so dread that it was still mythological. To the public, as it gradually heard about him, he seemed a magician. To scientists, from the first, he seemed a master.[62]

If we look at the issue symbolically, we can trace the connection between Franklin's work in lightning and his late work as a diplomat. Major Arcana #16 from the Tarot Deck helps us make this transition. It shows lightning striking a tower and is traditionally called "The House of God" (and sometimes simply "The Tower"). Barbara Walker offers one medieval interpretation:

> If the crumbling structure represented the Holy Roman Empire, which was sometimes called "the proud tower," the card could be seen as a graphic version of the popular underground prophecy of this Empire's downfall. It was said that as long as the Empire stood intact, Antichrist could not come to the world.[63]

Walker also notes that if the card was intended to portray an oncoming doomsday, "the two figures falling from the tower would have been emperor and pope, the combination of church and state," and that the card also suggests the replacing of one god with another:

> The biblical God himself was called a "high tower" (2 Samuel 22:3). The lightning bolt attacking the tower signified the god of the future destroying the god of the past: a classic Oedipal

---

62 Ibid., p. 170.
63 Barbara G. Walker, *The Secrets of the Tarot* (HarperSanFrancisco, 1984), p. 115.

drama in metaphor. Significantly, the lightning spirit's first appearance in the Bible was as a "son of God" (Job 1:6).[64]

Of course, Franklin's lighting rods would have been most useful on the tallest buildings available, the church towers, but ecclesiastical authorities resisted the idea offered by the "arch infidel" as being an ungodly solution to the problem.[65] This seems symbolically apt, as it was in part the stranglehold of the "church state complex" that the lightning bolt of freedom and revolution (which Franklin, with his Jupiter-Sun opposition, was quite fit to wield!) threatened to bring crashing down.

According to Carl Jung, Nostradamus predicted great tribulations for 1792: a time in which Bibles would be burned and paganism would return. A new age would dawn; or, rather, a renovation of the prevailing Age of Pisces. Jung notes that the period was significant astrologically partly because it was "the moment when the precession of the equinoxes reached the tail of the second fish."[66]

The period before 1792 brought the Anti-Christ, which in socio-political terms seems to be Reason. The transition brought us the so-called Enlightenment with its decidedly un-Christian sentiments,[67] and Franklin, one of the period's characteristic figures, is seen as a threat, as one who meddles in the doings of God. First he brings lightning from the skies, then he threatens (as it was imagined) to topple kingdoms (ruled by God's purported proxies) hither and yon.

Uranus seems the significant symbol here, partly because it was discovered in 1781, and partly because its movement into a Grand Trine with Neptune and Pluto marks a turning point in the relations between the colonies (and therefore Franklin) and the British. As we have seen, Neptune and Pluto remained in a trine aspect through around 1790, when Neptune began to move out of orb. (By 1800 the aspect was definitely over, with Neptune at 15–17 Scorpio and Pluto back at 2–5 Pisces; and it is significant that during the 1790's there was in the United States a severe conservative

---

64 Ibid., p. 116.
65 Ibid., p. 117.
66 C. G. Jung, *Aion* (Princeton: Princeton University Press, 1959), p. 98.
67 See Jung, op. cit., p. 43.

backlash—sometimes called the Federalist Reign of Terror, which signaled the end of the creative dynamism of the trine.)

By 1768, Uranus had moved into orb for the Grand Trine in earth signs, and remained there through the early part of 1775. Through much of this period, the trine centered very close to Franklin's Sun-Jupiter opposition. Transiting Pluto opposed his Jupiter in 1774–6 and had moved to conjoin his Sun in 1776–7; Uranus trined his Sun from Taurus in 1773–4; Neptune did so from Virgo in 1777–8. The transiting planets combined with Franklin's natal opposition to form a kite—the second of three kites to catapult him to the forefront of international affairs![68]

Franklin, having defended colonial rights against the incursions of the Stamp Tax, began to see that full independence from Britain was necessary and unavoidable, even if not entirely desirable. The astrological point to be made here is that on a collective level *Uranus' aspects with Neptune and Pluto catalyzed the revolutionary fervor of the late 1760s and early 1770s* (the period of the collective grand trine), and that the conjunction of Pluto with Franklin's Sun gave Franklin extraordinary power to influence the course of events—which is to say, enormous influence over the collective thought-stream. Pluto conjoining an 11th House Sun will perhaps wish to alter irrevocably the course of political events; Jupiter as ruler of the MC will do so through work that is publicly recognized (and, as noted, Sagittarian in nature).

The 1723 transit of Saturn over the 10:05 MC occurred on February 24, May 23, and November 20. Franklin left Boston in late September of that year, breaking his indenture with his brother James. He arrived in Philadelphia by November. In Boston he had been working with his brother's paper, *The Courant*, writing under the name Silence Dogwood (the first of his many female pseudonyms, suggesting a 10th House Venus). The Silence Dogwood papers helped *The Courant* to thrive, but Benjamin's brother and father at first did not know their source. However, after hearing so much favorable comment upon his work, Benjamin divulged his secret—and received some beatings from his broth-

---

68 The first was the electrical kite of 1752. The third was the astrological kite formed by SA Uranus 1775-79.

er. Franklin commented, years later in his *Autobiography:*

> I fancy his harsh and tyrannical treatment of me might be a means of impressing me with that aversion to arbitrary power that has stuck to me through my whole life. Thinking my apprenticeship very tedious, I was continually wishing for some opportunity of shortening it, which at length offered in a manner unexpected.[69]

In January 1723, James was taken up before the Assembly because something in the paper had been politically out of line, and he was imprisoned for a month. During that time, Benjamin managed the paper and "made bold to give our rulers some rubs" which led some people to "consider me in an unfavorable light as a young genius that had a turn for libeling and satire."[70] When there came an order from the House, upon James' release, that the paper could no longer be printed in his name, he decided (February 1723) that it would

> ... be printed for the future under the name of "Benjamin Franklin"; and to avoid the censure of the Assembly that might fall on him as still printing it by his apprentice, the contrivance was that my old indenture should be returned to me with a full discharge on the back of it ...[71]

New indentures were written up in secret, however, which led to additional bad blood between the two brothers (Mercury, ruling the third and square Saturn), and Benjamin, shortly after acting as editor of a paper and having one published in his name, decided to assert his own freedom. His brother saw to it, however, that he would find no work in other local printing houses, so Benjamin decided to leave Boston, intending first to go to New York, but ending up eventually in Philadelphia where he had to begin anew. He left Boston in secret in September (transiting Pluto opposing ASC September 25), arriving in Philadelphia probably in November (transiting Pluto square MC/IC; Saturn's final conjunction to MC).

---

69 Franklin, op. cit., p. 17.

70 Ibid., p. 17.

71 Ibid., pp. 17-18.

The chain of events has all the marks of Saturn's transit over the MC: success, then a fall from grace; resistance from authority figures, and, from the point of view of many people of the time, actions not entirely ethical (indentures being agreements not lightly broken). In leaving Boston, Franklin, having come to a temporary peak in his fortunes with the publication of his first significant writings and, for a time, being editor of a newspaper, had to start over again. The temporary success recalls what Hand tells us about Saturn's transit over the MC; the need for re-orientation recalls the words of Erin Sullivan about the same transit:

> As Saturn transits the MC and moves into the 10th House, a new force seizes the individual. A complete re-evaluation of his effectiveness is in order. Frequently this will manifest in an abrupt ceasing of one form of activity and an impulse to move into a new mode of behavior. The person experiencing this transit feels the need to test himself and his knowledge of the familiar in order to reassure himself of his potency in the world. It often results in a major step forward that challenges previous security patterns. The modern hero will often take on a new job, move across the country, face his peers in a new and authoritative way or perhaps move out of an academic or learning mode into a more professional mode. Though events are certainly not consistent or clearly defined, it is assured that a shift in inner perspective will take place over the year that follows the transit.[72]

She calls this transit "the call to adventure," which seems a fairly succinct description of what Franklin was experiencing at the time.

A piece of corroborative evidence is that at just about the time Benjamin left Boston in late September, Mars was transiting in the final degrees of Sagittarius, conjoining the 10:05 IC and suggesting conflict with the father and with "the home-ground" generally. This transit can also symbolize a temporary low ebb in one's professional fortune. Both of these seem to apply. The strength of the transit was increased by Mars retrograde station in mid-November, 1723 at 9+ Capricorn, in Franklin's 4th House.

---

72 Erin Sullivan, *Saturn in Transit* (New York: Arkana, 1991), p. 170.

The retrograde took it back over the 27+ Gemini IC right around Christmas time, and again in early March, reiterating the need for new beginnings.

Jupiter conjoined the 10:05 MC on January 27, 1723, just before Benjamin took over the paper. It returned very close to the MC, stationing at 28+ Sagittarius at the end of August, suggesting restlessness and a definite headiness; certainly not a transit designed to produce acquiescence, particularly as Uranus was in the final phase of its triple transit square Franklin's Sun. (The previous two phases had been at the end of 1722 and in April of 1723.)

Certainly a personal revolution was at hand; a revolution against the father's law (Capricorn Sun), and a revolution which produced travel (Jupiter) and new vistas (MC). Finally, Pluto's transit over the 10:05 Descendant on September 25, 1723 suggests power-struggles in relationships. The closely coinciding square to the MC/IC axis (November 27) suggests a death-rebirth experience related to the home and vocational direction. The timing, particularly of the conjunction to the Descendant, is notable. Pluto's natal placement in the 6th House suggests that these developments would be related to some sort of unequal relationship such as master-apprentice, and that Franklin would be required to find new work to meet his survival needs.

While Uranus' transit square the Sun strongly suggests a break from the father's authority (reiterating some of the possibilities of the Saturn transit) which would occur at the same time regardless of birth time, I don't think it accounts for all of the events that occurred. Though both Saturn and Uranus have indirect connections to the home in Franklin's chart (i.e., both aspect Mercury, IC ruler), and while these connections might well arise with a strong transit, the Saturn and Pluto transits, being to angles, seem more powerfully to indicate the new home that Franklin went to. The Saturn transit symbolizes, in a way the Uranus transit does not, the peak in Franklin's fortunes (in publishing: Sagittarius) followed by a sharp fall and then a new beginning. Pluto's square to the MC/IC axis in October and November precisely coincided with Franklin "dying" in his old home, after a struggle with a dominant parent, and giving birth to a new one. Recall Hand:

> ... changes are needed ... Perhaps you need to move. Sometimes this transit coincides with a change of residence, which

enables you to see what to do more easily because your new surroundings reveal previously hidden problems. You need not expect catastrophe with this transit by any means, but do not shrink from the challenge of change. Only in this way can you keep your life vigorous and challenging.[73]

In Franklin's case, the move did indeed reveal "previously hidden problems"—which were also potentials. Once in Philadelphia, he began to manifest in himself the moralistic tendencies of his father. (We might say that the projection of these upon his father was no longer effective.) Franklin had to "re-collect"[74] these tendencies to himself. The results of this re-collection were the moral codes and systems which set Franklin on his way to fame, influencing the collective in such uncanny ways.

Some other correlations to the 10:05 horoscope might help us to think that we are, at the very least, "in the ball-park." One is that in 1728, with Saturn transiting his 12th House, following his first, quasi-abortive journey to London (1724–6), Franklin, in a state of discouragement over past failures, crafts out his Program for Moral Perfection. The program arises because Franklin is haunted by a sense of failure, and desires to reform: fitting developments for a 12th House Saturn transit. In 1729, with Saturn still in the house of secrets, his illegitimate son William is born.

The 12th House transit's pains are somewhat ameliorated by Franklin's Jupiter Return in 1729. Franklin contributes (again under a pseudonym) several articles to one of the other newspapers in the Philadelphia, and then, on October 2, having (with financial assistance) bought out the editor, issues the paper under a new title (*The Pennsylvania Gazette*) and under his own name. As the Jupiter return took place at the end of August, the timing seems about right. However, though the paper was his, he announced it to the public as a partnership. He did not announce himself as sole owner until *after Saturn had entered the 1st House in 1731*. (The partnership was actually dissolved on July 14, 1730, with Saturn stationing in the 12th at 21+ Pisces, square Mars.

---

73 Hand, op. cit., p. 520.

74 The term is borrowed from Marie Louise Von Franz's *Projection and Recollection in Jungian Psychology* (London: Open Court, 1978).

Franklin kept this development secret, however, as he felt people might question a young man without obvious means standing forth as publisher. The first edition to appear under Franklin's name was dated May 11, 1732.)

During the 12th House transit, Benjamin also decided to make more money, his discontent bringing Saturn's natal placement to the fore:

> He has been a little frightened by his repeated failures; he resolves upon success. He has been forcibly reminded of the disadvantages incurred by lack of money; he therefore resolves to get some. He is the proprietor of his own business, but in name only; he wishes to pay off the loans advanced by Grace and Coleman as quickly as possible and stand forth as his own untrammeled boss. He therefore gives himself entirely to the mastery of external things; he becomes the complete extrovert and model bourgeois.[75]

He was twenty-four years old at the time; the year was 1730; Saturn made the previously mentioned station in Pisces closely square Mars, suggesting a determination to master the world before him. Mars as ruler of intercepted Aries suggests the release of heretofore unused capabilities. Franklin became more direct, more organized; "the model bourgeois."

Saturn crossed the 10:05 ASC in April, 1731 and came back to station at 27+Pisces in early December, squaring the MC/IC axis later that month. During July of that year, Franklin founded the first subscription library in North America. (The doors didn't open until 1732, with Saturn entering intercepted Aries, because books had to be purchased from England: Aries ruled by 9th House Mars in Sagittarius.)

Franklin also arranged for his printing press to print the paper money approved by Congress. The process had been set in motion by a piece Franklin had written some time before, advocating paper money. Having been one of the colonies first advocates of paper currency (and inflation), he was offered the job printing it, for much of the credit for passing the bill went, rightfully, to him. (Franklin's essay on the subject was first presented

---

75 Russell, op. cit., p. 120.

to Franklin's Junto, a philosophical "think tank" he organized, again reflecting the importance of his 11th House planets.) The printing took place in the summer of 1731, with Saturn now securely in his 1st House. This job enabled him to pay his debts and stabilize his life:

> He procures the printing of the laws and votes of the provincial government; opens a stationer's shop, and is soon able to hire a compositor and an apprentice ... the strain of earning a mere living is considerably eased. He commands more leisure than formerly. He now stands solidly on the first rung of the ladder of success.[76]

Franklin was on his way indeed, building his life in true Saturnian fashion. *Poor Richard's Almanac* was advertised in late 1732 and printed early the following year. Before long he was financing journeymen printers and reaping a share of their profits in recompense. The result was financial security—and eventually a considerable fortune:

> It was this method of sending out young revenue producers that helped to lay the foundations for Franklin's fortune, which later invested in land, grew to considerable dimensions and enabled him to make an early retirement from money-making. For business he had an acquired rather than innate taste, and he was glad to be rid of it.[77]

The period after this marks a sharp turning point in Franklin's career. Having achieved, around the time of his Saturn return in 1734-5, the financial success which was one goal of his 2nd House Saturn, he underwent a shift in values toward the more social concerns that occupied him for much of the rest of his life. When he was thirty (Saturn transiting in the 3rd), he was elected to his first political post as clerk of the Pennsylvania General Assembly. The work bored him: he made magic squares while waiting through the long-winded discussions, but the post was the first of many public trusts offered him. With Saturn moving into the 3rd House, he learned to communicate his new values to the world.

---

76 Ibid., p. 123.
77 Ibid., p. 143.

In general, this period between Saturn's transit of the ASC and its conjunction with his IC in 1738 might seem to be, as Grant Lewi put it, "a period of obscurity." The obscurity was relative, of course. Franklin was quite active in the public life of Philadelphia, becoming, in fact, the most highly regarded figure in that developing city. At the same time, however, with Saturn in the first three houses we might expect that he would be remaking himself in some way, first through the new and more professional persona he developed, then through a shift of values, and finally by finding more organized ways to communicate to the world. As we will see when we turn to the Solar Arc directions (and the progressed New Moon) related to his Freemasonry, this rebuilding was apparently quite significant indeed.

Rectification Polish

The material presented so far, dealing as it does with transits, does not provide a precise Midheaven or birth time, howevermuch it suggests that the 10:05 time is probably extremely close. To determine the time more precisely, we now turn to Solar Arc directions. As above, our primary interest will be in directions to the angles.

Franklin left on his first voyage to London November 2, 1724. The voyage was inspired by Governor Keith, who had promised to send letters of introduction which would enable Benjamin to purchase printing equipment which would set the young printer up with a business of his own. Franklin sailed for England fully expecting that the letters were on board, only to find out, on his arrival, that they were not. He also found out that false promises were not out of character for the good governor, and that he had been rather cruelly used. Franklin left London to return to Philadelphia on July 23, 1726, arriving in Philadelphia on October 11.

The promises that sparked his departure involved Franklin's prospects as a printer, a vocational matter. Though Franklin left Philadelphia on November 2, his ship didn't sail for "several months yet."[78] The SA MC squared Franklin's natal Neptune on February 15 of that year, about the time of the original proposal. The symbolism is appropriate: the SA MC suggests the career hopes Franklin cherished; Sagittarius suggests publishing and long journeys; Neptune suggests deception. Natal Neptune in intercepted Aries prods Franklin to leap before he looks (a practice he overcame as his life went on, getting a better and better hold on the intercepted sign until it became a gift instead of a liability). The SA Moon's trine of Jupiter (January, 1725) might more aptly symbolize the voyage itself and the temporary change of home, but the entire venture was colored by Neptune and by false hopes regarding vocation, set in motion at the time of the aspect.

Franklin's return from London in July, 1726 also provides interesting evidence. On January 20 of that year, the SA ASC conjoined natal Neptune. It was followed by the conjunction between the SA Moon and the 10:05 ASC on September 11. Though the latter aspect is quite easy to trace in Franklin's return home to Philadelphia, the former is a bit more challenging.

The SA ASC-Neptune aspect seems to reflect, not one event, but the general tendency of Franklin's life in London. In his essay "A Dissertation on Liberty and Necessity" (early 1725), Franklin claimed that there were no vices or virtues, and that men did what they must and that they deserved, for that, neither praise nor blame. The mark of Neptune seems to be on the document. Franklin may have found this waywardness of principle useful, for his life at that time was hardly exemplary. In addition, he was badly used by his best friend Ralph, who borrowed money which he never returned, and generally lived a parasitic life with Benjamin as host. Franklin even contemplated a career as a swimming instructor! It was this Neptunian quality, evident in all the forgoing, suggested in the natal chart by the 12th House Pisces Moon and the Pisces Ascendant, brought to the fore by the progression to Neptune, that Franklin eschewed in several ways in the years following.

As noted, the conjunction of SA Moon with the natal ASC seems quite appropriate to a return home, particularly as this return, though it was followed by a a serious illness (pleurisy: transiting Saturn was conjoining natal Mercury (lungs) spring, 1727), nonetheless inaugurated a new relationship with the public. To achieve this required discipline, symbolized by transiting Saturn's conjunction with Franklin's Sun. If the SA Moon's con-

---

78 Ibid., p. 59.

junction with the ASC symbolized Franklin's return home and his longing to start anew, transiting Saturn symbolized the structured way Franklin approached the problem. On the voyage home, he gave initial form to his desire for reform:

> 1. It is necessary for me to be extremely frugal for some time, till I have paid what I owe.

> 2. To endeavor to speak truth in every instance, to give nobody expectations that are not likely to be answered, but aim at sincerity in every word and action; the most amiable excellence in a rational being.

> 3. To apply myself industriously to whatever business I take in hand, and not to divert my mind from my business by any foolish project of growing rich suddenly; for industry and patience are the surest means of plenty.[79]

Franklin's road to reform takes some interesting turns. Before long, the turn becomes markedly religious as transiting Neptune squares Franklin's Moon and as Saturn moves into the Neptunian 12th House in the developments discussed above. In 1728, with Saturn now securely ensconced in that 12th House, he pens "Articles of Belief and Acts of Religion" (1728), addressed to "the Deity" ("O Father ..."), who

> abhorrest in thy creatures treachery and deceit, malice, revenge, intemperance, and every other hurtful vice; but thou art a lover of justice and sincerity, of friendship and benevolence, and every virtue; thou art my friend, my father, and my benefactor.[80]

He also fashions for himself a new creed for behavior. A few samples will demonstrate its flavor, and show that a new leaf had indeed been turned over. He petitions God:

> I may be preserved from atheism, impiety, and profaneness; and in my addresses to Thee, carefully avoid irreverence and ostentation, formality and odious hypocrisy ...

---

79 Quoted in Russell, ibid., p. 82.
80 Quoted in Russell, ibid., p. 95.

> That I may be loyal to my prince, and faithful to my country, careful for its good, valiant in its defense, and obedient to its laws, abhorring treason as much as tyranny ...

> That I may be just in all my dealings, temperate in my pleasures, full of candor and ingenuousness, humanity and benevolence ... Help me, O Father ....[81]

He found, however, that resolutions to be virtuous, as found in the "Articles," were "not sufficient to prevent our slipping" into its lack. So, at about the same time[82] he produced his thirteen moral principles as part of a program for moral perfection.

The document receives much discussion in the *Autobiography*. To some, it serves as "a perfect map of the tendencies of Franklin's character,"[83] Franklin developed a scheme in which he could keep track of his transgressions through a schemata of thirteen areas in which vice was to be avoided and virtue cultivated. He designed a ledger to keep track of his transgressions. This was the outline of the moral teachings, developed later through the preaching of Poor Richard, which Lawrence scorns in the quotation beginning this essay.

If the square from transiting Neptune to Franklin's Pisces Moon (1726–8) suggests the religious idealism of "Articles of Belief," Pluto's coinciding square of Venus certainly suggests that Franklin's passions were running high. That these two squares occurred simultaneously reflects the ongoing trine between Neptune and Pluto: the collective *Zeitgeist* was moving Franklin, at this time, toward the reform of his moral character. Without these reforms, he probably would not have achieved what he did, for the reforms led to Poor Richard, to the practical success (Saturn transiting into the first, discussed above) which was the necessary groundwork for the scientific work and statecraft which followed.

It will be helpful to the rectification process to contrast Franklin's return from England in 1726 with his return from France in 1785. The first, as we have seen, coincides with the SA Moon conjoining the ASC. The conjunction, along with the Sat-

---

81 Quoted in Russell, ibid., p. 95-96.
82 Franklin, op. cit., p. 75.
83 Russell, op. cit., p. 100.

urn-Sun transit, brings to the surface Franklin's reaction to the disorderliness of that 12th House Moon: he undertakes a program of reform. The 1785 return, however, reflects Franklin's 10th House Venus; and not surprisingly, there is a significant astrological correlation, as SA Venus conjoined Franklin's ASC on March 20, 1786, a few months after his return.

By 1785, Franklin was perhaps the most famous man in America, highly honored not only by the French, but by the English as well. His reputation as a diplomat preceded him. He was saluted by adoring crowds as he left France, and again a few weeks later at the waterside in Philadelphia. The period has the marks of the 10th House Venus: honors, valuation, reputation.

Franklin's departure from France on July 28, 1785 seems to reflect, in part, Jupiter's transit over the 10:05 ASC in April. The transiting Sun conjoined his Jupiter just a few days after he left his residence in Passy in early July. The Secondary Progressed Moon sextiled the ASC in mid-July and conjoined the natal Sun in August. Behind all of these factors, however, lies SA Venus on the ASC.

The apparent discrepancy in time might be accounted for by the nature of a 10th House Venus in Capricorn, which we would hardly expect to manifest solely through adulation received at leisure. Franklin's honors quickly took the form of new professional responsibilities. He hadn't been in Philadelphia very long before he was besieged by offers (not to say demands!) to participate in local and national affairs. These offers-cum-demands culminated in Franklin's contribution to the Constitutional Convention (SA Venus sextile Sun).

Franklin's work on himself in 1726–8 began under the influence of a progression (SA Moon on ASC), but the results of this work didn't stabilize until transiting Saturn crossed the ASC in 1731. That year and the next brought what was apparently another important inner change in Franklin; or, more precisely, an inner change with definite consequences in Franklin's behavior, and in fact his view of his life mission as a whole. He became a Freemason.

This element of Franklin's life is given short shrift by some of his biographers. Some don't mention it at all, and even the usually exhaustive Van Doren never probes the effect of Freemasonry on Franklin's thinking. Still, there's good reason to think that Freemasonry played a vital role in Franklin's development, and therefore in the American drive for independence.

The first known lodge in America dates from 1730. It was in Philadelphia, but Franklin was not a member. In his *Gazette*, however, there appeared at the end of 1730 "an article pretending to reveal the Masonic mysteries."[84] He became a Mason in February, and in May admitted that his December article had been in error. In June, 1732, he wrote the chapter's by-laws, and on the 24th of the month became a warden. Precisely two years later he became Grand Master of St. John's Lodge in Philadelphia, just after he had printed the *Constitutions*, the first Masonic book in America.[85] Some years later, he was elected Grand Master of the province.

Saturn conjoined the 10:05 ASC on March 31, 1731, just after Franklin formally joined the Lodge. He printed his repudiation in May, so it may well be that in April he was reconsidering what he'd said earlier. We might reasonably surmise, then, that he was coming to new understandings of Freemasonry. The Saturn-ASC transit suggests that these understandings might serve as guidance for the next nearly three decades.

Also in 1731, as Franklin was apparently delving into the principles of Freemasonry, SA Jupiter conjoined natal Pluto, suggesting a new awareness of social power (the power of ethics, justice and principle, ideas at the base of Freemason thought at the time) coming through philosophical or religious principles, and setting in motion a vision for his vocation or mission (Sagittarius, Jupiter) that would make him a conduit for the transformative idealism of the age (the important Neptune-Pluto trine discussed above).

The progressed New Moon (September 17, 1732), which occurred just after Franklin became a warden and printed the by-laws, reiterates the importance of this period. It occurred in his 12th House (secrecy) in Aquarius (groups), opposing his 6th House Pluto, which, in Leo and the 6th house, suggests the power of the individual in battling inequalities that have become ritualized into social forms. The opposition suggests an increased awareness, on Franklin's part, of his own power to bring about change; and the power seems to be rooted in the promulgation of ideas held firmly by a secret society. That Franklin at first manifested this power in very ordinary ways seems quite in keeping with the 6th House emphasis.

---

84 Van Doren, op. cit., p. 132.
85 Ibid., p. 132.

On January 18, 1732, the SA IC conjoined natal Jupiter. On November 9, 1734, the SA MC conjoined the natal Sun. The former date again approximates Franklin's printing of the by laws and becoming a warden; the latter date is fairly close to the time he became Grand Master. The former suggests that Franklin was finding a new grounding (IC) in the world through imbibing new principles of social progress; the latter suggests religious or philosophical authority (here also connected with his present vocation as a printer as he printed the *Constitutions*).

When Franklin became Grand Master of the province in 1749 (June 10), Jupiter was just past a conjunction to the 10:05 ASC on June 7, and approaching a square to the MC on June 29.

Van Doren, often considered Franklin's foremost biographer, claims that Freemasonry in America had been "social and local, with little influence in politics,"[86] a statement which would certainly be disputed by other authorities,[87] who would point out that Hancock, Washington, and Franklin all took their Freemasonry quite seriously. Nine signers of the Declaration were definitely Freemasons (possibly ten), as were at least two of the five men who drafted the document. The army was "almost entirely in Freemasonic hands."[88] Furthermore, Franklin's influence with John Paul Jones and Lafayette quite likely came through Freemason connections, as did the influence of several other foreign military leaders who aided the revolutionary effort.[89]

Though Franklin said little about his Freemasonry (its affairs being secret, after all), he retained his Freemason affiliations throughout his life. In France to negotiate aid for the revolutionary effort, he was elected Grand Master of the exclusive "Neuf Soeurs" ("Nine Sisters") Lodge, whose membership also included Voltaire and John Paul Jones, and he later became a member of the *Royale Loge des Commandeurs du Temple a l'Ouest de Carcassonne* ("Royal Lodge of Commanders of the Temple West

---

86 Ibid., p. 687.

87 The material that follows draws heavily from *The Temple and the Lodge* by Michael Baigent and Richard Leigh (New York: Arcade, 1989). The authors present what appears to be a balanced account of Freemasonic influence in the Revolution, neither claiming that there was a Freemasonic conspiracy nor denying the Freemasonic influence entirely. They provide much interesting evidence on, among other matters, the "field lodges" found in the armies of both sides.

88 Ibid., p. 239.

89 Ibid., p. 241.

of Carcassonne"), a more mysterious Freemason enclave.[90]

Freemason societies were one of the few organizations of the period who elected their leaders and who felt that power should reside in the position, not in the man:

> ... Freemasonry was one of the few eighteenth-century institutions in which the principle [separation of man from office] did function effectively and enjoyed a degree of respectability. Masters and grand masters were elected from and by their peers for a stipulated tenure. They did not exercise autocratic power. On the contrary, they could be, and often were, held accountable. And when they were deemed unworthy of the office to which they had been elected, they could be impeached or deposed—not by revolution, "palace coup" or any other violent means, but by established administrative machinery. Nor would the dignity of the office be diminished.[91]

Thus was paved the way toward some of the guiding principles of the American Constitution.

This is not to say that the Revolution was a Freemason conspiracy as some have claimed. It may be more reasonable to claim, as Baigent and Lewis do in *The Temple and the Lodge,* that Freemasonry provided

> ... an ambience, a mentality, a hierarchy of attitudes and values for which Freemasonry provided a particularly efficacious conduit. The Freemasonry of the age was a repository for an imaginatively stirring and potent idealism, which it was able, in a fashion uniquely its own, to disseminate. Most colonists did not actually read Locke, Hume, Voltaire, Diderot or Rousseau, any more than most British soldiers did. Through the lodges, however, the currents of thought associated with such philosophers became universally accessible. It was largely through the lodges that "ordinary" colonists learned of that lofty premise called "the rights of man." It was through the lodges that they learned the concept of the perfectibility of society. And the New World

---

90 Ibid., p. 234.
91 Ibid., pp. 257–8.

seemed to offer a species of blank slate, a species of laboratory in which social experiment was possible and the principles enshrined by Freemasonry could be applied in practice.[92]

This description seems to reflect the astrological symbolism of Neptune and Pluto; their trine certainly suggests an "imaginatively stirring and potent idealism" which was disseminated to influence the collective mind and turn it toward active change.

However, we would be wrong to assume that Freemasonry was always insisting on revolution. By and large, and particularly early on, Freemasonry seemed to provide a restraining influence, not an inflammatory one. As late as 1777, even Franklin was "prepared to renounce all thoughts of independence if the grievances which had precipitated the war were redressed."[93] The same was apparently true for Washington and Joseph Warren (Grand Lodge of Scotland's Grand Master for North America):

> Most of the non-Freemasons among the defiant colonists— men such as John and Samuel Adams—were already [in 1775] demanding more radical measures [than a mere refusal to submit to tyranny]. As we have noted, however, Warren, in declaring his continued allegiance to the crown, if not to Parliament, expressed the position of most Freemasons.[94]

Just a few years earlier (in 1771) Franklin wrote of his hope— which he had less and less faith in—that wise action might "destroy those seeds of dis-union, and both countries might thence continue much longer to grow great together, much more secure by their united strength and more formidable to their common enemies."[95] (The grand trine among Uranus, Neptune, and Pluto stirred people toward independence, but not, it seems, toward anarchy. This seems much in keeping with the nature of the grand trine. As for Franklin, his drive for independence was always moderated by his Saturnian need for order.)

Given all this—Freemasonry's influence on the Revolution and later Constitution, and Franklin's long and loyal association

---

92 Ibid., p. 211.
93 Ibid., p. 219.
94 Ibid., p. 217.
95 Quoted in Van Doren, op. cit., p. 388.

with it—we might well ask whether Franklin's entry into the Philadelphia Lodge was perhaps more important in his development than first appears. It also seems to me, in looking over Franklin's life, that the years before 1730–1733 were devoted largely to making his own way in the world, the years after that were increasingly devoted to the improvement of society. The entry in Freemasonry may well have been a causal factor in this, or it may be simply a correlative (though the nature of Freemasonry suggests that it was at least partially causal, possibly significantly so, even if we consider Freemasonry to be one cause among many).

Conclusion: The "So What?" Proposition

To what purpose do we engage in such an investigation? No doubt *astrologers* care about what time of day Benjamin Franklin was born, though even among us it's hard to see what *practical* benefit might come of it. (This last is certainly a point Mr. Franklin would have stressed, and I confess to having Venus in Capricorn within 6 degrees of Franklin's!) We might certainly answer, "Curiosity is enough! We simply wish to investigate, to know the truth!" And we do, but mightn't there be more than that? While these questions probably come under the purview of our editor, it might be a good idea to pursue the idea a bit here.

The most intriguing element of this study—to me, at any rate—has to do not with getting the rectification right, but in watching how Franklin responded to collective trends.

As Franklin's Freemasonic affiliations were apparently interwoven with the work he did later, his earlier development, symbolized by arcs and progressions, reflects an inner growth which manifested through collective affairs, symbolized by outer planet transits. Franklin's "electric spark" seems not only a matter of drawing literal lightning down from literal skies, but also a matter of sparking or catalyzing important reactions in the sociopolitical arenas of his day.

After the creative Neptune-Pluto trine was over, there was the strong reaction (noted above) of the Federalist Reign of Terror, and even, some would claim, of the Constitution itself, which, while providing for new governmental operations, said nothing about the rights of the individual. (We might remember, too, that the ink on the Bill of Rights was barely dry when the Sedition Act was passed.) Those people who wanted to change society for the better had to strike, it seems, while the iron was hot.

We are in a similar situation now with the ongoing "long sextile" between Neptune and Pluto, and we need to take advantage. Again we seem to be in a "seed time" (to borrow, I think, a phrase from Rudhyar). We, too, stand on a threshold, though it often seems like the edge of an abyss. Though this matter might be discussed from many points of view, I would like to stress only one: the symbolism of Pluto.

About the time of Pluto's discovery, Carl Jung wrote that whatever is not acknowledged as part of the self is experienced in the world as an event.[96] That is, we experience unacknowledged elements of ourselves *as projections.* If enough people reject the same sort of elements (i.e., the Pluto within), then the world becomes filled with images which reflect those rejected elements; and, because those elements have been rejected or "negativized," they appear in the world as *immense problems.* Thus: the Plutonic images that confront us on all sides. Unlike Franklin, if we wish to change the world around us effectively we cannot simply deal with Pluto as an *external* force.

Franklin's 6th House Pluto suggests not only the power that came from his programs of self-improvement, but also his powerful undermining of collective inequality and an attempt to establish a new, more powerful sense of individual dignity (Leo). And he could do this by dealing effectively with *those* restrictive powers, residing in royalty and its ministers (e.g., in England), that made individual dignity subservient to hierarchical power.

Our situation is similar, yet significantly different. Like Franklin, those alive now experience a quickly moving Pluto. People are generally confronted with Plutonic forces early in life. We, too, see individual dignity subservient to hierarchical power. To us, however, with Pluto now discovered, these energies must be dealt with as psychological forces first and foremost, a personal responsibility to acknowledge the dark or primitive parts of

---

96 I have discussed the relationship between Pluto and Jung's work—Pluto as symbolizing the inseparability of mind and phenomena—at more length in "The Dynamic of Pluto," *The Ascendant,* Spring, 1993. (*The Ascendant* is the publication of the Oregon Astrological Association, PO Box 6771, Portland, OR 97228.)

ourselves. Rejected, these energies appear in the world in forms with which we are all too familiar.

Moralistic programs like Franklin's may look somewhat ridiculous to anyone who has experienced Pluto's demand for a full acknowledgement of these psychic elements.[97] At the same time, we may look with a kind of nostalgic amazement at a man who could have such a genial control over the destiny of world events. To us, the trend of events seems more overwhelming, less amenable to practical solutions—demanding, instead, a change of consciousness. (Of course, our diplomats and leaders often seem to be completely devoid of any moral convictions. However ridiculous Franklin's moral program might seem, it may be a ridiculousness we would like to see our leaders cultivate!)

To Franklin, virtue might be attained *by systematically altering one's relationship to phenomena,* whether through moral program or political reform. To us, virtue *must first be found within, by battling inner dragons,* by acknowledging even the most degrading elements of who we are. Only then will we be able to withdraw the destructive projections from the external world for which we are all (ever since the discovery of Pluto) personally responsible.

Moral programs aside, Franklin might, in all this, *be a model* for us, not in the specifics of his approach, but in his general attitude toward phenomena altogether. He was always curious to see how things worked and how he might improve that workability. He did his work with the phenomena themselves.

On the other hand, while we must be just as curious, we won't get as far by dealing with the course of events alone. We must, instead, deal with the source of those events in the collective unconscious or, more precisely, through our awareness of those collective demands *as elements of our own minds.*

To such an investigation, we might apply Franklin's constant curiosity, even if what we find is disturbing; for curiosity, while it may have killed a cat or two, is probably our saving grace when dealing with a world that is only *apparently* dualistic. Curiously enough, curiosity sows those small seeds that may grow into plants capable of enveloping and devouring tyranny in whatever form.

---

97 Consider, for example, D. H. Lawrence with his close Mercury-Pluto square!

Bibliography

Baigent, Michael and Richard Leigh. *The Temple and the Lodge*. New York: Arcade, 1989.

Barbour, Brian M., ed. *Benjamin Franklin: A Collection of Critical Essays*. Englewood Cliffs, NJ: Prentice-Hall, 1979.

Burt, Kathleen. *Archetypes of the Zodiac*. St. Paul: Llewellyn, 1988.

Erlewine, Stephen. *The Circle Book of Charts*. Tempe, AZ: American Federation of Astrologers, 1982.

Franklin, Benjamin. *Autobiography and Other Writings*. Boston: Houghton Mifflin, 1958.

Franklin, Benjamin. *Fart Proudly: Writings of Benjamin Franklin You Never Read in School*. Columbus, OH: Enthea Press, 1990.

Franklin, Benjamin. *The Wisdom of Benjamin Franklin: Political and Economic Essays*. New York: G. P. Putnam's and Sons, 1927.

Greene, Liz. *Saturn*. New York: Samuel Weiser, 1976.

Hand, Robert. *Planets in Transit*. Rockport: Para Research, 1976.

Jung, C. G. *Aion*. Princeton: Princeton University Press, 1959.

Keyes, Nelson Beecher. *Ben Franklin: An Affectionate Portrait*. Surrey: Kingswood, 1913.

Melville, Herman. *Israel Potter: His Fifty Years of Exile*. New York: Dolphin, 1965.

Oken, Alan. *Alan Oken's Complete Astrology*. New York: Bantam, 1988.

Rudhyar, Dane. *An Astrological Mandala*. New York: Vintage, 1974.

Russell, Phillips. *Benjamin Franklin: The First Civilized American*. New York: Brentano's Publishers, 1926.

Sullivan, Erin. *Saturn in Transit*. New York: Arkana, 1991.

Tierney, Bil. *Dynamics of Aspect Analysis*. Reno: CRCS, 1983.

Van Doren, C. G. *Benjamin Franklin*. New York: Viking Press, 1938.

Von Franz, Marie Louise. *Projection and Re-collection in Jungian Psychology*. London: Open Court, 1978.

Walker, Barbara G. *The Secrets of the Tarot*. San Francisco: HarperSanFrancisco, 1984.

White, Charles W. *Benjamin Franklin: A Study in Self-Mythology* New York: Garland Publishing, 1987.

Marc Penfield

Marc Penfield, a double Scorpio with Gemini rising, has been an astrologer since 1964. Known primarily as an historian and researcher, he satisfied his interest in geography by being a travel agent for many years. Marc has one of the largest private collections of birth data on famous persons, as well as cities, states, and countries. He specializes in Mundane or Geopolitical Astrology, as well as Rectification and Astrological Relocation.

Marc is the author of *An Astrological Who's Who* (Arcane, 1972), *America: An Astrological Portrait* (Vulcan, 1976), *The Nadi System of Rectification* (Vulcan, 1977), *The Penfield Data Collection* (Vulcan, 1977), *Horoscopes of the Western Hemisphere* (ACS, 1984), and *Bon Voyage* (AFA, 1992), which deals with relocation techniques.

Marc Penfield

Lincoln, the South, and Slavery

 The first permanent English settlement in America was established at Jamestown, Virginia on May 23, 1607 (NS). According to *The Old Dominion* by Thomas Nelson Page, the colonists arrived at 4 P.M. I've rectified the chart to one-half hour earlier (see chart, page 424). This chart illustrates quite well the Southern way of life.

Libra rising shows a region where grace, elegance, and refinement prevailed, at least on the surface. It was an area famous for good manners, courtesy, and charm, not to mention hospitality. The South is a region which was romanticized and idealized, a part of America famed for its antebellum mansions surrounded by huge oaks laden with moss. The leisurely pace and reputation for taking things easy do not indicate laziness, despite the high temperatures and humidity during the summer; Southerners were by nature more relaxed and laissez-faire about most issues than were their Northern cousins.

The South, in theory, was a place where cavaliers paid homage to women whom they protected, worshiped, and adored. Especially in Virginia, the first settlers desired to establish a democratic republic in which superior beings would rule the many. They believed intensely in liberty, but despite the Libran Ascendant, the issue of equality was something often ignored in their pursuit of excellence. This disparity was felt not only from

229

the whites to the blacks but also from rich landowners to poor farmers.

Cancer at the Midheaven indicates a region where family is king. In some small towns, everyone seems to be related to each other. Southerners are passionately interested in genealogy, your pedigree, where you come from, and how long you have been in a particular place. There's a strong dynastic streak in Southern life, especially in politics, where the leading authority figure, Big Daddy, is often quite patronizing and condescending. With the exception of New Orleans and Charleston, most communities in

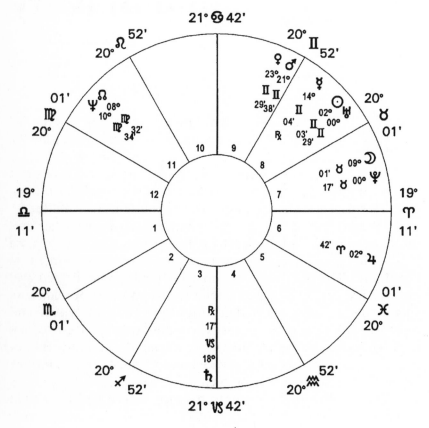

The South
May 23, 1607, 3:30 p.m. LMT
Jamestown, Virginia
76W47 37N13
Porphyry Houses

Source: *The Old Dominion*, by Thomas Nelson Page, says 4 P.M.

the South were, in the past, anything but cosmopolitan or sophisticated; it was a region of small towns with provincial outlooks. After all, Southerners liked their contented life and were averse to upsetting the status quo and traditional standards.

The Moon in Taurus indicates that the South was an agricultural region, unlike the North which was highly-industrialized. [The chart for the Northern way of life is set for the moment the Pilgrims stepped off the Mayflower at Plymouth, Massachusetts, at 9 A.M. on December 21, 1620 (NS), according to the Massachusetts Historical Society.] There is an attachment to the land down South and all it stands for (viz. Scarlett O'Hara and Tara) and, like most farm types, the only change they wish to deal with concerns the weather. With that Moon conjunct Pluto, Southerners detest outsiders telling them what to do and how to live their lives. Stubborn and conservative to the nth degree, what was good enough for their forefathers was good enough for them. The depth of Southern emotions was frightening at times: they could be as intense and volcanic as one would expect, with Pluto keying the Scorpio influence upon the Moon. With the Moon trine Neptune, the Southerner was an idealist, adamant, intractable, unyielding, and unbending. This aspect also indicates a strong nostalgia for the good old days, a glamorous illusion at best but one still portrayed in books and movies.

The Sun and Uranus in Gemini illustrate the high degree of independence and individualism in the South: they're not called rebels for nothing! Not overly concerned or influenced by what others think of them, there's a strong streak of eccentricity and unconventionality lurking just under the surface. The Uranian influence might presuppose a democratic and egalitarian way of life, but the flip side emerged instead, due to the highly perverse side of Uranus. Thus there exists in the South a dichotomy between the conservative side of the Moon in Taurus and the Cancer Midheaven and the Sun-Uranus desire to do one's own thing. The Sun-Uranus conjunction sextiles Jupiter, indicating a region where religion is important, where beliefs are taken seriously and with great zeal, since Jupiter sits in a fire sign. But sometimes, Southerners can be overly self-righteous, rewriting the Scriptures to account for their inhumane treatment of the Negro, for example. This anomaly comes from the Sun-Uranus *square to Neptune,* the planet of distortion and lies.

Mercury occupies Gemini as well: Southerners love to talk and talk and can ramble on and on for hours, seldom getting to the point in record time. Their method is highly expressive, their delivery flowery, and their way with similes truly amazing. One often wonders, however, if the truth has not been embellished for the sake of a good story as Neptune squares Mercury. Thus are the legends and myths born which exist to this day. Mercury in a double-bodied sign might also account for why so many Southern men and women have two "first names"! But then, the Southern way of life was dualistic from its very inception.

The conjunction of Venus and Mars in Gemini brings out the romantic nature just as the Libran Ascendant does, which they trine. Southerners have a reputation for being sexy, and they seem to mature earlier than do their Northern cousins. The lack of inhibitions sometimes carries them to the heights of depravity; Southerners are hedonistic and rather self-indulgent by nature. There's a relaxed acceptance of sexual matters down South which is obvious throughout literature. The plays of Tennessee Williams, the novels of Erskine Caldwell are rife with eroticism; the music world of jazz and the blues gave voice to yearnings for love and affection. Venus and Mars in a flirtatious sign, however, indicate that one must not always take those interests or invitations as anything more than mere friendliness or politeness. Southern love affairs were often tempestuous, volatile, and highly unpredictable, and Gemini is prone to the double standard. Mistresses were quite common for those men who could afford them, and sometimes they were of a different race, as well. Southerners are passionate and unbridled due to Venus and Mars semisquaring the Moon. Always exciting and restless, Rebs are spontaneous and versatile, always seeking stimulus and variety.

Jupiter in Aries indicates a people who are freedom-lovers par excellence. Trying to appear confident and self-assured at all times, Southerners act in ways that are often rash and impetuous. Always ready for a fight, their sense of pride is strong, their sense of honor never questioned, their behavior usually gallant and knightly. But as Aries is an adolescent sign, very youth-oriented, many up North feel that those down South never really grew up to accept the fact they can no longer live in the past.

Saturn in Capricorn near the 4th cusp indicates the love of tradition, conservatism, and worship of the past found so often south of the Mason-Dixon line. Like the positions of the Moon and Midheaven, Saturn abhors change for its own sake, especially at the top rung of the ladder. Saturn often adopts the attitude of "noblesse oblige," which some call snobbishness. Only recently has the South reclaimed its heritage as something more than just a tourist attraction or a place of refuge for those tired of cold winters. Saturn is ambitious, doubly so in Capricorn, but it's also suspicious of anyone or anything which tries to upset the status quo. Even after the Carpetbaggers left the South, ending the period called the Reconstruction, many of the old ways returned. With Saturn, tradition dies slowly, if at all. As ruler of the the 4th cusp, which governs one's homestead and landholdings, the foundation of one's existence, the need for security, stability, and permanence in one's life, is powerfully grounded.

Slavery

In my professional opinion, *both* Neptune and Pluto rule slavery. Neptune's connection is obvious, as it rules the natural 12th House which deals with prisons and places of confinement. Pluto's connection comes from the coercion, duress, pressure, and intimidation used to subjugate people one considers inferior. The connection of the Moon and Pluto to the Lunar Nodes ties the South to this ignoble way of life; doubly so as the Moon rules the Midheaven which indicates the Southern way of life and its reputation in the eyes of the world. The Nodes often indicate fate, karma, and one's destiny, which any entity must acknowledge or fade into oblivion.

When the Civil War began, the progressed Midheaven for this chart of Southern civilization was conjunct Jupiter, the planet of high hopes, idealism, and self-righteousness. The Ascendant was opposing Saturn, the planet of tradition and ruler of the 4th House, i.e., their lifestyle and reason for being. The South actually believed they could win a war against the North, which had twice the population and superior military might. Transiting Uranus at the Sun/Mercury midpoint semisquared the Midheaven and transiting Neptune was sextile Uranus, enlarging the vision of indomitability and invulnerability. The Rebs actually thought they could lick the Yankees in a few months and be home for Christmas, but Pluto was crossing the South Node, an ominous warning that their way of life was about to be irrevocably transformed, eliminated, and eradicated.

On the day Ft. Sumter was fired upon—April 12, 1861—the transiting Sun at 21 Aries was square the Midheaven, indicating the fight for honor to protect the sovereignty and autonomy of the Confederacy. Saturn was retrograding back to square the Sun and Uranus in the 8th House, thus placing a time limit on how long the South could hold out against the enemy. All the South seemed to have in abundance were high hopes, empty boasts and a lot of long-winded enthusiasm. When Mars semisquared the Midheaven the die was cast, since Mars rules the 7th House of conflict and war. The South probably knew it would be a losing battle, but it was better to die fighting for their beliefs than to surrender their honor and dignity to the Yanks they so despised.

Slavery has been around since the beginning of time. Ancient history was rife with tales of slave revolts like those of Spartacus and Moses. Modern European slavery began in the fifteenth century, when Portuguese traders began importing Negroes from West Africa, and by the time Columbus sailed for the New World, a large percentage of Lisbon was black. Trading posts were built along the African coast, from Senegal to Angola. Slaves from the Gold Coast generally went to North America or the Caribbean: those further south went to Brazil or South America. Slave agents, known as *caboceers*, rounded up suitable prospects, branded them with the name of the shipping company and then sold them to the highest bidder.

The journey to America took eight to ten weeks. Many slaves tried to jump overboard; those who refused to eat were force-fed. After all, a loss of life meant loss of revenue to the shippers. Captains realistically planned on a few deaths due to natural causes or suffocation, since slaves were packed like sardines in the bowels of ships, with few sanitary facilities. When the slaves arrived in the New World, they were broken in by being forced to work twelve-hour days. The original slaves were native tribes of the Caribbean, but they were killed off by diseases brought in by the Europeans. Many slaves wouldn't or couldn't adjust to their new surroundings. The food was horrible and unfamiliar to them, and their living and working conditions deplorable. Between the beginning of the sixteenth century and the Civil War, nearly fourteen million Africans were imported as slaves. Most worked on vast plantations that shipped sugar cane to New England where it was turned into rum which was then sold to buy more slaves.

Slaveowners were constantly aware of their need to protect themselves against their charges, living in constant fear of slave rebellion. Slave Codes were introduced which 1) required a slave to carry a pass at all times; 2) removed punishment from slave owners if they beat a slave; 3) required slaves to be beaten if they struck a Christian; 4) removed punishment from a slave owner if slave property was destroyed; 5) forbade a slave to testify in court; 6) forbade slaves from congregating in groups of more than five; 7) forbade a slave from reading or writing; 8) forbade a religious service unless a white person was present. To keep the slaves in line, severe treatment and threat of harsh punishment were used. White owners developed the belief that because of the Negro's supposed inherent inferiority, they were justified in their treatment of the blacks. By the time the American Revolution began, a real dichotomy existed in the South. Colonists were rebelling against the strong-armed tactics of their British overlords, yet were applying those same methods of treatment to black people in their own back yard.

The first slaves came to America as indentured servants who would work for a specified period of time (usually four to seven years) and then gain their freedom. But after a decade or so, Virginia abandoned this program in favor of outright slavery. As tobacco became more and more profitable, the demand for slaves increased. They became a commodity, less than human but more valuable than livestock.

Slave markets existed not only in Southern cities like New Orleans, Charleston, and Richmond but also up North in Philadelphia and Newport, Rhode Island. At first, the North condoned slavery; since most blacks were house servants, their owners did not witness the uglier side of servitude. In New England, slaves were often allowed to educate themselves. Down South, two ranks of slaves existed: field hands led a harsh and stressful existence and were jealous and envious of house servants who clearly had the better life. One group was distrustful of the other.

Children of mixed liaisons took the status of their mothers regardless of how light their skin was. Those with fifty percent "black blood" were called mulattos, those with twenty-five percent black blood were quadroons, those with one-eighth black blood were octoroons. Slaves could marry, but their unions were not legal in the eyes of the church. Slave children, like their parents, could be sold and were often separated from their families. Children were listed under "stock" in the ledger books. Some slaves did manage to gain their freedom upon the death of their masters, and others simply ran away and obtained what freedom was available up North. By the time of the Civil War, over 500,000 freed slaves existed, equally distributed between North and

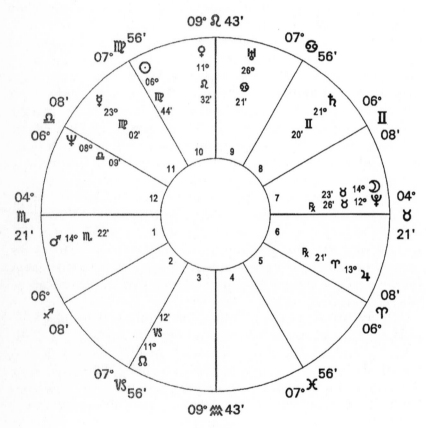

Slavery
Aug. 30, 1619, 10:15 A.M. LMT
Jamestown, Virginia
76W47 37N13
Porphyry Houses
Source: Rectified from nautical tables

South. But even their newfound freedom restricted their movements, and their civil rights were limited. In order to conduct a business, they had to obtain special licenses and their papers had to be with them at all times in case a white person demanded to know their status.

The first slaves arrived in America at Jamestown on August 30, 1619, on a ship the Dutch had highjacked from the Spanish. According to contacts well-versed in nautical matters, the ship docked at high tide which was about 10 A.M. that late summer's day. I've rectified the time fifteen minutes later. The first boatload contained twenty indentured black servants who were to work for seven years to gain their freedom.

Virginia legalized slavery in 1661 and Maryland followed two years later. In 1688, Quakers in Pennsylvania denounced slavery as the progressed Sun conjuncted Mars and opposed the Moon. Note that Mars rules the 6th House and the Moon governs the 9th House, thus the conflict between labor and philosophical belief systems. In 1712, a slave revolt erupted in New York City and fires broke out. In the end, twenty-one were hanged as the Midheaven opposed Pluto (repression) and the Ascendant inconjuncted Saturn (law and order). Another slave revolt threatened to erupt in New York City in 1741 but before it could take place, 200 were arrested, eighteen were hanged, and thirteen burned at the stake as the Sun squared Neptune (slavery) and the Midheaven inconjuncted Pluto, ruler of the Ascendant.

In 1774, Rhode Island and Connecticut banned slavery as the Sun opposed Venus, ruler of the 12th House. Two years later, the Declaration of Independence was written by Thomas Jefferson who inserted an anti-slavery clause but *had to delete it* due to lobbying by Southern representatives. That year the Sun squared the Moon and Mars. During the Revolution, America refused to recruit blacks into the armed forces, but changed their minds when Britain promised freedom to any slave who fought on their side.

In 1777, Vermont became the first state to abolish slavery in its Constitution; it favored gradual emancipation rather than outright abolition. As new states entered the Union, the question of their becoming a slave state or a free state remained. Whites outside the South were largely hostile toward slavery, but were ambivalent on the question of equality. By 1786, slavery was forbidden throughout the Northern colonies: the following year the newly-created Northwest Territory completely forbade slavery within its boundaries as the progressed Sun inconjuncted Uranus.

At the Constitutional Convention in Philadelphia during the summer of 1787, representatives counted slaves as sixty percent of the white population for census purposes and, in Article I – Section IX, slavery would be permanently abolished twenty years after ratification of the Constitution. By the first census of 1790, only ten percent of the slaves in the North were not free, while ninety percent of those in the South were still in chains. Over forty percent of the South's total population was of African origin.

With the invention of the cotton gin by Eli Whitney in 1793, the Southern economy really took off, as the "slavery" Midheaven squared the natal Ascendant and the Ascendant trined Mercury, the planet of commerce. In 1790, there were 700,000 slaves in America: four decades later, nearly two million existed. By the time the Civil War broke out, one in every seven persons in the United States was a slave. By 1808, twenty years after the Constitution was ratified, slavery was indeed abolished as the Ascendant sextiled Venus, ruler of the 12th House.

The Missouri Compromise of 1820, promoted by Henry Clay, allowed Missouri to come into the Union as a slave state in exchange for Maine entering as a free state. Slavery was forbidden north of the 36°30' latitude, as the Sun trined Uranus, ruler of the 4th House of territory. The Ascendant was conjunct Saturn, the planet of limits and restrictions.

In 1831, two major events occurred as the Sun opposed Neptune and the Midheaven sextiled Pluto. Nat Turner, a slave from Virginia, fomented a rebellion against his master and then went on a rampage, killing sixty people, including his master and family. The Abolitionist movement also began under William Lloyd Garrison, who founded the anti-slavery movement. Also about this time, the Underground Railroad began to emerge. During the next three decades, over 75,000 slaves *escaped* from the South. In reality, the railroad was the work of blacks in the South; individuals like Harriet Tubman, a former slave, repeatedly entered the South and brought out parties of fugitive slaves, leading them from one station to another some ten-twenty miles apart. Some slaves decided to leave America altogether and fled to neighboring Canada.

The Compromise of 1850 allowed California to enter the Union as a free state, even though much of it was below the boundary line outlined in the Missouri Compromise. The "slavery" Sun in 26 Aries was now squaring Uranus. No decision was made on other territories gained from the Mexican War. That same year, the Fugitive Slave Law automatically assumed the guilt of any black person aspiring to escape to a free state who could then be returned back to his former master.

With the passage of the Kansas-Nebraska Act in May 1854, which revoked the Missouri Compromise, the kettle really began to boil. Congress left the question of slavery up to the individual territories, thus giving birth to "Bleeding Kansas" where men like John Brown, fighting on the side of the Abolitionists, succeeded in keeping slavery from the mid-portion of the country. Two years earlier, Harriet Beecher Stowe's novel, *Uncle Tom's Cabin,* was published and an uproar not heard since the Revolution reverberated throughout the country. When Lincoln met Stowe some years later, he said "So you're the little lady who started the war."

In March 1857, a few days after Buchanan's inauguration, the Supreme Court handed down its infamous Dred Scott decision as the Sun opposed the Ascendant, the Midheaven opposed Neptune, and the Ascendant sextiled Mars. Dred Scott was a slave from Missouri who sued for his freedom after his master took him into a free territory. The court, under Chief Justice Taney, ruled that since blacks were not citizens, they could not sue in court. He ruled that Congress could not bar slavery from any territory as it violated the 5th Amendment by depriving slave owners of their right to enjoy property without due process of law. Scott was returned to his former owner, sending further shock waves throughout the land.

In October 1859, John Brown, the Abolitionist from Connecticut, conducted a raid on the Federal Arsenal at Harper's Ferry, West Virginia in hopes of starting a slave revolt. He was captured soon after and hanged in December 1859 as the Sun trined its own position and the Midheaven at 9 Aries trined its own position as well.

But hope loomed on the political horizon. With the birth of the Republican Party in 1854, slavery was now an issue that would be dealt with at the ballot box. With the nomination of Abraham Lincoln in 1860 for the Presidency, drumbeats began to rattle down

South, since Lincoln was known to have anti-slavery feelings. When Lincoln was elected, the South was both outraged and frightened. On December 20, 1860, South Carolina seceded from the United States and, within six weeks, the Confederacy was formed. On April 12, 1861, the Civil War began at Fort Sumter, as the Sun was inconjunct Neptune (slavery), the Midheaven trined Venus (ruler of the 7th House of war) *and the Ascendant was applying to conjunction with Uranus, the planet of rebellion.* No one doubted the outcome of the war would determine forever whether or not slavery would be allowed to continue in this country.

At first, Lincoln avoided upsetting the South any more than he already had by being elected, but it soon became apparent that if the North was going to win the war, then slavery would have to be abolished permanently. On September 22, 1862, Lincoln issued his Emancipation Proclamation which stated that, if those states now in rebellion against the United States did not surrender, Lincoln would sign another proclamation freeing the slaves altogether. Since the South did not comply, Lincoln *signed the document,* on New Years' Day, 1863, freeing all slaves in the Confederacy. Those 800,000 slaves in the border states of Delaware, Maryland, Kentucky, and Missouri would have to wait until ratification of the 13th Amendment in December 1865 to gain their freedom. When Lincoln signed the Emancipation Proclamation, there was remarkable astrological witness: the 244 years progressed Sun was in 10 Taurus squaring the Midheaven of the slavery chart, the Midheaven was conjunct Jupiter, the planet of freedom, and the progressed Ascendant was conjuncting Uranus, the planet of independence!

The South had been defeated both politically and economically. Prior to the Civil War, this region had the greatest wealth per capita in the country: after the war, it ranked at the bottom of the list. Before Lincoln took office, half our Presidents had come from the South. Since that time, only *four* Chief Executives have been elected from the South: Andrew Johnson, Lyndon Baines Johnson, Jimmy Carter, and Bill Clinton.

The slavery chart on page 428 shows Scorpio rising, the sign of intense love or hatred, and irrevocable issues that can transform society. It is also the sign of other people's money, those trusts and legacies left for future generations. The two rulers of Scorpio, Mars and Pluto, oppose each other from angular houses, one of the most difficult aspects one can have in a chart, in my opinion. It indicates violence, subjugation, pressure, and intimidation. With Scorpio in a fixed sign, slavery would become a permanent fixture for two-and-a-half centuries. Southerners believed firmly that it was their right to hold others against their will as the Moon (ruler of the 9th House of belief systems) conjuncts Pluto (ruler of the Ascendant) and opposes Mars (ruler of the 6th House of workers, "servants"). Anyone who felt different was openly confronted as the Mars-Pluto opposition is also part of a T-square involving Venus, ruler of the 7th House of warfare. But Venus also rules the 12th House of secret enemies and plots, so the relationship between slavery (Ascendant) and its detractors (Descendant) *was set on a course of conflict from the very beginning.*

The Moon sits in Taurus, just as it does in the chart for the South (see page 422). Taurus resists change and worships tradition for its own sake. I find it interesting that the ruler of the 9th House (Moon) in this T-square squares not only the ruler of the 7th House (Venus) but also the ruler of the 12th House. A pattern evolved over the years where both open *and* secret enemies fought each other on the moral issue of slavery. With the Moon and Pluto conjunct, this way of life was firmly entrenched. The trine of Moon-Pluto to Neptune shows the misguided notion that the South was in the right to hold others against their will.

The Sun in Virgo, as ruler of the Midheaven, indicates that slavery was based on work and labor. Slaves were vital to the South, for their labor supported the economy. Without slaves, the South's agricultural superiority and subsequent financial wealth would have been considerably less. Virgo is also the sign of discrimination, a way of life that, unfortunately, most descendants of slaves endure to this day. Virgo is also a critical sign, so many people were indeed judgmental about this ignoble institution. Virgo is also the sign of perfection, so slaves were chosen not just for their beauty and potential usefulness, but also for their physical prowess. Only the healthiest were chosen; since Virgo is a practical sign, this was simply good business.

As ruler of the 2nd House, Jupiter in the 6th House shows the financial assets behind slavery. But as Jupiter is retrograde, slaves were not paid for their service. Jupiter trines Venus at the Midheaven but with Venus involved in the aforementioned T-square, *Jupiter really led to the downfall of the South.* Slavery became a self-destructive mechanism for an entire civilization. Jupiter opposes Neptune indicating *the issues of morality* which were conveniently overlooked in the rush for profits. Religious and ethical issues seemed to be at odds with Neptune in the 12th House of secret enemies.

Saturn in the 8th House again indicates the financial strength slavery held for the plantation owners. By the time the Civil War began, there were about 350,000 slave owners, holding four and a half-million slaves. Few owners held more than fifty, and only a handful held more than a hundred. Mercury, as ruler of the 8th House, squares Saturn, showing great fear and apprehension among the slaves themselves. Saturn governs guilt and shame, so this attitude about slavery (3rd House rules attitudes) was fraught with embarrassment from its beginning. The fact that the Mercury/Saturn midpoint falls only 2 degrees from the Midheaven indicates the extensive need for protection and security against the very people those slaveowners had hired to do their dirty work. The square of Mercury to Saturn, as ruler of the 3rd House, also indicates the prohibition against educating the blacks, except in New England where schooling was allowed, if not directly encouraged. Mercury, as ruler of communication, sextile Uranus might also indicate the unique dialect spoken by most blacks from the Atlantic to the Pacific, regardless of where they were born. Uranus rules the 4th House and is placed in the 9th House so the origin of American slavery came from a foreign land, a region thought by Ptolemy to have been ruled by Cancer.

When the Dred Scott decision was rendered in 1857, transiting Pluto was crossing the Descendant of the slavery chart, laying the framework for the bloody conflict which followed. When the Civil War began, transiting Pluto was conjunct the progressed Sun at 8 Taurus, the midpoint between the Descendant and Pluto. Pluto had already semisquared Saturn at the time Lincoln was elected thus threatening the status quo. Uranus was trine Neptune at the time the war began, indicating eventual freedom (Uranus) for the slaves (Neptune). The progressed Midheaven conjunct Jupiter and the Ascendant conjunct Uranus the following year brought slavery to an end. When General Robert E. Lee surrendered to General U. S. Grant at Appomattox in April 1865, transiting Pluto was within minutes of its natal position. *Thus the end of slavery occurred on a Pluto return.* Unfortunately, things didn't work out as planned by Lincoln, and history may well have to wait for another Pluto return before the promise envisioned a century ago comes to fruition.

The National View

When the Declaration of Independence was drawn up in the summer of 1776, the responsibility was left to Thomas Jefferson to state the American case against the British. Despite Jefferson being a Southern plantation owner and a holder of slaves, he inserted a clause *against* slavery, which was deleted at the behest of other slaveholders before they would sign the document. God only knows whether the Civil War would have occurred had that original anti-slavery clause been left in the Declaration of Independence as Jefferson had desired.

Comparisons between the Declaration (United States) chart and the South are formidable (page 436). The U.S. Sun opposes the South's Saturn, showing the conflict between governmental authority and state's rights. The U.S. Jupiter squares the South's Jupiter, polarizing moral and ethical issues. The U.S. Ascendant at 8 Scorpio opposes the South's Moon and Pluto, indicating the high degree of emotion between the two parts of our country. The fact that the U.S. Ascendant is in the same sign as the Ascendant for the slavery chart (page 428) indicates that neither side would budge an inch and each side felt it was in the right.

The U.S. Mercury sits on the South's Midheaven, which opposes the U.S. Pluto again showing considerably strong feelings which would lead to conflict if the opposition could not be ameliorated. The U.S. Sun sextiles the South's Neptune pointing to the interference of Southern representatives who didn't want their livelihood threatened just to get rid of the British.

Ties between the U.S. chart and the chart for slavery are even more potent (see chart, page 428). The U.S. Sun squares slavery Jupiter (moral issues) and the U.S. Midheaven is squared by the slavery Moon and Pluto, indicating the conflict of lifestyles. The U.S. Mercury sits on slavery Uranus which opposes the U.S. Pluto, a strong indication of pressure, tension, and coercion. The U.S. Neptune sits on the slavery Mercury, showing why our founding fathers simply looked the other way when the mention

Outer Chart
The South
May 23, 1607, 3:30 p.m. LMT
Jamestown, Virginia
76W47 37N13
Inner Chart
The Declaration of Independence
July 4, 1776, 2:19 P.M. LMT
Philadelphia, Pennsylvania
75W10 39N57
Porphyry Houses

Sources: *Patriot in Purple* by Allan says "shortly after 2 P.M." Diary of John Hancock corroborates. U.S. State Department and the White House also give the time of 2 P.M. Articles in *Harper's* magazine from the mid-nineteenth century give eye-witness accounts from people who said it was around 2 P.M.

of slavery was brought up in Congress. One must remember that the U.S. Neptune also squares slavery's Saturn, an aspect of frustration, sickness, and debility. The U.S. Neptune also squares the U.S. Mars, thus placing Mars on top of slavery Saturn in the 8th House of death and annihilation.

[These many synastric contacts to the charts of "The South" and "Slavery" would be present with any "Declaration" chart on July 4, 1776, except for the reference to its angles, and in some to the Moon. — Ed.]

I've often wondered why so little was done about slavery until Lincoln's administration. Years ago, I noticed that practically *every* President had had a planet at either 8 degrees of fixed or 22 degrees of mutable signs: both positions aspect the U.S. Ascendant of the 2:19 P.M. chart, Mars and Neptune. All Presidents during the 1850s (except Pierce) had Jupiter at 22–23 of a mutable sign. Fillmore had Saturn at 8 Leo (square the U.S. Ascendant) tying his hands and limiting his effectiveness. Buchanan had Uranus at 10 Leo, also squaring the U.S. Ascendant, so he detached himself from the furor that was bubbling under the surface.

Lincoln was the first President to have his natal Uranus, *the planet of freedom, independence and revolution,* on the U.S. Ascendant; the job of dealing with this touchy subject sat on his shoulders. Lincoln was also our first President to have his natal Pluto conjunct the Midheaven of the inauguration chart (March 4, 1861, at noon), so his administration accomplished what previous administrations felt beyond their comprehension. Clearly, Lincoln was the right man at the right moment in history, answering the call to eradicate a way of life that had been infecting American life for generations.

The U.S. progressed chart for the Civil War shows the Sun at 5 Libra squaring natal Jupiter pointing to the moral and ethical impetus for the war. Progressed Saturn was trining Mars showing the conflict between tradition and authority would be successfully concluded, and Progressed Mercury (ruler of the 8th House) was squaring Pluto, ruler of the Ascendant. But the most remarkable thing to me was the progressed Midheaven at 7-1/2 Scorpio approaching the natal Ascendant and squaring our Nodes which brought in the issues of fate, karma and destiny.

The U.S. progressed Ascendant at 13-1/2 Capricorn was opposing our natal Sun, indicating the country needed surgery, or a repair job at best, in order for us to survive. Our authority (the Sun) was being questioned and our reputation was suffering as a result. Transiting Pluto at 8 Taurus was opposing our natal Ascendant which is inconjunct Uranus and semisquare Neptune. This position and aspect of Neptune indicate that the issue of slavery would be an irritant, something one craved to attend to and eradicate, but something in our early history we simply learned to live with.

In late 1853, the progressed Midheaven entered the sign of Scorpio, to remain there for nearly three decades. During this period, slavery issues came to the fore and threatened to tear the country apart (Scorpio rules the 1st House of the United States chart. After the Civil War, the period called Reconstruction (a typically Scorpionic word) took place. It was a sad and tumultuous time until 1877 when the U.S. progressed Ascendant moved out of Capricorn and into Aquarius.

Six weeks after Lincoln's election, the legislature of South Carolina voted to secede from the United States, the political beginning of the Civil War. The date was December 20, 1860, the time was 1:15 P.M., the place was Charleston. The Fire Grand Trine among the Sun, Jupiter, and the Ascendant indicates great optimism, high hopes, and *self-righteousness*. Little thought was given to the square of the Sun to Neptune which blinded their ambition and blew hopes for victory all out of proportion in the face of superior forces up North. Mercury opposed Uranus, the axis squared by Saturn, pointed to the lack of a strong, industrial base to support the conflict that would come; hopes for foreign support also fell flat.

Venus, ruler of the Descendant, trine Neptune and square Jupiter, made South Carolina's decision to secede a matter of honor, however misguided its intentions may have been. Venus trine Mars as well would seem to indicate potential victory *until one sees that Venus rules the 7th House, the house of one's opponents.* Thus the other side would win. Mars sextile the Midheaven indicated the *spirit* to fight, which was second to none, but the T-square (Mercury-Uranus and Saturn) illustrated that, despite the noblest ambitions, the South just couldn't endure the rigors a long war would entail.

The secession Ascendant squares the U.S. Pluto (see page 436), ruler of the U.S. Ascendant, and the secession Midheaven opposes the U.S. Sun, ruler of the U.S. Midheaven. The T-square in the secession chart ticks off the U.S. Uranus, which rules the U.S. 4th House of territory. The midpoint pictures in the secession chart really tell a story. Sun/Jupiter = Ascendant shows the high spirits that day in Charleston, but Saturn/Neptune= Mars points to huge losses and numerous casualties. Mars/Neptune=Pluto is an even worse omen of futility and desecration, which would obliterate and annihilate an entire civilization. Clearly, *secession was something doomed from its inception.* The Confederacy was spinning its wheels, fighting a losing battle.

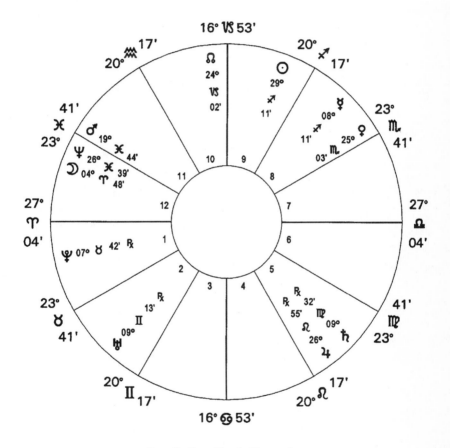

South Carolina's Secession
Dec. 20, 1860, 1:15 P.M. LMT
Charleston, South Carolina
79W56 32N46
Porphyry Houses
Source: *The Charleston Mercury.*

I wondered why South Carolina was the *first* state to secede. I knew the state had been a thorn in the government's side in Washington for several decades. Back in 1832, South Carolina issued its Nullification Proclamation against what they called the Tariff of Abominations issued by Congress. South Carolina felt it was their right to pick and choose which laws from Washington they would or would not obey. It came as no surprise to find that this state was the only one in the South which had Mars sitting at

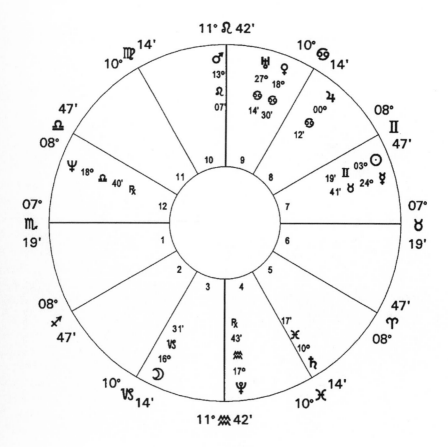

South Carolina
May 23, 1788, 4:48 P.M. LMT
Charleston, South Carolina
79W56 32N46
Porphyry Houses
Source: The South Carolina Historical Society says 5 P.M.

the top of the chart, a truly warlike and highly independent position. Mars is co-ruler of South Carolina's Ascendant and its other ruler, Pluto, at 17 Aquarius opposes the Midheaven of the United States. Thus the midpoint between South Carolina's Mars and Pluto *squares* the U.S. Midheaven. The Palmetto State was the instrument of the South's destruction, being a powder keg and hotbed of revolution since its admission into the Union. Transits to the South Carolina chart for the beginning of the Civil War (see

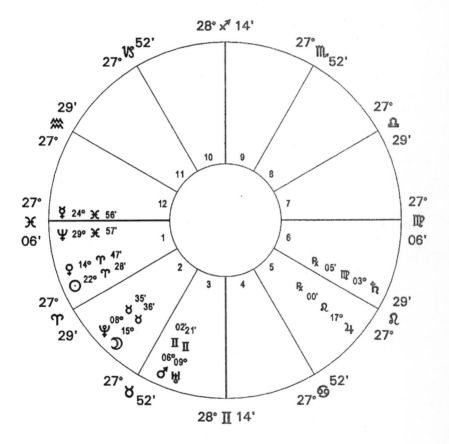

Civil War Begins at Fort Sumter
Apr. 12. 1861, 4:30 A.M. LMT
Charleston, South Carolina
79W56 32N46
Porphyry Houses
Source: Bruce Catton, historian of the Civil War.

below and page 440) show Pluto opposing its Ascendant, just as it was in the U.S. chart, and Saturn was opposing itself, indicating a conflict between authority and tradition.

Since this first war action took place in Charleston, not the capital of South Carolina anymore, I wondered if that *city's* chart had encouraged secession. Known as the "fightingest city in the South" due to its Sun and Moon at 29 Aries at its Midheaven, its Ascendant at 7 Leo squares the U.S. and South Carolina Ascendant and sits *right on the U.S. Nodal axis* (not shown here)!

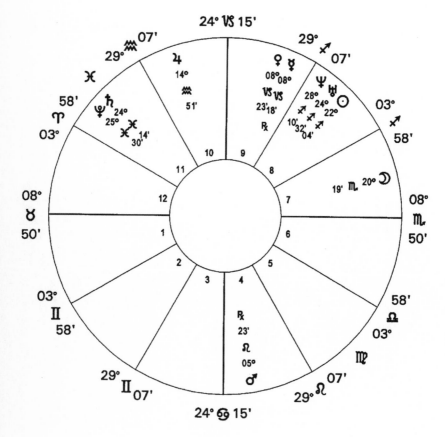

Alabama
Dec. 14, 1819, 2:14 P.M. LMT
Huntsville, Alabama
86W35 34N44
Porphyry Houses
Source: The Alabama Historical Society says "mid-afternoon." Rectified.

Charleston's progressed Ascendant that fateful December day of secession was 4 Scorpio, the same degree as the Ascendant of the slavery chart. Coincidence? I think not.

From Charleston, the action then moved to Montgomery, Alabama where the Confederacy was founded six weeks later (see chart, page 444). Montgomery, which was founded eleven days before Alabama came into the Union, has Mars at 5 Leo, conjuncting the U.S. Nodal axis and squaring the U.S. Ascendant. The state of Alabama (see chart, page 442) also has Mars at 5 Leo and its Ascendant at 8 Taurus opposes the U.S. Ascendant and squares the Nodal axis. Just as in the U.S. chart, Pluto was transiting this horizon, this time on the Ascendant. Alabama's natal Sun at 22 Sagittarius opposes the U.S. Mars and squares the U.S. Neptune, indicating conflicting ideals and aspirations which would lead to war. Among the charts of South Carolina, Charleston, Montgomery, and the state of Alabama are numerous contacts to that *all-important 8th degree axis of Taurus and Scorpio which activates our national rising degree.* I think it was no accident that the events surrounding the Civil War took place in these locales, for they were tied into each other in ways that clearly were karmic.

The Civil War, or War Between the States, began on April 12, 1861 at 4:30 A.M. when Southern guns fired on Federal troops stationed at Ft. Sumter in the harbor outside Charleston. The chart (page 441) shows doom from the word go, and nobody in his or her right mind would have picked a chart like this to begin a war, unless one expected or planned to lose. Late Pisces rises, not the strongest sign for victory, and Neptune, its ruler, sits in the last degree of its own sign. Neptune rising certainly indicates misguided ambition and false dreams of victory and, obviously, no astrologer was consulted to set up an election chart!

The Confederacy came into being at high Noon on February 4, 1861, in Montgomery, Alabama (chart, page 444). The Sun exactly opposes the U.S. Midheaven showing the conflict of governments. When the progressed Moon trined Mercury, ruler of the Ascendant, the capital moved from Montgomery to Richmond, Virginia where it remained for the duration of the war. The Confederacy was born on a U.S. Uranus return, indicative of the feeling of separativeness occurring at that time in this country. With Uranus in Gemini, a dual sign, ruling the 4th cusp (the IC) of the U.S. chart, *two nations would one day vie for supremacy.*

The Confederacy ended on April 2, 1865, when Jefferson Davis fled Richmond, which was in flames set by its own people. One week later, Lee surrendered to Grant.

The man on whose shoulders fell the burden of saving this nation was born in a log cabin on the banks of Nolin Creek, a few miles south of Hodgenville, Kentucky on the morning of February 12, 1809. Sources such as Doris Chase Doane, Lois Rodden and T. Pat Davis have advocated birth times ranging from 2 A.M. to 9 A.M. with rising signs of Sagittarius, Aquarius, or Aries. After

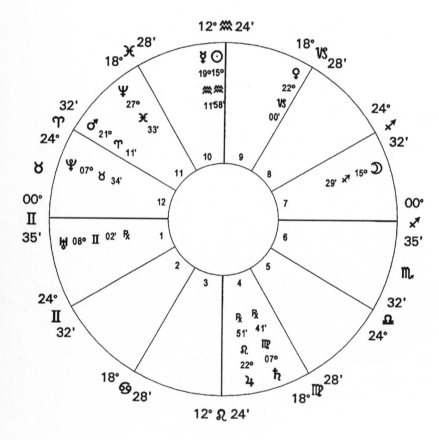

The Confederacy
Feb. 4. 1861, Noon LMT
Montgomery, Alabama
86W19   32N23
Porphyry Houses
Source: *Book of World Horoscopes* by Nicholas Campion.

hours and hours of research, I've rectified Lincoln's birth time to 7:20 A.M. LMT (7:37 A.M. CST) giving the sixteenth President the first degree of Pisces on the Ascendant. Earlier charts placed the Saturn/Neptune conjunction either on the Ascendant or at the Midheaven: my version places them *square the Ascendant* in the 9th House, with the Sun in the 12th House where history tells us it belongs. In order for a chart to really work, one must look not only at progressions and transits, but also view *the relocated charts for the places where important events took place.* No other birth time

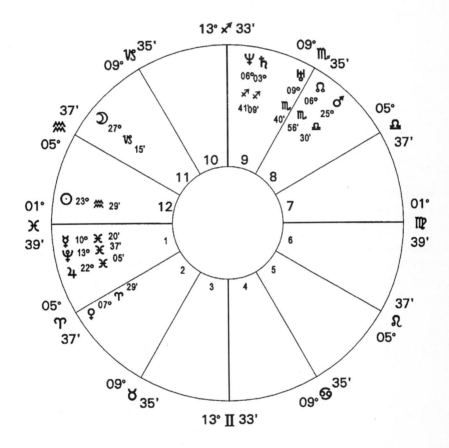

Abraham Lincoln
Feb. 12. 1809, 7:20 A.M. LMT
Hodgenville, Kentucky
85W45 37N30
Porphyry Houses
Source: Rectified from sources which state Lincoln was born "in the morning."

during the morning hours fits all the above criteria as does the one used here.

Pisces rising indicates an individual who would become known not only for his or her compassion and understanding of complex issues but also for martyrdom, adulation, and hero-worship. No other President in our history has been so revered or deified as was Lincoln, the subject of more biographies than any other person with the exception of Christ and Napoleon. Getting behind the myths and legends is another matter, especially with the Sun placed in the 12th House.

Lincoln loved solitude: he was a loner at heart who loved to go on long walks, despite continuing problems with his feet, which are ruled by Pisces. Often people with the Sun in the 12th House have to bide their time until the Universe needs their services at a crucial moment in history. Many times those individuals feel as if they are being used for some higher purpose over which they have no control. Lincoln was the vehicle designated to save this country; he was the only one who could heal and bind its wounds. Twelfth-House types also have an innate empathy for those less fortunate than they, those underdogs society has pushed to the back of the bus.

A real dichotomy exists for those with the combination Lincoln had: his Piscean Ascendant caused Honest Abe to resign himself to his fate, yet he had to remain emotionally detached while controlling events from behind the throne. Nonetheless, he bore his burden with dignity, probably feeling as if he were the sacrificial lamb or puppet for higher forces.

The classical, physical description of a Pisces doesn't apply to Lincoln. The ruler of his Ascendant, Neptune, lies in *Sagittarius*, a tall and lanky sign, and Neptune sits in the 9th House as well. Its conjunction to Saturn made Lincoln gaunt and haggard-looking and, despite his great height, he seldom weighed more than 160 pounds. (I've seen a few very tall and rangy Pisces Ascendants such as the playwright and actor, Sam Shephard.) There was an inner beauty, almost poetic, when one gazed upon his face. Lincoln was an old soul, filled with wisdom and tenderness.

Lincoln's Midheaven in Sagittarius points to an individual who would be a seeker for truth and justice. Besides the law, he could have entered the ministry, become a philosopher or teacher, or become involved in any occupation which desired to better the human condition. The two keywords for Sagittarius are often intertwined with Aquarius: freedom and independence. Lincoln's belief system was non-sectarian, his interests wide-ranging and eclectic. His philosophy was aesthetic, his overall tone one of idealism and inspiration.

With Neptune, the ruler of the Ascendant, conjunct Saturn in the 9th House, Lincoln always sought the deeper meaning of things. Sagittarian types are known for their honesty, but they manage to get to the heart of an issue in record time and still retain the goodwill and affection of the person they are addressing. Lincoln's views on life were universal but, with Saturn conjunct Neptune in the house of philosophy, he sought *practical solutions*, not just window-dressing that might fall apart later down the road; *Saturn yearns for durability and permanence.* Lincoln was probably a spiritualist: all we know is that he belonged to no specific Protestant denomination. His mission was to strip away the veneer and facade, to clarify issues and to take stands on issues others preferred to ignore.

Mercury and Pluto rising point to a man who would influence many, a person who sought verbal simplicity, a man who often talked in parables, thus making difficult concepts simple and easily understood. His "House Divided" speech during the debates with Douglas got right to the heart of the issue of slavery while his second inaugural speech where he prayed "with malice towards none and charity for all" is a testament to the power and influence of these Piscean planets. His most famous and very short speech at Gettysburg was largely ignored by the press and was a disappointment to those who had just finished listening to a two-hour oration by the long-winded Senator Everett. When his Gettysburg Address ended with the statement that "the government of the people, by the people and for the people shall not perish from the earth," few could have thought those words would become so enshrined in our nation's consciousness. This speech was one of the most heartfelt, emotionally-stirring and poignant orations ever delivered, brief yet passionate, evocative yet simple. Mercury and Pluto rising in Pisces made Lincoln a self-taught man who read by the fireside when young and a man who read anything he could lay his hands on during his early adult years. He studied law in his spare time and managed to pass the bar examination after only five years of study.

Jupiter is also rising, as ruler of the Midheaven and co-ruler of the Ascendant. Jupiter made Lincoln a great story teller. His sense of humor was rather self-deprecating, but he never stooped to denigrate his audience by playing to the lowest common denominator. Lincoln always presented himself with dignity and grace, his nobility shining forth for all to see. Despite his apparent self-confidence and self-assuredness, Lincoln was rather shy and unassuming at first until he got to know the other person better. He probably felt it was wiser to remain silent on things he knew little about than to state his opinions which might alienate outsiders. Lincoln learned things by keeping his eyes and ears open to the mood and feelings of the people around him; he did not allow himself to be used for purposes beyond his control or comprehension.

Mars in the 8th House indicates a passionate man, or one who would evoke strong feelings in others. He was a man who would have to deal with issues of death, transformation and regeneration. Mars in this house also suggested a quick and sudden death, often a violent one at the hands of someone venting their anger fighting for a cause. Had Lincoln lived to complete his second term, his desire to heal the wounds the country had endured during four long years of war might have left the South in an entirely different state than it became under successive administrations.

Mercury also rules his 7th House, the area of partnerships and his marriage to Mary Todd. Mercury conjunct Pluto indicates a tempestuous marriage fraught with many emotional scenes. His wife often went over the edge emotionally to the point that ten years after Lincoln's assassination, her son, Robert, was forced to have her committed to an insane asylum for four months before she could get back on track. Most of the time, Lincoln simply let his wife have her way: he had resigned himself to her outbursts and simply left the house for a while, walking down the street with his head bowed, his wife screaming out the door in very colorful language no Southern lady should be caught uttering. Simply put, his wife was a nag and a shrew. Note that the ruler of Lincoln's Ascendant squares the ruler of his Descendant, so whether Lincoln could ever have had a happy marriage is something for historians to ponder.

The Moon, ruling the women in Lincoln's life, is squared by Mars. Mary Todd was a fiery and passionate woman whose temperamental outbursts were legendary. She was highly jealous of her husband, whom she felt flirted too much with the ladies. With the Moon in Capricorn, his wife would also be ambitious, not just for herself but also for her husband. Mary had her Sun in Sagittarius conjunct Mars *right on Abraham Lincoln's Midheaven.* Her Sun also squared Saturn making her stop at nothing until she got to the top of the ladder. Most historians agree that if it hadn't been for his wife, Lincoln would have been content to remain a country lawyer back in Illinois. Mary pushed Abe into the White House.

Additionally, Lincoln's Moon in Capricorn indicated severe bouts of depression, not only at the death of his mother and Ann Rutledge, but also at the death of his sons, Eddie and Willie. The square of the Moon to Mars indicates anger but its outlet is limited since Mars occupies the 8th House of secrets and repression.

Lincoln's Venus in Aries also describes his wife. Since Venus inconjuncts Uranus, their relationship was on-again, off-again in the beginning and afterwards it became a roller-coaster ride. Mary had her Sun conjunct Uranus which was squared by Pluto, indicating compulsiveness and obsessiveness about money. With Venus in Lincoln's 2nd House, his wife spent extravagantly, as if money were burning a hole in her pocket, on items of finery and adornment. Her bills from dressmakers, milliners, and glove-makers were the scandal of Washington. She felt that, since she was the First Lady of the land, it was her duty to be the best-dressed woman in the country. Political satirists said the only reason Lincoln was re-elected was so he could pay for the huge bills his wife was running up trying to look good! When Mary left the White House, she was thousands of dollars in debt; it took a while to pay them off, and some debts were simply absorbed.

With Lincoln's Moon ruling his 5th House of children, Lincoln suffered the death of his children. Of his four sons, only Robert lived to maturity: Eddie died at age four, Willie at eleven, his son Tad at eighteen.

There is one more thought to ponder: Lincoln's Sun, Moon, Mercury, Venus, and Mars are in either the signs of their detriment or fall. Jupiter occupies its own sign and both Uranus and Neptune are exalted. Not that many charts have this much power and ability to affect history.

Lincoln in Development

In December 1816, Thomas Lincoln moved his family to southern Indiana as his son's progressed Sun conjuncted his natal Ascendant and the progressed Moon opposed Uranus, the planet of change. In October 1818, Abe Lincoln's mother, Nancy Hanks, died of milk fever as his Sun was squaring Saturn and his Moon was square the Ascendant. The Midheaven square Jupiter also indicated the loss of a parent since Jupiter rules the Midheaven. In December 1819, his father remarried a woman named Sarah Bush Johnston, a widow whom Lincoln came to adore. The feeling was mutual, and her influence on young Abe was strong. Lincoln's Progressed Moon was conjunct his Midheaven semisquare Uranus, indicating the sudden entrance of a new mother.

In January 1828, his sister, Sarah, died in childbirth. Three months later, Lincoln left on a flatboat for New Orleans where he came into contact with slavery for the first time, as the Moon squared his Midheaven and the Sun squared the Midheaven. In March 1830, the Lincoln family moved again, this time to a farm outside Decatur, Illinois, as the Moon trined the Ascendant. A year later, in April 1831, Lincoln moved away on his own to New Salem, a small village northwest of Springfield as the Ascendant inconjuncted Uranus and transiting Pluto was crossing his progressed Ascendant. During his six-year stay in New Salem, Lincoln managed a general store and held the position of Postmaster. The latter job gave him much free time to study, mostly books on the law, a career he had decided to pursue.

Lincoln first ran for public office in the summer of 1832, shortly after his brief stint in the Black Hawk War. When the election returns came in, Lincoln was defeated as his Moon conjuncted Saturn. But Lincoln persisted, and in August 1834, he was elected to the state legislature in Vandalia as the Moon sextiled his Ascendant and the Midheaven sextiled Uranus, ruler of his Sun sign. Pluto was trining the Midheaven thus planting the first of many seeds that one day would carry him into the White House.

Despite his first political success, his *personal* life was falling apart. His business partner at the store died in January 1835, leaving Lincoln deeply in debt. Later that summer, in August 1835, his close friend and possible paramour, Ann Rutledge, died as his Moon semisquared Saturn. Some say that Ann was the only woman Lincoln ever loved. That may be so, but a year later, he proposed to a heavy-set woman named Mary Owens. She turned him down.

On March 1, 1837, Lincoln was admitted to the bar, and six weeks later he moved to Springfield, the new capital of Illinois. He became partners with William Herndon and, for a while, shared a room with Joshua Speed.

The fated day of December 16, 1839 was one Lincoln would long remember. It was on that night at the home of Ninian Edwards, a former Governor of Illinois, that Abe met Mary Todd, whose sister was married to Edwards. Lincoln's Sun was sesquare Uranus, his Moon conjunct Pluto. His Ascendant moving into an opposition of Mars made the young lawyer smitten with this witty, charming, and vivacious woman from Kentucky. Their courtship was up and down, and many times Lincoln probably thought of calling it off. When the wedding day of January 1, 1841 came, *Lincoln did not show up for the ceremony.* He remained in his room all day in a severe state of depression. His Ascendant was squaring that Moon in Capricorn.

Eventually, they started courting again, and on November 4, 1842, at 5 P.M., Abraham Lincoln and Mary Todd were married in the front room of the Governor's Mansion. With Lincoln's progressed Ascendant in the last degree of Aries, it was a "last ditch effort": if he didn't marry her then, it would be permanently over. His Ascendant also semisquared progressed Pluto lending an aura of compulsiveness and urgency to the situation. His progressed Midheaven semisquare Saturn introduced the sense of duty and obligation and his Moon sesquisquare transiting Neptune probably caused him to resign himself to his fate.

On August 1, 1843, their first son, Robert Todd Lincoln, was born in a room on the second floor of the Globe Tavern. Lincoln's Ascendant sextiled its own position and the Moon sextiled the natal Ascendant. It was a joyous occasion as transiting Jupiter was sitting on Lincoln's Sun. Their second son, Edward Moore, was born in March 1846 as his progressed Moon squared the Ascendant and Jupiter opposed his Uranus and transiting Saturn crossed his Ascendant. Eddie died of a fever one month short of his fourth birthday as Jupiter opposed its own position and transiting Neptune squared his Saturn. Pluto was also opposing Mars in his 8th and the Moon sesquared Saturn, the planet of grief and sorrow.

In November 1846, Lincoln was elected to the U.S. House of Representatives as his Midheaven semisquared Neptune, ruler of the Ascendant and Saturn crossed the Sun. Lincoln wasn't overly popular in Washington where he fought against the Mexican War, so when his term ended in August 1848, he was glad to return home to Springfield. With his Ascendant now opposing Uranus, he was tired of politics and would not seek office for another decade.

In late December 1850, his third son, William Herndon, was born as the Progressed Moon sesquisquared the Midheaven. Less than a month later, in January 1851, Lincoln's father, Thomas, died as the Midheaven squared Mars in the 8th House and semi-squared Mercury, ruler of the 4th House. Lincoln refused to go to the funeral since old memories had surfaced concerning his relationship with his father, whom Lincoln preferred to ignore. His ambivalent feelings were shown by the Progressed Moon inconjunct the Ascendant and transiting Uranus and Pluto squaring his natal Moon. In April 1853, his fourth and final son, Thomas (nicknamed Tad) was born with a cleft palate; the Midheaven conjoined the Moon and the Ascendant sextiled Pluto. Lincoln loved Tad best, shown by his progressed Sun conjunct Venus that year and transiting Jupiter was sextiling his Sun and Mars.

When the Kansas-Nebraska Act was passed in 1854, Lincoln's interest in politics resurfaced. Four years later, he decided to run for the U.S. Senate against Stephen A. Douglas, a former suitor of his wife. The first of many debates took place in July 1858 as Lincoln's Midheaven sextiled Saturn and his Ascendant sextiled Jupiter. His Sun was also trining the Midheaven. If one had looked only at the progressions, one would have predicted victory for Lincoln. His *defeat* in November that year occurred due to transiting Jupiter opposing itself, Saturn inconjuncting Uranus, Uranus squaring his Ascendant, and Pluto crossing the South Node.

In May 1860, the Republican Party nominated Lincoln on the third ballot at Chicago. Lincoln's progressed Midheaven was 4 Aquarius, squaring the Ascendant of the slavery chart (see chart, page 430) and his progressed Ascendant at 24 Taurus was still within orb of squaring his natal Sun. The Moon was 2 degrees shy of crossing his Midheaven, and Jupiter was trining its own position. In November 1860, Lincoln won the election with forty percent of the popular vote, with the Democratic party having split into three factions. Transiting Jupiter on election day sextiled Lincoln's Mars, a sure-fire indication of victory.

Lincoln left Springfield for Washington in February 1861 and was sworn into office as our 16th President on March 4th as his Progressed Moon squared Jupiter. Lincoln's relocated chart was clearly more favorable in Springfield than it was in Washington. In Illinois, the relocated Midheaven at 9 Sagittarius conjuncts Neptune, ruler of his Ascendant, squares Mercury, ruler of his Descendant and 4th, and trines Venus. This was where he fell in love, got married, and raised a family. The relocated Ascendant at 24 Aquarius *conjuncts his natal Sun and trines his Mars,* indicating the feeling of belonging and having the ability to make an impact on his community.

In Washington, however, his relocated Midheaven at 21 Sagittarius squares his natal Jupiter, ruler of his Midheaven, but also sextiles both the Sun and Mars. Thus the equation becomes Midheaven = Sun/Mars/Jupiter, a lucky and forceful combination which enabled him to keep the Union together because of a single-minded determination. Lincoln's relocated Ascendant in Washington was *conjunct his Pluto.* I've noticed that whenever a political figure has Pluto on an angle, *their life is placed in jeopardy in that locale.* Kennedy had Pluto on the Midheaven in Dallas, Ford had Pluto on the 4th cusp in San Francisco and Martin Luther King had Pluto on the 4th cusp in Memphis. Reagan had Pluto squaring his relocated Midheaven in Washington and he survived.

In 1861, Washington was the most heavily-fortified city in the world, protected by sixty forts and military posts. When Lincoln took office, his Moon was crossing the relocated Midheaven. Since the Moon rules women, his wife came under attack for her Southern sympathies. Most of his wife's kinfolk fought on the Confederate side and many Americans considered her a traitor or even worse, a spy for the South. Either way, she couldn't win, and she became an unpopular First Lady despite her beauty and charming manners.

With his Pluto on the Ascendant in Washington, life there was no bed of chocolates for the President. Besides having to deal with one ineffective general after another, Lincoln fought with his Cabinet and had to suspend some Constitutional guarantees, such as Habeas Corpus, since this was wartime and the country was largely under martial law. Lincoln wielded his newfound authority wisely; desperate times require desperate methods. In the middle of this turmoil, Lincoln's son, Willie, died of typhoid as Lincoln's Sun sesquisquared the Ascendant and transiting Uranus opposed his Midheaven.

Despite his aversion to slavery, Lincoln thought it wise not to interfere with the issue when first taking office. However, he soon changed his mind when he realized that if the North were going to win the war, *then the slaves would have to be freed.* Lincoln waited for a major victory before making his announcement, and a few days after Antietam, Lincoln issued the Emancipation Proclamation on September 22, 1862. He signed the document at 3 P.M. on New Years' Day 1863 in the White House to free nearly four million blacks.

Against overwhelming odds and skepticism, Lincoln was re-elected in November 1864. His position was tenuous at best until news from the front indicated that Sherman had captured Atlanta, thus splitting the South. Besides, political pundits thought it unwise to change horses in mid-stream at such a trying time in our history. Five weeks after his second inaugural, Lee surrendered to Grant on Palm Sunday, April 9, 1865 at 4 P.M. The war was over at long last, and the nation went wild with victory celebrations.

But the jubilation was not to last for long. On Good Friday, April 14, 1865, Lincoln attended a stage-drama performance at Ford's Theatre in Washington with his wife. John Wilkes Booth, an actor with strong Southern sympathies, entered the Presidential box, put a derringer behind Lincoln's left ear and pulled the trigger. The bullet lodged behind Lincoln's right eye and doctors refused to consider an operation. His body was moved across the street to the Peterson House where, at 7:22 A.M. on April 15, 1865, Abraham Lincoln passed into eternity. A doctor took two coins from his pocket and placed them on Lincoln's eyes. Then Stanton, the Secretary of War, said those famous words, "Now he belongs to the ages." His funeral cortege wound its way from Washington through Baltimore and Philadelphia to New York where his body lay in state for some time. Then on to Cleveland, Indianapolis, and Chicago, and finally to Springfield, where he was entombed in the Oak Ridge Cemetery north of town.

Lincoln's progressed Midheaven at 9-1/2 Aquarius was squaring natal Uranus, ruler of his Sun sign and governor of the 12th House of secret enemies and conspiracies. Lincoln's Sun was still within orb of an opposition to progressed Mars in the 8th House of death. Mercury, ruler of the end of life 4th House, was in opposition to natal Jupiter, ruler of his Midheaven and co-ruler of the Ascendant. Progressed Venus, ruler of the 8th House, was applying to an opposition of Saturn, "the grim reaper." Transiting Jupiter at 29 Sagittarius had just inconjuncted his progressed Ascendant at 0 Gemini, and transiting Saturn was squaring the Moon from the 8th House. Pluto at 12 Taurus was within orb of inconjuncting the Midheaven, thus sealing his place in the pantheon of history.

Lincoln's life contains many what-ifs and suppositions since subconscious forces seemed to direct his life from one stage to another. Lincoln was more than just mortal, for in the eyes of history, he was the vehicle to give birth to a new nation, conceived in liberty and dedicated to the proposition that all men are created equal. What if he had been allowed by the gods to marry Ann Rutledge? Would she have propelled Lincoln to reach for the stars as did his wife, Mary? What if by some fluke he had won that Senate seat and Douglas had faded into oblivion? Would he have even thought of running for the Presidency, or would the Republican Party have been so keen to nominate a dark horse? What if the Democratic Party had not split into three factions that fateful year of 1860? Would South Carolina and other states still have felt it imperative to secede and form their own country? Would Lincoln have been as well-remembered as a peacetime President, or was his moment in history to be defined by the bloodiest conflict our nation has ever had to endure? What if he had not gone to Ford's Theatre that night or the guard hired to guard the Presidential box not taken leave of his post and gone next door to get a drink?

Would Lincoln's treatment of the South really have been as humane as we would like to think, or a milder version of what occurred under the administrations of Johnson and Grant? Would black people have had to wait as long for their civil rights to be restored or recognized had Lincoln lived longer and become the elder statesman? Clearly, Abraham Lincoln had no say in the above matters, for the Almighty had decided on a different course for our country.

Lincoln's death made him the most honored, revered, beloved, and admired President in our history, a man who, to this day, still brings tears to the eyes of those who gaze upon his craggy face at his Memorial in Washington. Those who read his speeches remember the simple statements of truths that are universal and immutable, regardless of culture, ethnic background, or religion. Few persons have come so far from such humble beginnings to rise to such heights of power in order to save the very nation that gave them birth.

Ours was a nation that, during Lincoln's lifetime, was being torn apart, limb by limb, its heart bleeding from wounds few mortals could heal; a heart without a soul. Lincoln healed those wounds as best he could. Had he lived, he could have bound up the scars of recovery as well. Lincoln not only preserved this nation but as well he saved America from the worst proclivities of its people.

STAY IN TOUCH

On the following pages you will find some of the books now available on related subjects. Your book dealer stocks most of these and will stock new titles in the Llewellyn series as they become available. We urge your patronage.

To obtain our full catalog, to keep informed about new titles as they are released, and to benefit from informative articles and helpful news, you are invited to write for our bimonthly news magazine/catalog, *Llewellyn's New Worlds of Mind and Spirit*. A sample copy is free, and it will continue coming to you at no cost as long as you are an active mail customer. Or you may subscribe for just $10.00 in the U.S.A. and Canada ($20.00 overseas, first class mail). Many bookstores also have *New Worlds* available to their customers. Ask for it.

Llewellyn's New Worlds of Mind and Spirit
P.O. Box 64383-K868, St. Paul, MN 55164-0383, U.S.A.

* * *

TO ORDER BOOKS AND TAPES

If your book dealer does not have the books described, you may order them directly from the publisher by sending the full price in U.S. funds, plus $3.00 for postage and handling for orders *under* $10.00; $4.00 for orders *over* $10.00. There are no postage and handling charges for orders over $50.00. Postage and handling rates are subject to change. We ship UPS whenever possible. Delivery guaranteed. Provide your street address as UPS does not deliver to P.O. boxes. Allow 4-6 weeks for delivery. UPS to Canada requires a $50.00 minimum order. Orders outside the U.S.A. and Canada: Airmail—add retail price of book; add $5.00 for each non-book item (tapes, etc.); add $1.00 per item for surface mail.

FOR GROUP STUDY AND PURCHASE

Because there is a great deal of interest in group discussion and study of the subject matter of this book, we offer a special quantity price to group leaders or agents. Our special quantity price for a minimum order of five copies of *Astrology Looks at History* is $70.80 cash-with-order. This price includes postage and handling within the United States. Minnesota residents must add 6.5% sales tax. For additional quantities, please order in multiples of five. For Canadian and foreign orders, add postage and handling charges as above. Credit card (VISA, MasterCard, American Express) orders are accepted. Charge card orders only ($15.00 minimum order) may be phoned in free within the U.S.A. or Canada by dialing 1-800-THE-MOON. For customer service, call 1-612-291-1970. Mail orders to:

LLEWELLYN PUBLICATIONS
P.O. Box 64383-K868, St. Paul, MN 55164-0383, U.S.A.

Prices subject to change without notice.

COMMUNICATING THE HOROSCOPE
Noel Tyl, editor

Help your clients reach personal fulfillment through thoughtful counseling! Each person's unique point of view functions as a badge of identification that can alert you to what you should listen for during a consultation. The horoscope presents a portrait of each person's perspective, which the successful consultant will use to communicate and counsel clients more effectively.

Communicating the Horoscope presents the viewpoints of nine contributing astrologers on factors crucial to a client's successful analysis: the importance of the timing of the consultation for both client and astrologer; how to help clients explore major issues and how to use the insights of their charts to sort out problems; suggestions for reading the client's behavior and unspoken messages; ways to simplify chart interpretations for clients unfamiliar with astrology and translate the horoscope into terms they can grasp; techniques for empathetic listening; and how interpreting the chart in terms of its possibilities opens clients to making the changes necessary for their own growth. Includes many insightful chart examples.

- One's Point of View: So Close to the Sun – Noel Tyl
- The Magic of the Consultation Moment – Christian Borup
- Creative Listening and Empathy – Haloli Q. Richter
- A Communication Model for Astrologers – Diana Stone
- Solving Problems: Key Questions to Ask Yourself and the Client – Donna Cunningham
- When the Client Avoids the Issue – Karen M. Hamaker-Zondag
- Bottom-Line Astrology – Susie Cox
- Telling Stories to Make Your Point – Jeff Jawer
- Working with Measurement, Memory and Myth – Wendy Ashley

ISBN: 1-56718-866-4, 6 x 9, 256 pp., charts, softcover $12.00

SEXUALITY IN THE HOROSCOPE
Noel Tyl, editor

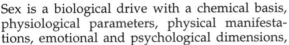

To empower clients to be more successful and satisfied in every area of life is the astrologer's legitimate aim. You might specialize in relationships or finance, but you cannot ignore the rest of a client's life if you intend to enhance the whole person. You must be willing and able to deal with the private and the often painful, the repressed as well as the blissful.

Sex is a biological drive with a chemical basis, physiological parameters, physical manifestations, emotional and psychological dimensions, and sociological implications. It involves our states of self-awareness and self-esteem, our capacity for communications, and parental influence. At the most basic physical level, it is friction. At the most spiritual level, it is merging into transcendental oneness.

The experience of sexuality is complex in its manifestation in life and in its occurrence in the horoscope. As they explore charts of the famous, infamous, and everyday persons, ten well-known astrologers share insights into the following intriguing topics:

- Classic Scenarios of Psychosexual Development – Noel Tyl
- Pluto Pathology: The Dark Side of Human Sexuality – Glenn Perry, Ph.D.
- Relationship Dynamics and Their Sexual Reality – Marion D. March
- Sexual Energy & Creativity – Gina Ceaglio
- Imagination/Fantasy: Sexuality's Escape Valve – John Townley
- Homosexuality in the Horoscope – J. Lee Lehman, Ph.D.
- Freeing the Spirit: Getting Beyond Denial – Ted Sharp
- Integrating the Sexual Profile for Wholeness – Jayj Jacobs
- Sexual Repression – Anthony Louis, M.D.
- AIDS: An Astro-Medical Perspective – B. F. Hammerslough
- Includes the charts of famous personalities

ISBN: 1-56718-865-6, 6 x 9, 336 pp., softbound   **$14.95**

PREDICTION IN ASTROLOGY
A Master Volume of Technique and Practice
by Noel Tyl

No matter how much you know about astrology already, no matter how much experience you've had to date, you'll be fascinated by *Prediction in Astrology,* and you'll grow as an astrologer. Using the Solar Arc theory and methods he describes in this book, the author was able to accurately predict the Gulf War, including the actual date it would begin and the timetable of tactics, two months *before* it began. He also predicted the overturning of Communist rule in the Eastern bloc nations nine months in advance of its actual occurrence.

Tyl teaches through example. You learn by doing astrology, not just thinking about it. Tyl introduces Solar Arc theory in terms of "rapport" measurements, which you begin to do immediately, without paper, pencil, or computer, dials, or wheels. Just with your eyes! You will never look at a horoscope the same way again!

Tyl, in his well-known, very special way, also gets personal. He presents 30 Aphorisms, the keenest of maxims, the most practical of techniques, to create predictions from any horoscope. And as if this were not enough, Tyl then presents 20 Aphorisms for Counseling. Look for Tyl's "Quick-Glance" Transit Table, 1940-2040, to which you can refer more quickly than a computer. The busy astrologer will use this Appendix every day for many years to come.

0-87542-814-2, 360 pgs., 6 x 9, softcover   **$17.95**

THE MISSING MOON
by Noel Tyl

This delightful collection of ten short stories illustrates principles of astrological counsel and practice with deliciously absurd wit. Read about the mysterious man whose horoscope has no Moon, and learn what the famous poem "Casey at the Bat" really means!

Follow Tyl's hero-astrologer, Michael Mercury, through a series of trials and misadventures on his journey around the horoscope. This is exact astrology presented through exhorbitant humor. You'll enjoy so much while you check your techniques as you solve mysteries, locate Plutonium, follow heroine Atlantia Lemuria into hypnosis . . .

0-87542-797-9, 180 pgs., 5 1/4 x 8, illus., softcover   **$4.95**

SYNTHESIS & COUNSELING IN ASTROLOGY
The Professional Manual
by Noel Tyl

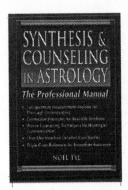

One of the keys to a vital, comprehensive astrology is the art of synthesis, the capacity to take the parts of our knowledge and combine them into a coherent whole. Many times, the parts may be contradictory (the relationship between Mars and Saturn, for example), but the art of synthesis manages the unification of opposites. Now Noel Tyl presents ways astrological measurements—through creative synthesis—can be used to effectively counsel individuals. Discussion of these complex topics is grounded in concrete examples and in-depth analyses of the 122 horoscopes of celebrities, politicians, and private clients.

Tyl's objective in providing this vitally important material was to present everything he has learned and practiced over his distinguished career to provide a useful source to astrologers. He has succeeded in creating a landmark text destined to become a classic reference for professional astrologers.

1-56718-734-X, 924 pgs., 7 x 10, 115 charts, softcover   **$29.95**

HORARY ASTROLOGY
The History and Practice of Astro-Divination
by Anthony Louis

Here is a how-to guide for the intermediate astrologer on the art of astrological divination. It's the best method for getting answers to questions of pressing personal concern based on the planets' positions at the time of inquiry. Delves deeply into the heritage and the modern applicability of the horary art. Author Anthony Louis is a practicing psychiatrist, and he brings the compassion and erudition associated with his field to this scholarly textbook.

Written beautifully and reverently in the tradition of William Lilly, the book translates Lilly's meaning into modern terms. Other features include numerous case studies; tables; diagrams; and more than 100 pages of appendices, including an exhaustive planetary rulership list, planetary key words and a lengthy astrological/horary glossary. Dignities and debilities, aspects and orbs, derivative houses, Arabic parts, fixed stars, critical degrees and more are explored in relation to the science of horary astrology. Worksheets supplement the text.

0-87542-394-9, 592 pgs., 6 x 9, illus., softcover   **$19.95**

INTIMATE RELATIONSHIPS
the Astrology of Attraction
edited by Joan McEvers

Explore the deeper meaning of intimate relation-ships with the knowledge and expertise of eight renowned astrologers. Dare to look into your own chart and confront your own vulnerabilities. Find the true meaning of love and its place in your life. Gain new insights into the astrology of marriage, dating, affairs and more!

In Intimate Relationships, eight astrologers discuss their views on romance and the horoscope. The roles of Venus and the Moon, as well as the asteroids Sappho, Eros and Amor, are explored in our attitudes and actions toward potential mates. The theory of affinities is also presented wherein we are attracted to someone with similar planetary energies.

Is it a love that will last a lifetime, or mere animal lust that will burn itself out in a few months? Read *Intimate Relationships* and discover your *natal* attractions as well as your *fatal* attractions.

0-87542-386-8, 240 pgs., 6 x 9, softcover **$14.95**

HOW TO MANAGE THE
ASTROLOGY OF CRISIS
edited by Noel Tyl

More often than not, a person will consult an astrologer during those times when life has become difficult, uncertain or distressing. While cri-sis of any type is really a turning point, not a disaster, the client's crisis of growth becomes the astrologer's challenge. By coming to the astrologer, the client has come to an oracle. At the very best, there is hope for a miracle; at the very least, there is hope for reinforcement through companionship and information. How do you as an astrologi-cal counselor balance a sober discussion of the realities with enthusias-tic efforts to leave the client feeling empowered and optimistic?

In this, the eleventh title in Llewellyn's New World Astrology Series, eight renowned astrologers provide answers this question as it applies to a variety of life crises. *How to Manage the Astrology of Crisis* begins with a discussion of the birth-crisis, the first major transition crisis in every-body's life—their confrontation with the world. It then discusses signif-icant family crises in childhood and healing of the inner child . . . mental crises including head injuries, psychological breakdown, psychic expe-riences, multiple personalities . . . career turning points and crises of life direction and action . . . astrological triggers of financial crisis and recent advances in financial astrology . . . astrological maxims for relationship crises . . . and the mid-life crises of creative space, idealism, and con-sciousness.

0-87542-390-6, 224 pgs., 6 x 9, charts, softcover **$12.00**

HOW TO USE VOCATIONAL ASTROLOGY
FOR SUCCESS IN THE WORKPLACE
edited by Noel Tyl

Announcing the most practical examination of Vocational Astrology in five decades! Improve your astrological skills with these revolutionary NEW tools for vocational and business analysis! Now, in *How to Use Vocational Astrology for Success in the Workplace*, edited by Noel Tyl, seven respected astrologers provide their well-seasoned modern views on that great issue of personal life—Work. Their expert advice will prepare you well for those tricky questions clients often ask: "Am I in the right job?" "Will I get promoted?" or "When is the best time to make a career move?" With an introduction by Noel Tyl in which he discusses the startling research of the Gauquelins, this ninth volume in Llewellyn's New World Astrology Series features enlightening counsel from the following experts: Jayj Jacobs, Gina Ceaglio, Donna Cunningham, Anthony Louis, Noel Tyl, Henry Weingarten, and Bob Mulligan. Read *How to Use Vocational Astrology* today, and add "Vocational Counselor" to *your* resume tomorrow! Includes the complete 1942 classic by Charles E. Luntz *Vocational Guidance by Astrology.*

0-87542-387-6, 384 pgs., 6 x 9, illus., softcover $14.95

ASTROLOGY'S SPECIAL MEASUREMENTS
How to Expand the Meaning of the Horoscope
edited by Noel Tyl

Every new student of astrology looks with bewilderment at that first horoscope and asks, "What's it mean when there's nothing in my 7th house? Won't I ever get married?" The student feels the strong need to *measure*. He needs something to define the space in the house and give meaning to the picture. Measurements are the lenses that help us see nearer, farther, and with greater contrast and clarity. In the process of analysis, measurement becomes diagnosis.

In this volume, ten experts discuss the finer points of measurement and meaning, analysis and diagnosis. How many measurements do you need? How many should fortify you for meaningful conversations with clients? Not all measurements work in every horoscope or for every astrologer—and too many can present so much data that you lose confidence within the multiplicity of options. Furthermore, no matter how precise the measurements, they still rely on the astrologer to adapt them to the human condition. *Astrology's Special Measurements* will be a tremendous resource for putting those special measurements to work easily and without fear.

ISBN: 1-56718-864-8, 6 x 9, 352 pgs., charts, tables, softbound $12.00

Prices subject to change without notice.

THE HOUSES
Power Places of the Horoscope
Edited by Joan McEvers

The Houses are the departments of experience. The planets energize these areas—giving life meaning. Understand why you attract and are attracted to certain people by your 7th House cusp. Go back in time to your 4th House, the history of your beginning. Joan McEvers has ingeniously arranged the chapters to show the Houses' relationships to each other and the whole. Various house systems are briefly described in Joan McEvers' introduction. Learn about house associations and planetary influences upon each house's activities with the following experts.

- Peter Damian: The First House and the Rising Sun
- Ken Negus: The Seventh House
- Noel Tyl: The Second House and The Eighth House
- Spencer Grendahl: The Third House
- Dona Shaw: The Ninth House
- Gloria Star: The Fourth House
- Marwayne Leipzig: The Tenth House
- Lina Accurso: Exploring Your Fifth House
- Sara Corbin Looms: The Eleventh: House of Tomorrow
- Michael Munkasey: The Sixth House
- Joan McEvers: The Twelfth House: Strength, Peace, Tranquillity

0-87542-383-3, 400 pgs., 5 1/4 x 8, illus., softcover $14.95

EXPLORING CONSCIOUSNESS IN THE HOROSCOPE
edited by Noel Tyl

When Llewellyn asked astrologers across the country which themes to include in its "New World Astrology Series," most specified at the top of their lists themes that explore consciousness! From shallow pipedreaming to ecstatic transcendence, "consciousness" has come to envelop realms of emotion, imagination, dreams, mystical experiences, previous lives and lives to come—aspects of the mind which defy scientific explanation. For most, consciousness means self-realization, the "having it all together" to function individualistically, freely, and confidently.

There are many ways to pursue consciousness, to "get it all together." Astrology is an exciting tool for finding the meaning of life and our part within it, to bring our inner selves together with our external realities, in appreciation of the spirit. Here, then, ten fine thinkers in astrology come together to share reflections on the elusive quicksilver of consciousness. They embrace the spiritual—and the practical. All are aware that consciousness feeds our awareness of existence; that, while it defies scientific method, it is vital for life.

0-87542-391-4, 256 pgs., 6 x 9, tables, charts, softcover $12.00

SPIRITUAL, METAPHYSICAL & NEW TRENDS IN MODERN ASTROLOGY
Edited by Joan McEvers

This is the first book in Llewellyn's New World Astrology Series. Edited by well-known astrologer, lecturer and writer Joan McEvers, this book pulls together the latest thoughts by the best astrologers in the field of Spiritual Astrology.
- Gray Keen: Perspective: The Ethereal Conclusion
- Marion D. March: Some Insights Into Esoteric Astrology
- Kimberly McSherry: The Feminine Element of Astrology: Reframing the Darkness
- Kathleen Burt: The Spiritual Rulers and Their Role in the Transformation
- Shirley Lyons Meier: The Secrets Behind Carl Payne Tobey's Secondary Chart
- Jeff Jawer: Astrodrama
- Donna Van Toen: Alice Bailey Revisited
- Philip Sedgwick: Galactic Studies
- Myrna Lofthus: The Spiritual Programming Within a Natal Chart
- Angel Thompson: Transformational Astrology

0-87542-380-9, 264 pgs., 5 1/4 x 8, softcover   **$9.95**

THE ASTROLOGY OF THE MACROCOSM
New Directions in Mundane Astrology
Edited by Joan McEvers

Explains various mundane, transpersonal and worldly events through astrology. The perfect introduction to understanding the fate of nations, weather patterns and other global movements.
- Jimm Erickson: A Philosophy of Mundane Astrology
- Judy Johns: The Ingress Chart
- Jim Lewis: Astro*Carto*Graphy—Bringing Mundane Astrology Down to Earth
- Richard Nolle: The SuperMoon Alignment
- Chris McRae: The Geodetic Equivalent Method of Prediction
- Nicholas Campion: The Age of Aquarius—A Modern Myth
- Nancy Soller: Weather Watching with an Ephemeris
- Marc Penfield: The Mystery of the Romanovs
- Steve Cozzi: The Astrological Quatrains of Michel Nostradamus
- Diana K. Rosenberg: Stalking the Wild Earthquake
- Caroline W. Casey: Dreams and Disasters—Patterns of Cultural and Mythological Evolution into the 21st Century

0-87542-384-1, 420 pgs., 5 1/4 x 8, charts, softcover   **$14.95**

SIGNS OF LOVE
Your Personal Guide to Romantic and Sexual Compatibility
by Jeraldine Saunders

Unlimited love power can be yours through an intimate knowledge of your horoscope, your numerical birth path, and other vitally important signs and signals that lead the way to loving relationships.

Now in an irresistible approach to the human heart, Jeraldine Saunders, a noted authority on the mystic arts, shows you how to look for love, how to find it, and how to be sure of it. With the aid of astrology, graphology, numerology, palmistry, and face reading, you will discover everything you need to know about your prospects with a given individual. You will learn the two enemies of love and how to eliminate them; the characteristics of all twelve zodiacal signs; the signs that are compatible with yours; the secrets behind your lover's facial features.

Signs of Love is the ultimate guide for gaining a better understanding of yourself and others in order to create a meaningful love life and attain lasting happiness.

1-56718-602-5, 320 pgs., mass market, illus.   **$6.99**

NAVIGATING BY THE STARS
Astrology and the Art of Decision-Making
by Edith Hathaway

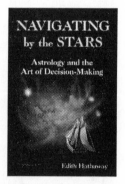

This book is chock full of convenient shortcuts to mapping out one's life. It presents the decision-maker's astrology, with the full range of astrological techniques.

No other one source presents all these cutting edge methods: Uranian astrology, the 90° dial, astro-mapping, Saturn quarters, hard aspects, angular relationships, the Meridian House System, secondary progressions, solar arc directions, eclipses, solstice and equinox charts, transiting lunation cycles, monthly kinetic mundascope graphs, among others.

To illustrate the immediate applications of the techniques, the author examines many charts in depth, focussing on study of character, destiny, timing cycles, and geographical location. She draws from 45 wide-ranging personal stories, including famous figures from history, politics, show business, the annals of crime, even corporations.

0-87542-366-3, 320 pgs., 6 x 9, softcover   **$14.95**

SPIRITUAL, METAPHYSICAL & NEW TRENDS IN MODERN ASTROLOGY
Edited by Joan McEvers

This is the first book in Llewellyn's New World Astrology Series. Edited by well-known astrologer, lecturer and writer Joan McEvers, this book pulls together the latest thoughts by the best astrologers in the field of Spiritual Astrology.
- Gray Keen: Perspective: The Ethereal Conclusion
- Marion D. March: Some Insights Into Esoteric Astrology
- Kimberly McSherry: The Feminine Element of Astrology: Reframing the Darkness
- Kathleen Burt: The Spiritual Rulers and Their Role in the Transformation
- Shirley Lyons Meier: The Secrets Behind Carl Payne Tobey's Secondary Chart
- Jeff Jawer: Astrodrama
- Donna Van Toen: Alice Bailey Revisited
- Philip Sedgwick: Galactic Studies
- Myrna Lofthus: The Spiritual Programming Within a Natal Chart
- Angel Thompson: Transformational Astrology

0-87542-380-9, 264 pgs., 5 1/4 x 8, softcover   **$9.95**

THE ASTROLOGY OF THE MACROCOSM
New Directions in Mundane Astrology
Edited by Joan McEvers

Explains various mundane, transpersonal and worldly events through astrology. The perfect introduction to understanding the fate of nations, weather patterns and other global movements.
- Jimm Erickson: A Philosophy of Mundane Astrology
- Judy Johns: The Ingress Chart
- Jim Lewis: Astro*Carto*Graphy—Bringing Mundane Astrology Down to Earth
- Richard Nolle: The SuperMoon Alignment
- Chris McRae: The Geodetic Equivalent Method of Prediction
- Nicholas Campion: The Age of Aquarius—A Modern Myth
- Nancy Soller: Weather Watching with an Ephemeris
- Marc Penfield: The Mystery of the Romanovs
- Steve Cozzi: The Astrological Quatrains of Michel Nostradamus
- Diana K. Rosenberg: Stalking the Wild Earthquake
- Caroline W. Casey: Dreams and Disasters—Patterns of Cultural and Mythological Evolution into the 21st Century

0-87542-384-1, 420 pgs., 5 1/4 x 8, charts, softcover   **$14.95**

SIGNS OF LOVE
Your Personal Guide to Romantic and Sexual Compatibility
by Jeraldine Saunders

Unlimited love power can be yours through an intimate knowledge of your horoscope, your numerical birth path, and other vitally important signs and signals that lead the way to loving relationships.

Now in an irresistible approach to the human heart, Jeraldine Saunders, a noted authority on the mystic arts, shows you how to look for love, how to find it, and how to be sure of it. With the aid of astrology, graphology, numerology, palmistry, and face reading, you will discover everything you need to know about your prospects with a given individual. You will learn the two enemies of love and how to eliminate them; the characteristics of all twelve zodiacal signs; the signs that are compatible with yours; the secrets behind your lover's facial features.

Signs of Love is the ultimate guide for gaining a better understanding of yourself and others in order to create a meaningful love life and attain lasting happiness.

1-56718-602-5, 320 pgs., mass market, illus.   **$6.99**

NAVIGATING BY THE STARS
Astrology and the Art of Decision-Making
by Edith Hathaway

This book is chock full of convenient shortcuts to mapping out one's life. It presents the decision-maker's astrology, with the full range of astrological techniques.

No other one source presents all these cutting edge methods: Uranian astrology, the 90° dial, astro-mapping, Saturn quarters, hard aspects, angular relationships, the Meridian House System, secondary progressions, solar arc directions, eclipses, solstice and equinox charts, transiting lunation cycles, monthly kinetic mundascope graphs, among others.

To illustrate the immediate applications of the techniques, the author examines many charts in depth, focussing on study of character, destiny, timing cycles, and geographical location. She draws from 45 wide-ranging personal stories, including famous figures from history, politics, show business, the annals of crime, even corporations.

0-87542-366-3, 320 pgs., 6 x 9, softcover   **$14.95**

ASTROLOGICAL COUNSELING
The Path to Self-Actualization
Edited by Joan McEvers

This book explores the challenges for today's counselors and gives guidance to those interested in seeking an astrological counselor to help them win their own personal challenges. Includes articles by 10 well-known astrologers:

- David Pond: Astrological Counseling
- Maritha Pottenger: Potent, Personal Astrological Counseling
- Bill Herbst: Astrology and Psychotherapy: A Comparison for Astrologers
- Gray Keen: Plato Sat on a Rock
- Ginger Chalford, Ph.D.: Healing Wounded Spirits: An Astrological Counseling Guide to Releasing Life Issues
- Donald L. Weston, Ph.D.: Astrology and Therapy/Counseling
- Susan Dearborn Jackson: Reading the Body, Reading the Chart
- Doris A. Hebel: Business Counseling
- Donna Cunningham: The Adult Child Syndrome, Codependency, and Their Implications for Astrologers
- Eileen Nauman: Medical Astrology Counseling

0-87542-385-X, 304 pgs., 5 1/4 x 8, charts, softcover   **$14.95**

PLANETS: The Astrological Tools
Edited by Joan McEvers

Explains various mundane, transpersonal and worldly events through astrology. The perfect introduction to understanding the fate of nations, weather patterns and other global movements.

- Jimm Erickson: A Philosophy of Mundane Astrology
- Judy Johns: The Ingress Chart
- Jim Lewis: Astro*Carto*Graphy—Bringing Mundane Astrology Down to Earth
- Richard Nolle: The SuperMoon Alignment
- Chris McRae: The Geodetic Equivalent Method of Prediction
- Nicholas Campion: The Age of Aquarius—A Modern Myth
- Nancy Soller: Weather Watching with an Ephemeris
- Marc Penfield: The Mystery of the Romanovs
- Steve Cozzi: The Astrological Quatrains of Michel Nostradamus
- Diana K. Rosenberg: Stalking the Wild Earthquake
- Caroline W. Casey: Dreams and Disasters—Patterns of Cultural and Mythological Evolution into the 21st Century

0-87542-381-7, 384 pgs., 5-1/4 x 8, softcover   **$12.95**

HOW TO PERSONALIZE THE
OUTER PLANETS
The Astrology of Uranus, Neptune & Pluto
Edited by Noel Tyl

Since their discoveries, the three outer planets have been symbols of the modern era. Representing great social change on a global scale, they also take us as individuals to higher levels of consciousness and new possibilities of experience. Explored individually, each outer planet offers tremendous promise for growth. But when taken as a group, as they are in *Personalizing the Outer Planets*, the potential exists to recognize *accelerated* development.

The seven prominent astrologers in *Personalizing the Outer Planets* bring these revolutionary forces down to earth in practical ways.
- Jeff Jawer: Learn how the discoveries of the outer planets rocked the world
- Noel Tyl: Project into the future with outer planet Solar Arcs
- Jeff Green: See how the outer planets are tied to personal trauma
- Jeff Jawer: Give perspective to your inner spirit through outer planet symbolisms
- Jayj Jacobs: Explore interpersonal relationships and sex through the outer planets
- Mary E. Shea: Make the right choices using outer planet transits
- Joanne Wickenburg: Realize your unconscious drives and urges through the outer planets
- Capel N. McCutcheon: Personalize the incredible archetypal significance of outer planet aspects

0-87542-389-2, 288 pgs., 6 x 9, illus., softcover **$12.00**

WEB OF RELATIONSHIPS
Spiritual, Karmic & Psychological Bonds
edited by Joan McEvers

The astrology of intimacy has long been a popular subject among professional astrologers and psychologists. Many have sought the answer to what makes some people have successful relationships with one another, while others struggle. *Web of Relationships* examines this topic not only in intimate affiliations, but also in families and friendships, in this eighth volume of the Llewellyn New World Astrology Series.

Editor Joan McEvers brings together the wisdom and experience of eight astrology experts. Listen to what one author says about the mythological background of planets as they pertain to relationships. Discover how past life regression is illustrated in the chart. Consider the relationship of astrology and transactional analysis. *Web of Relationships* explores the karmic and mystical connections between child and parent, how friends support and understand each other, the significance of the horoscope as it pertains to connections and much more. Each chapter will bring you closer to your own web of relationships and the astrology of intimacy.

0-87542-388-4, 240 pgs., 6 x 9, softcover **$14.95**

Prices subject to change without notice.

YOUR PLANETARY PERSONALITY
**Everything You Need to Make Sense of
Your Horoscope
by Dennis Oakland**

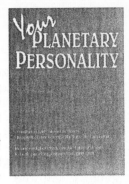

This book deepens the study of astrological inter-pretation for professional and beginning astrologers alike. Dennis Oakland's interpreta-tions of the planets in the houses and signs are the result of years of study of psychology, sciences, symbolism, Eastern philosophy plus the study of birth charts from a psychotherapy group. Unlike the interpretations in other books, these empha-size the life processes involved and facilitate a greater understanding of the chart. Includes 100-year ephemeris.

Even if you now know *nothing* about astrology, Dennis Oakland's clear instructions will teach you how to construct a complete and accurate birth chart for anyone born between 1900 to 1999. After you have built your chart, he will lead you through the steps of reading it, giving you indepth interpretations of each of your planets. When done, you will have the satisfaction that comes from increased self-awareness *and* from being your *own* astrologer!

This book is also an excellent exploration for psychologists and psychia-trists who use astrology in their practices.

0-87542-594-1, 580 pgs., 7 x 10, softcover $19.95

ASTRO-ECONOMICS
**A Study of Astrology and the Business Cycle
by David Williams**

This informative, comprehensive volume combines history, theory, astrology, and finance to form a systematic predictive science of the business cycle.

Following a review of economic thought pertaining to this cycle, the author examines possible planetary causes of heavy sunspot activity and its correlation to business cycles. Major economic turns and geocentric planetary aspect data have been compiled with Jupiter-Uranus, Jupiter-Saturn and Saturn-Uranus conjunctions coinciding with depressions or low business activity in America. Uranus moving into the sign of Gemi-ni, however, has come to be a predictor of a major liberating event.

An extensive discussion of the nullification of unfavorable aspects by more powerful favorable aspects (and vice versa) is also presented. Numerous tables, charts and wheels graphically represent such find-ings. A great introduction to financial astrology for the novice, as well as a wonderful reference book for any financial analyst.

0-87542-882-7, 64 pgs., 8 1/2 x 11, charts, softcover $3.00

THE ASTROLOGICAL THESAURUS, BOOK ONE
House Keywords
Michael Munkasey

Keywords are crucial for astrological work. They correctly translate astrological symbols into clear, everyday language—which is a never-ending pursuit of astrologers. For example, the Third House can be translated into the keywords "visitors," "early education" or "novelist."

The Astrological Thesaurus, Book One: House Keywords is a the first easy-to-use reference book and textbook on the houses, their psychologically rich meanings, and their keywords. This book also includes information on astrological quadrants and hemispheres, how to choose a house system, and the mathematical formulations for many described house systems.

Astrologer Michael Munkasey compiled almost 14,000 keywords from more than 600 sources over a 23-year period. He has organized them into 17 commonplace categories (e.g., things, occupations and psychological qualities), and cross-referenced them three ways for ease of use: alphabetically, by house, and by category. Horary users, in particular, will find this book extremely useful.

0-87542-579-8, 434 pgs., 7 x 10, illus., softcover   **$19.95**

ASTROLOGY AND THE GAMES PEOPLE PLAY
A Tool for Self-Understanding
in Work & Relationships
by Spencer Grendahl

Expand your self-awareness and facilitate personal growth with the Astro-analysis approach to astrology! Astro-analysis is a completely new and unique system that enables you to combine simple astrological information with the three-ring model of basic ego states—Parent, Adult and Child—used in popular psychology. This easy-to-follow technique makes available to the average person psychological insights that are generally available only to 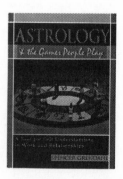 astrologers. Not only is it easy to transcribe your horoscope onto Astro-analysis' three-sphere diagram, but you will find that this symbolic picture provides accurate and meaningful perceptions into the energy patterns of your personality, clearly delineating the areas that may be "overweighted" or most in need of balance. This material is enhanced by examples and explanations of horoscopes of actual people.

Astro-analysis is a powerful self-help tool that will quickly make you aware of the basis for your behavior patterns and attitudes, so you can get a new perspective on your relationships with others and determine the most promising strategies for personal growth.

1-56718-338-7, 224 pgs., 7 x 10, softcover   **$12.95**